How to Raise a Wild Child

HOW TO RAISE
A WILD CHILD

The Art and Science of
Falling in Love with Nature

SCOTT D. SAMPSON

HOUGHTON MIFFLIN HARCOURT
BOSTON   NEW YORK
2015

Library of Congress Cataloging-in-Publication Data is available.
ISBN 978-0-544-27932-2

NOTE: Readers and the children they mentor should give due regard
to safety in all interactions with nature.

"Ich lebe mein Leben . . . / I live my life in widening," from *Rilke's Book of
Hours: Love Poems to God* by Rainer Maria Rilke, translated by Anita Barrows
and Joanna Macy, translation copyright © 1996 by Anita Barrows and Joanna
Macy. Used by permission of Riverhead Books, an imprint of Penguin Group
(USA) LLC.

Book design by Victoria Hartman

Printed in the United States of America
DOC 10 9 8 7 6 5 4 3 2 1

In wildness is the preservation of the world.

— HENRY DAVID THOREAU

For my mother, Catherine June Sampson,
nature mentor extraordinaire,
and
for my sister, Kerry Dawn Sharpe,
who taught me how to live with grace and grit.
I miss you both terribly.

Contents

Preface

LIKE MANY CHILDREN, I developed a passion for dinosaurs as a kid. Without exaggeration, *paleontology* was one of the first words I learned to spell. By the tender age of four, I had memorized dozens of multisyllabic names of prehistoric creatures. I dug for fossils in the backyard (unsuccessfully) and came home from family camping trips with assortments of rocks (and occasional fossils), most of which were banished to the backyard. A black-and-white photo taken when I was four years old shows me hugging a cement *Stegosaurus*—true love.

Unlike most children, I never lost my passion for dinosaurs. Some say I never really grew up. After contemplating several alternative careers, I eventually chose to pursue a doctorate in zoology at the University of Toronto. My dissertation involved naming and describing two previously unknown horned dinosaurs discovered in Montana.

In 1999, I accepted a dual position at the University of Utah in Salt Lake City as a paleontology curator at the Utah Museum of Natural History (now the Natural History Museum of Utah) and an assistant professor in the Department of Geology and

Geophysics. It was a dream job for a dino-guy like me, with museum resources for fieldwork and fossil preparation, access to graduate students, and plenty of amazing fossils to be discovered within a day's drive. I also took advantage of opportunities to hunt dinosaurs (or at least their fossilized bones) in far-off lands, enjoying many seasons in Africa and elsewhere. It seemed I was set for life.

But in 2007, now a tenured professor and museum chief curator, I gave it all up. Well, most of it. I kept fossil hunting in Utah, but my wife Toni and I decided to move to northern California, where I devoted the bulk of my energies to public science education and fostering nature connection. Many colleagues thought I was nuts, and so did I for a while. Why make such a drastic change?

It came down to a pair of compelling insights. First, the current disconnect between kids and nature threatens the health of children. A childhood lived almost entirely indoors immersed in technology is an impoverished childhood, with numerous negative impacts on growth—physical, mental, and emotional. Second, the current trend toward denaturing childhood also threatens the places we live and perhaps even the future of humanity. We likely have about one generation (some say less, some say a little more) to make profound changes and set ourselves on a sustainable course. After that—well, nature, as they say, bats last.

If sustainability depends on transforming the human relationship with nature, the present-day gap between kids and nature emerges as one of the greatest and most overlooked crises of our time, threatening people and countless other species. Helping children fall in love with nature deserves to be a top national priority, on par with reducing greenhouse gas emissions and preserving species and wild places. Having spent much of my adult life communicating science to nonscientists, including kids, I felt the need to contribute more directly to this urgent effort.

Since then, my work has taken several forms, including writing, speaking, and various media projects. The most high-profile example has been *Dinosaur Train*, a PBS KIDS television series produced by the Jim Henson Company that, as of this writing, airs daily across the United States and in many other countries around the world. I serve as the show's science advisor and host, consulting on scripts and helping to craft the stories for the animated characters, including Buddy, a young *T. rex,* and Tiny, a kid *Pteranodon* (flying reptile). At the end of each episode, I appear on camera to talk about the science behind the stories, making connections between the prehistoric world of dinosaurs and our present-day world. My enthusiastic tagline at the end of every show is, "Get outside, get into nature, and make your own discoveries!"

Dinosaur Train has been a roaring success, as well as a lot of fun, reaching millions of children and parents. Through my writing and speaking events, the show has also afforded me terrific opportunities to promote the cause of connecting children with nature. Yet a few years ago, a fundamental question hit me like a *T. rex* thighbone to the gut: *Exactly how do kids connect with nature, and how does this process change as they grow up?* I had some ideas, but really didn't know the answer.

Surely, I presumed, with so many organizations engaged in nature connection, there must be a bevy of books on the topic. A rigorous search revealed no shortage of offerings on outdoor activities for kids, from birding to gardening, and plenty of volumes devoted to environmental education. Yet with few exceptions, these books did not delve directly into nature connection, let alone how this process changes with the age of the child. No one would argue that toddlers and teenagers engage with nature in different ways, but exactly what are those ways? Digging further, I found a stream of academic papers, most written in the past couple of decades, addressing this very issue. Yet until now these results have not been summarized in a single volume for a general audience.

Ultimately, the search for answers took me far beyond the scientific literature, into backyards, classrooms, school gardens, urban parks, nature centers, museums, and out into the wilderness. I've studied nature mentoring, learned "bird language" with my daughter Jade, and spent time with kids in wild places. Along the way, I was embarrassed to discover that my own sense of nature connection was—it has to be said—pitiful. So, while writing this book, I sought to deepen this connection, both for Jade and for myself. Ultimately, all this research has led me to a series of conclusions about how nature connection actually works, and how the process changes as children grow. The implications of these findings get to the very heart of parenting and teaching, and of childhood itself. *How to Raise a Wild Child* is that story, aimed at everyone interested in the art and science of helping children fall in love with nature. If you're interested in becoming a nature mentor to the children in your life, this is the book for you.

In 2013, just as I began writing this volume in earnest, I moved with my family from the seaside village of Muir Beach, California, to Denver, Colorado, to take on another opportunity. The Denver Museum of Nature & Science offered me an executive position, with the potential to tackle important work on an urban scale. Now well into my second year, I'm excited to be at such a forward-thinking institution endeavoring to make a difference. And, thanks to input from numerous new colleagues and friends, the move to Denver greatly altered the content of this book.

In the end, the writing of *How to Raise a Wild Child* was bookended by sadness. Just as I began to crank out the first chapters, the greatest nature mentor of my life, my mother, passed away after a lengthy downward spiral in the wake of a major stroke. Then, about a year later and just a few weeks prior to completing the manuscript, my sister Kerry died rather suddenly following a two-year bout with cancer. These deep losses have only cemented in me the need to push through the daily noise and focus on the things that matter most. It's my deep personal hope that this book is one of those things.

Acknowledgments

How to Raise a Wild Child is my attempt to build on and synthesize numerous insights from those who have come before me. Among the most influential have been Thomas Berry, Fritjof Capra, Rachel Carson, Loren Eiseley, Richard Louv, Joanna Macy, David Orr, David Suzuki, and Henry David Thoreau. David Suzuki and Richard Louv, in particular, have been major inspirations. Suzuki, that great Canadian environmentalist, has been a huge mentor in my life, a scientist who has always advocated for integrating people with nature. Louv helped launch the burgeoning children and nature movement and has served as its strongest voice; he also kindly took time to be interviewed for this book.

I am grateful to the following individuals who offered important input before and/or during the writing process: Lise Aangeenbrug, Kenny Ballentine, Adam Bienenstock, Cindy Bowick, Michael Bucheneau, Susan Daggett, Sharon Danks, John Demboski, Chris Dorsey, John Gillette, David Hage, Mary Ellen Hannibal, Patricia Hasbach, Governor John Hickenlooper, Kirk Johnson, Michael Kaufman, Margaret Lamar, Stephen

LeBlanc, Juan Martinez, Ian Miller, Rachel Neumann, Antonio Pares, Dale Penner, Laurette Rogers, Judy Scotchmoor, Dondre Smallwood, David Sobel, George Sparks, Mark Stefanski, Jeff Su, Brian Swimme, Mary Evelyn Tucker, Nancy Walsh, and Tim Wohlgenant.

I'm deeply indebted to the generous folks—friends, colleagues, scientists, scholars, and practitioners of nature connection—who offered advice on sections, chapters, or the book as a whole: Michael Barton, James Bartram, Tim Beatley, Louise Chawla, Chip Colwell, Sharon Danks, Stacie Gilmore, Andréa Giron, José Gonzalez, Alison Gopnik, Gregor Hagedorn, Peter Kahn, Richard Louv, Martin Ogle, Zach Pine, Dan Rademacher, Toni Simmons, Jeff Su, Doug Tallamy, and Jon Young.

A special thank-you to Jon Young, expert nature mentor, and to all of the 2014 Art of Mentoring staff and participants, who, among other things, helped me to truly understand the role of community in fostering nature connection.

Many thanks to my literary agent, Esmond Harmsworth of Zachary Shuster Harmsworth, and to my editor, Lisa White of Houghton Mifflin Harcourt, for their skillful shepherding of this project. Lisa's editorial efforts greatly improved the manuscript. I'm especially pleased to publish this book with Houghton Mifflin Harcourt, home of numerous important nature books, including Rachel Carson's *Silent Spring*. Although Carson never had the chance to write her "wonder book" about connecting kids with nature, I like to think that she would approve of this one.

I am grateful to the entire community—humans and nonhumans alike—of Muir Beach and the surrounding Marin Headlands for nurturing my connection to people and nature over most of the past decade. Many ideas presented in this book were generated and honed while walking those seaside hills.

Warm thanks to Tim Moore and Earl Howe for sharing in my childhood explorations of nature on the west side of Vancouver.

My family—mother, father, and sisters—helped instill a love of nature in me as a child. Christy, thanks for being my companion in those early years. Dad, you showed me how to be confident in nature. Mum, you were my stalwart mentor.

My adult daughter Twan has been an indefatigable source of emotional support throughout the writing of this book, and many years before that.

My younger daughter Jade has taught me far more than I've taught her. She is the light that shines from the future, drawing me forward into deeper nature connection and inspiring me to undertake projects like this one.

Finally, I'm at a loss to express the gratitude I feel for my beautiful wife, Toni Simmons, whose unwavering support carried me through all the tough times. Tiger, without your nurturing, this book simply could not have happened.

Introduction

Bootful of Pollywogs

Rethinking Nature and Childhood in Perilous Times

The major problems in the world are the result of the difference between how nature works and the way people think.

— GREGORY BATESON

SUNSHINE AND SPRINGTIME are notoriously rare bedfellows in Vancouver, British Columbia. One day when I was four or five years old, my mother took me into the forest a few blocks from home. She'd heard that the "frog pond," as it was known, was brimming with tadpoles. Cinching the deal that fateful day were scattered, caressing rays of sun.

The event, one of my earliest memories, began with a brief, loamy walk down a forest trail. The trees were thick with moisture, still dripping from the relentless, drizzling rains. Arriving at the pond, I scampered to the water's edge and squatted down, staring intently. It was a few moments before I realized that each of the frenetic black blobs before me was a distinct life form. Wearing tall black rubber boots, I stepped tentatively into the water, captivated by the larval swarm. I bent over and scooped up several with my hands to get a closer look. Bulging eyes, bloblike bodies, and long, slimy, transparent tails worked madly against my fingers.

Captivated, I inched out farther, and farther still, gasping as the water suddenly overtopped a boot. (Many years later, my mother told me that she started to object but thought better of it.) After hesitating briefly, imagining the tadpoles now darting around my sock, I took another willful step into the muck. The second boot flooded.

I was really in it now, sharing this pond-universe with jillions of frogs-to-be. Stepping gingerly so as to avoid any inadvertent amphibicide, I eventually found myself at the pond's center, the water now above waist level. The sense of wonder and the smile across my face grew in tandem as I picked up handful after handful of squirming tadpoles. Immersed in that miniature sea of pollywogs, I felt, perhaps for the first time in my life, a deep and ecstatic sense of oneness with nature.

Through the late 1960s and 1970s, I escaped into that forest on Vancouver's west side whenever possible, often in the company of my friend Tim. Our local elementary school backed up against the forest, and the forward-thinking administrators established an "Adventure Playground" amidst a stand of hemlock, cedar, and Douglas fir abutting one of the playing fields. At recess and lunch, we would sprint for this natural wonderland, where a giant overturned cedar stump became cave, castle, and spaceship.

As adolescents, our forest excursions expanded exponentially as we discovered the full 2,000-acre extent of the University Endowment Lands. (For us, it was simply "the woods.") Canine companions joined us for this phase. I had a German shepherd named Rocky and Tim was accompanied by Raisin, a poodle–Siberian husky mix that resembled a four-legged ball of steel wool. (When queried about her breed, Tim would offer the same straight-faced reply: "Purebred Pooberian.")

Vision is the least intimate of human senses. In the forest, we were embraced by the sweet, almost citrusy fragrance of Douglas fir; the water-drenched autumn air that turned breath visible; the deep qworking of ravens perched high on cedar boughs; and the tangy sumptuousness of fresh-picked huckleberries. This multisensory milieu offered a safe place, a cocoon within the world, for adolescent males to talk out their social angst and ponder the future. Needless to say, the dogs loved it too, relishing the endless textures and scents. We explored trail after trail, with names like Sasamat, Hemlock, and Salish.

Often we avoided trails entirely, preferring to bushwhack through the dense coastal foliage, clambering over rotting logs and navigating rock-strewn streams thick with skunk cabbage, nettles, salal, and ferns. On these meandering excursions, the forest took on a wild and unpredictable flavor, with amazing discoveries possible at any moment: teeming ant colonies; deep and murky ponds like Japanese soaking tubs; raucous, foul-smelling bird rookeries; and humongous stumps, old-growth ghosts. Hours later, humans and canines alike emerged from the evergreen realm filthy, exhausted, and exhilarated.

We had no idea that this place was imprinting on our hearts and minds, that our pores were soaking up every moment.

After a big winter snowfall (also a rare occurrence), the forest transformed yet again. Blinding whiteness blanketed every branch, twig, and needle. What had seemed a shadowed, entangled, noisy place just the day prior was now a rolling, sun-drenched refuge of deep, cathedral-like silence—all edges gone.

Lighthearted, we punched through the heavy snow, stopping occasionally to lounge in cavelike snow-free zones beneath some of the larger trees.

In our mid-teenage years, testosterone overdoses manifested in the forest as a risky game dubbed "Deelo Wars." A deelo (etymology uncertain) was any piece of woody debris that you could heft at someone else. In essence, the strategy amounted to abandoning cover of tree or bush just long enough to hurl large sticks at several of your closest friends. Of course, they were busy doing the same—every man for himself. All of us sustained a few direct hits, but I'm happy to report that no serious injuries resulted. (No, I don't recommend trying this at home.)

I departed Vancouver in the mid-1980s to attend graduate school in Toronto, eventually earning a PhD and becoming a paleontologist. Tim, meanwhile, headed skyward, becoming a commercial airline pilot. In the succeeding decades, I've been fortunate enough to hunt for dinosaur bones in such far-flung locales as Zimbabwe, Mexico, and Madagascar. Cumulatively, I've spent years living in tents in remote places often referred to as "badlands." While out fossil hunting, I've had face-to-face encounters with an assortment of amazing and very much alive creatures, among them bear, elephant, hyena, cobra, moose, and crocodile. But the senses with which I've experienced these places and their inhabitants were attuned in that second-growth temperate forest on Vancouver's west side. Together with family camping trips, daily play in the wild corners of our neighborhood, and, later, long hikes in the Coast Range mountains, those countless treks in the Endowment Lands fostered in me a persistent passion for nature, undoubtedly influencing my career path. In recent years I've come to realize that I can't help but take that Pacific Northwest forest with me wherever I go. It is an indelible part of who I am, more like a lens on the world than a collection of memories.

The Extinction of Experience

My outdoor experiences mimicked those of many other 1960s and '70s children. Baby boomers like me love to wax nostalgic about being kicked outdoors after school, returning only at dark, often in response to a parent yelling for them to come home. We talk of weekends and holidays full of nature roaming, sometimes alone, sometimes with friends, but always autonomously.

Few twenty-first-century kids can cite similar experiences. During the past generation, childhood has undergone a profound and, until recently, largely ignored transformation. One study found that the average American boy or girl spends four to seven minutes a day outdoors. Another placed the estimate at about thirty minutes of daily, unstructured, outdoor play. Whatever the actual number is, it seems pretty clear that children today spend a tiny fraction of the time playing outdoors that their parents did as kids.

By comparison, those same average American kids devote more than seven hours daily to staring at screens, replacing reality with virtual alternatives. Most boys rack up more than 10,000 gaming hours before age twenty-one. Children can now recognize greater than a thousand corporate logos, but fewer than ten plants native to their region. The net result of these staggering statistics is what author Robert Michael Pyle has dubbed "the extinction of experience," highlighted by the gaping chasm between children and nature.

This indoor migration has been a massive, unplanned experiment with negative health consequences only now coming into view. During those marathon screen sessions, bodily exercise is restricted largely to thumb gyrations. Unsurprisingly, chronic physical and mental illnesses in children have skyrocketed. Today, about 18 percent of our kids six and older are obese, with diabetes, heart disease, and other ailments both rampant and on the rise. As of 2011, about 11 percent of American children four to seventeen years of age had been diagnosed with attention deficit hyperactivity disorder (ADHD). In 2014, nearly six million children in the United States, one in eight, took Ritalin, largely to combat ADHD. According to at least one U.S. surgeon general, the present generation of children may be the first of the modern age with a life expectancy less than that of their parents.

To be clear, this problem isn't restricted to the United States, or to North America. Recent surveys show the same rampant denaturing trend occurring throughout much of the developed world. Recognition of this issue is growing as well, with the majority of people strongly supporting the idea that children need more time in nature.

One survey, commissioned by The Nature Conservancy and funded by Disney, asked parents in five countries—Brazil, China, France, Hong Kong, and the United States—to describe their attitudes about children and nature. Among the findings were the following:

- Relatively few parents say that their children regularly spend time in nature. Fewer than one in four American parents—one in five in the other countries—reported that their children daily spend time in a park or natural area.
- The overwhelming majority of parents in all five countries view children's lack of time in nature as a major problem.

In the United States, 65 percent of respondents regarded this issue either as "very serious" or "extremely serious."
- Parents believe that developing a connection with nature is critical to a child's development. Among American parents, 82 percent regard time in nature to be "very important" to their children's development, second in priority only to reading.

The United Kingdom's National Trust recently published a lengthy report detailing the precipitous decline in children's time in nature and arguing for the numerous health benefits that will accrue if we can reverse this trend. Similarly, in 2012 the International Union for the Conservation of Nature (IUCN) adopted the resolution, "Child's Right to Connect with Nature and to a Healthy Environment," citing the growing gap between children and nature as a global issue of pressing importance.

In short, it is now broadly recognized that kids spend the great bulk of their time indoors, and that we need a widespread, concerted effort to reconnect children with nature.

So what happened?

Well, the digital revolution for one thing. Perhaps even more so than adults, children are highly susceptible to the hypnotic siren call of computers and handheld gadgets. Yet blaming technology is far too simplistic; many other factors have been involved. The fear factor, for example. Thanks to the media frenzy that now surrounds child abductions, parents are afraid to let their children play outdoors unattended. This is in spite of the fact that friends and relatives, rather than strangers, commit the great bulk of these crimes, and that the odds of your child being snatched are no greater than they were in 1950 or 1960. Another fear—this one of litigation—has driven many property owners to outlaw nature-related activities such as building tree forts.

And well-intentioned parents fearful of their children somehow falling behind or missing out have filled their schedules with sports, music lessons, academic tutoring, and other organized activities, with little time left for unstructured play.

Then there's the urban factor. The world's population has exploded in recent decades, with cities following suit to accommodate the growing throngs. Since late 2008, more than half of humanity's billions have inhabited urban areas. Like ravenous giants, expanding cities have swallowed up more and more nature, and degraded what's left behind.

In his 2006 bestseller, *Last Child in the Woods*, Richard Louv spotlighted the current alienation of children from the natural world—what he termed *nature-deficit disorder*—as well as the many health benefits of nature connection. In the tradition of Rachel Carson's *Silent Spring*, *Last Child* became a clarion call for change. The book catalyzed the children-in-nature movement, triggering new legislation in numerous states as well as the federal No Child Left Inside Act, approved by the House in 2008, but never voted on in the Senate. Grassroots efforts have been bolstered by federal initiatives like Michelle Obama's Let's Move! campaign, the United States Forest Service's Children's Forest initiative, and, most recently, President Obama's America's Great Outdoors campaign, now working with various state-level partners. Many related books and documentaries have appeared, alongside essays and letters to the editor. As far back as 2006, *USA Today* reported that "A back-to-nature movement to reconnect children with the outdoors is burgeoning nationwide." The Children & Nature Network, cofounded by Louv, now reports over 100 regional campaigns spanning the United States, Canada, Australia, New Zealand, Italy, Mexico, and Colombia; cumulatively, these efforts reach millions of children a year.

In the pages that follow, I summarize the result of recent research demonstrating that abundant time in nature is a critical wellspring of human health, with a deep and formative influence on children in particular. Nature's impacts extend far beyond physical fitness, encompassing intellectual and emotional health, self-identity, and basic values and morals. Health benefits of exposure to nature include enhanced healing, stress reduction, creativity, and self-esteem. Nature also has an unparalleled capacity to stir our emotions, fostering raw and powerful feelings of wonder, awe, mystery, joy—and, yes, fear. Smelling a wildflower in an alpine meadow, sprinting into the ocean surf, and sharing a face-to-face encounter with a coyote are all experiences that differ mightily from virtual alternatives.

The Other Side of the Human-Nature Relationship

There's another, equally compelling reason for us to reconnect with nature. Alongside declining human health, you've undoubtedly heard that nature's well-being is also on the wane, at least here on Earth. It's now scientifically documented and broadly known that human-induced effects such as global warming, habitat destruction, and species extinctions have driven Earth's living systems to a series of perilous tipping points. If current trends persist until the close of this century, the world's climate will warm an average of three or four degrees, triggering cataclysmic flooding of coastal regions and rampant desertification inland, displacing billions of people. During that same interval, we could drive about one-half of the planet's species diversity to extinction, an eco-evolutionary experiment last run 66 million years ago when the dinosaurs were all but extinguished. Humanity's persistence is at risk as well. At a minimum, our present course will generate human suffering on an unfathomable scale and rob future generations of a healthy biosphere.

The question asked all too rarely is, why? Why are we destroying so much of Earth's nature and threatening our own future? In particular, why does this destruction continue apace despite a mountain of scientific evidence heralding catastrophe?

Most who acknowledge the present eco-crisis see the prime causes as "out there" in the environment. They point to multiple culprits, or "sources"—for example, greenhouse gas emissions, toxic pollutants, and deforestation—often heaping blame on multinational corporations and their "greedy" CEOs. From this perspective, the solution is more and better technology—solar and wind power, hybrid vehicles, high-performance buildings, and the like—accompanied by "simpler" lifestyles and a "greening" of the economy. Some of this tribe goes further, arguing for a complete restructuring of industrial society, including our political democracy and capitalist economy.

Conversely, a smaller but fast-growing contingent—among them scientists, artists, indigenous leaders, educators, environmentalists, spiritual leaders, and philosophers—claim that greener technologies, simpler lifestyles, and restructured economies are essential, yet insufficient. Even if every adult in the industrialized world became a vegetarian, took three-minute showers, and reduced their garbage nearly to zero; even if we all installed solar panels, rainwater capture systems, and compact fluorescent bulbs; even if we converted to cloth shopping bags, mass transit, and ate only local and organic, they argue, we'd still be hell-bound. Exterior transformations, this second tribe argues, must be accompanied by an interior revolution in thinking.

I stand with the second group. New technologies alone simply won't cut it. What if tomorrow we somehow realized the dream of 100 percent "clean energy" regulated by "smart grids"? Would we suddenly cease decimating nature? Hardly. It seems more likely that the destruction would accelerate, as we channeled all that cheap, clean energy into the exploitation of "natural resources." As Albert Einstein famously claimed, "The significant problems we have cannot be solved at the same level of thinking with which we created them." Most of the external tools needed to set humanity on a new, sustainable path—knowledge, technologies, and wealth—are already available. Yet our response remains glacial relative to the urgent need for action. The most crucial unresolved sustainability issue, then, is a matter of mind and education rather than science and technology.

Our present dysfunctional worldview is founded on an erroneous perception: the existence of humanity outside nature. Despite the fact that nature provides the raw materials for our economy and that we clearly live on a finite planet, economists continue to regard the natural world as a subset of the economy, and speak of limitless growth. Yet the opposite is clearly true: our economy is a part of nature, as evidenced by the dramatic economic effects caused by topping ecological limits. A second, closely related perception is human dominion over the natural world. Seeing ourselves as external and superior to nature, we feel entitled to exploit natural "resources" at will. Adrift in a sea of objects, we're left without any meaningful home, let alone a desire to protect and nurture the places we live.

How did we get so far off track? How did nature become "Other," the ultimate big-box store for insatiable masses of shopaholics? On this question there's much disagreement. Some point to the origins of written language, which triggered the loss of oral traditions intimately tied to local places. Others blame our extreme manipulation of the natural world on the birth of agriculture. Still others point to the early Greek philosophers' separation of humanity from nature based on reason, or the religious positioning of humans as the dominant species at the apex of creation, or the scientific revolution's heightening of this sense of human dominion. Almost certainly our alienation from nature was progressive, punctuated by many historical forks in the road, including those listed above and many others.

Whatever the causes, the primary tactic used to address the sustainability crisis has been the rational "doom-and-gloom" approach. Surely, most scientists and environmentalists have thought, if folks just understood the facts, they'd change their behavior. (I should know; I've been part of this ineffectual echo chamber.) Yet it turns out that people are more likely to shut down or go into denial when presented with such daunting information, particularly when the bulk of it is so removed from our day-to-day lives. Think about how you felt after reading the first paragraph of this section. On the spectrum from depressed to inspired, I'll bet your reaction was closer to the former.

Marketing experts have long known that it's not the mind, but the heart, that offers the most potent pathway to shifting behavior. Car ads, for example, don't beat us over the head with statistics on horsepower or 0 to 60 acceleration times; instead we watch beautiful people driving through pristine landscapes. Understanding informed by emotional engagement—that's the key.

We need a radical reenvisioning of nature to include a strong sense of compassion. As the late evolutionary biologist Stephen J. Gould once claimed, "We cannot win this battle to save species and environments without forging an emotional bond between ourselves and nature—for we will not fight to save what we do not love." Embracing this approach, the IUCN has launched a "Love, Not Loss" campaign, arguing that we must replace the standard doom-and-gloom message with one of love. Our goal, they say, must be to help humanity to once again fall in love with nature. I couldn't agree more.

And the best time to initiate this love affair? Childhood.

Heading Off-Trail

Unlike many adults whose childhood nature haunts have been paved over, the forest of my youth remains. A portion of the Endowment Lands on Vancouver's west side has even been given a new name, Pacific Spirit Regional Park. The old trails remain, now well signed and groomed, some laced with wooden boardwalks to transport walkers, runners, and riders across muddier reaches. Professional dog-walkers leading ragtag packs of canines are frequent sightings. In recent years, terrific kids' programs have popped up, including day and night guided nature walks, something I would have relished as a boy.

Nevertheless, during my infrequent visits to this forest, I find myself disheartened by the dearth of young children, and the near absence of adolescents. Something else is wrong too: the magic of this verdant wood seems to have dissipated. Despite the sparkling new name, the forest feels tame, lacking in spirit. Perhaps it's just the cynicism that comes with age, but while walking those perfectly groomed paths I no longer sense the wildness that permeated my younger bones. "Stay on the Trail" signs offer frequent reminders that the old bushwhacking days are long gone.

Absorbing a place with all of one's senses means getting a little dirty, at least some of the time. The profound gap between on- and off-trail experiences is aptly summed up by mountain guide and philosopher Jack Turner:

> To walk a trail after bushwhacking is to cross mental borders:
> the border between lost and found, not knowing and knowing,
> nonhuman and human, wild and tame, hard and easy, danger-
> ous and safe, deciding and merely following . . . To walk a trail
> after bushwhacking is to dumb down.

I understand that there may be potential for serious ecological damage if we encourage mobs of kids to bushwhack through Pacific Regional Spirit Park as Tim and I once did (assuming one could actually find a youthful mob so inclined). But I wonder. Would it be too much to set aside a few sizable patches of forest, perhaps with a pond or two, as trail-free adventure playgrounds? The same could be said for urban green spaces everywhere. Nature connection is a contact sport, and nature can take it.

Equally important, of course, is actually getting kids into natural places. As summed up in a recent poster from the Child & Nature Alliance of Canada, "The best way to get a child outside is to go with them."

Too often we think of nature as something wholly separate from us, sequestered in national parks, forests, and seaside beaches that require organized trips. But nature is all around us, in backyards, schoolyards, gardens, and empty lots, relentlessly thrusting skyward through sidewalk cracks. If children are to grow into healthy, well-adjusted adults, nature needs to be integral to their everyday lives, from place-based learning at school to unstructured, unsupervised, even risk-prone play around home. Nature isn't just a bunch of far-off plants, animals, and landscapes to learn about and visit once or twice a year. It's an environment to be immersed in daily, especially during our childhood years.

You may recall the famous wild boy of Aveyron, the feral

child discovered in 1800 after living many years alone in the woods of southern France. Victor, as he was dubbed, failed to progress beyond a rudimentary level of speaking, reading, and writing, though there's suspicion today that he was autistic, and perhaps the victim of abuse in his earliest years. The point here is that a solo life in the wild does not produce a healthy, well-adjusted person with a deep nature connection. Instead, such isolation is likely to result in a broken, psychologically damaged individual.

In this book, my use of the term *wild child* refers to something entirely different—a child sharing deep connections with nature *and* people. Both kinds of connections are literally impossible without healthy mentoring from adults. We are social beings and, as we'll see, connections with the natural world are strongest when a youngster has multiple mentors. Nature connection thrives alongside people connection.

Returning to the frog pond story that began this chapter, the true hero was my mother. What if she had elected to stay home with me on that spring morning in 1965 instead of venturing into the local forest? Or what if, fearing risk or mess, she had prevented me from wading into that pond? I shudder to think how my life would be different if I'd been forbidden to enter the forest as an adolescent, or if our family vacations had not included hiking and camping. My mother made sure that I spent abundant time outdoors. By the time I was nine years old, she'd signed us both up as members of a local mountaineering club. We walked on a mountaintop glacier when I was ten, an icy image forever etched in my mind. She watched me carefully and asked questions about the things that most interested me. She told me nature stories great and small. And, until I was an adult, I had absolutely no clue that I was being mentored. I'm not even certain she thought of herself in this way.

Today, most kids face a denatured childhood, with potentially dire consequences both for them and the places they call home. We must find a way to turn the tide and reconnect children with nature. The indispensable key to success will be nature mentors—people just like you.

Many more kids need to experience a bootful of pollywogs.

The Goals and Plan of This Book

With *How to Raise a Wild Child*, I have three goals. The first is to ring the alarm bell and broaden awareness on a pressing issue—humanity's disconnect from nature. The current children-in-nature movement, although booming, is still largely a grassroots effort at the fringes of affluent white society. We have a long way to go before turning the corner on connecting kids with nature, let alone achieving sustainable societies. And, as noted, far more is at stake than how children spend their leisure time.

My second goal is to explore the process of nature connection. Critical questions include: Do we have a genetic propensity to form nature bonds? What kinds of knowledge are most effective in fostering a love affair with nature? How should the process change as children grow? What is the role of digital technologies? How can we engage kids, with their ever-shrinking attention spans, in the slow pace of nature? What kinds of nature—from television documentaries to city parks to wilderness expeditions—are most effective in forming lasting connections? How can we deepen nature connections for children in urban settings, and radically expand the movement to transcend socioeconomic and ethnic boundaries? Finally, given that the days of parents sending kids outside after school are gone, at least for the time being, how can we convince adults to join children outdoors?

Finally, my third and primary goal, comprising the bulk of the book, is to help parents, educators, and others become nature mentors for the children in their lives. Lasting, deep nature connection does not explode into one's consciousness in an "Aha!" moment. Nor does it come from learning a bunch of facts, equivalent to the rules of subtraction or grammar. Forming a deep connection with nature is an ongoing, multiyear process with multiple phases. Vital ingredients along the way include firsthand experiences in natural settings, learning through actively doing, storytelling, and understanding a few big ideas. To be most effective, all of these elements require mentoring, just as my mother provided for me.

We all live in some sort of relationship with the natural world—shallow, deep, or something in between. Today, the vast majority of us in developed societies are biased heavily toward the shallow side of this spectrum. Our challenge, then, is to raise a generation of children deeply connected with nature. Achieving this pressing goal simply cannot happen without the guidance of adult mentors. The ambition and promise of *How to Raise a Wild Child* is to empower those nature mentors.

The book is structured in four parts. Part 1, "Nature, Lost and Found," consists of two chapters that outline our problematic relationship with nature and the importance of firsthand experiences in local places. These chapters set the stage for the remainder of the book, focusing on the importance of experiential learning in nearby nature. Nevertheless, if you're anxious to get to more of the hands-on activities, feel free to skip to Chapter 3. In Part 2, "Essential Elements," we explore the key ingredients of nature connection, including the basics of nature mentoring and the role of a couple of big ideas to help scaffold learning. The third part, "Life Stages," includes a trio of chapters devoted to mentoring youngsters in early childhood, middle childhood, and adolescence, respectively, highlighting issues and useful strategies for each phase. Finally, "Obstacles and Solutions" tackles two of the greatest challenges facing nature mentors—digital technologies and urban environments—and offers productive avenues for addressing both. The book's final chapter provides a vision for how we might scale nature connection and transform cities along the way.

But, before setting off on this adventure, I must warn you: to be a truly effective mentor, you'll have to deepen your own level of connection with nature as well. And you'll need to open yourself up to new, more experiential forms of learning. The finest mentors learn as much or more from their mentees as the reverse. Nevertheless, if you follow the simple steps outlined here, I can all but guarantee that your life, as well as the life of your child, will forever be changed for the better. But please don't take my word for it. Read on and try it out!

Part I

NATURE, LOST
AND FOUND

1

Wilding the Mind

What Is Nature, and Do We Really Need It?

Nature is not a place to visit. It is home.

— GARY SNYDER

WE HUMANS HAVE a rather bizarre relationship with nature. We seek it out to stroll, run, swim, commune, and socialize in. Those with financial means bike, rollerblade, climb, skydive, surf, sail, bird-watch, whale-watch, and stargaze, spending billions of dollars a year gearing up for and traveling to these activities. While there, we collect bugs, rocks, driftwood, fossils, counts of bird species, or, most commonly these days, photographs. Closer to home, we grow nature in our gardens, place it in pots that adorn our homes, cherish it as pets, and hug stuffed versions of it to our sleeping bodies. Increasingly, we also consume digital versions—books, documentaries, movies, and videos—that allow us to travel to wild places without so much as stepping beyond the front door.

On the flip side, we also kill nature for sport and place it in cages for our amusement. We rip it from mountainsides, scrape it off the ocean's bottom, harvest it for raw materials, befoul it with toxins, and destroy it in vast quantities to accommodate humanity's sprawl. Most fundamental of all, we literally chew up and swallow substantial amounts of nature daily simply to fuel our bodily selves. How can we possibly eat nature and love it too (beyond the taste, that is)? What is this multifaceted thing called nature, and do we really need it to sustain our minds as well as our bodies?

Nature the Divine, or the Terrible?

Over most of the past decade, one of my favorite activities has been walking the hilly Marin Headlands close to my home in northern California. The patchy shrubs and grasslands afford spectacular coastal vistas and erupt into a kaleidoscope of wildflowers come springtime. The plentiful animal spottings include harrier hawks, coyote, alligator lizards, quail, mule deer, California newts, gray fox, blue-eyed dragonflies, ravens, and even rare gray whale spouts. Occasionally I've been startled by the last-second departure of a slithering garter snake or a bounding brush rabbit. Bobcats, in contrast, have sometimes sat a few feet off the trail, embodying that classic disinterested feline pose as I strolled past.

Here, the greatest threats to human life and limb are ticks and poison oak, or perhaps a sprained ankle. I'm told that mountain lions still prowl the headlands, but I have yet to glimpse one. (Oh how I would love to see a mountain lion.) In 2000, an errant black bear from farther north in Sonoma County wandered into our bailiwick, the first such occurrence in many years. Encounters with other humans are infrequent enough that it feels like I've temporarily escaped the anthropocentric world. In short, these bipedal excursions into the hills come close to epitomizing the idyllic nature outing—a gorgeous setting that replenishes body, mind, and spirit. I have been very fortunate.

Were I to have hiked this same spot 150 years ago—a span of only two human lifetimes—the experience would have been vastly different. That grizzly bear adorning California's state flag is no mere aesthetic add-on. For thousands of years, local indigenous peoples lived, and occasionally died, under the daily threat of grizzlies. Bears were still a dominant force when Europeans arrived. In 1602, the Spanish maritime explorer Sebastián Vizcaíno saw grizzlies feeding on a whale carcass and elected not to land at certain points along the California coast because of the sheer numbers of these giant bruins. As European settlements expanded in the ensuing centuries, the golden bears stood fast, killing livestock and looming large on the landscape. Somewhat ironically, given their name, gold was the bears' ultimate undoing. Within 75 years of the discovery of this precious metal in California—a single human lifetime—the state's grizzlies were wiped out, the final one in 1922. The last known human to die in a grizzly attack in California was lumber mill owner William Waddell, in 1875. A creek in Big Basin Redwoods State Park, near the site of the attack, still bears his name.

As I hike the trails near my home, I often imagine how the experience would change if there were a real chance of running into a grizzly—or wolves, which also lived here. Would I react differently to those rustling bushes? Would I pay greater attention to my surroundings? Would my sense of calm and relaxation be marred by that ever-present possibility of becoming another animal's next meal? You betcha. As author David Quammen notes in his wonderful book *Monster of God*, "Among the earliest forms of human self-awareness was the awareness of being meat." Having spent time searching for fossils in sub-Saharan

Africa—visiting places where lions, leopards, and hyenas still roam—I can attest to the spectrum of emotions felt when one is a potential link in the food chain. Living in cities devoid of big carnivores, we've forgotten that all but the last few generations of people lived with such threats daily.

When people first arrived in the northern California area around 13,200 years ago, they discovered a landscape more closely akin to the modern Serengeti than to present-day San Francisco. This was the tail end of the Pleistocene ice age, when the region was home to an array of awe-inspiring creatures: mammoths and mastodons, giant ground sloths and camels, broad-horned bison and horses, saber-toothed cats and dire wolves, American lions and short-faced bears. Of this mega-mammal menagerie, *Arctodus*, the short-faced bear, may have been the greatest terror. Weighing about 2,000 pounds and towering thirteen feet tall when rearing up, this massive carnivore would have dwarfed a grizzly. And unlike modern bears, *Arctodus* was long-legged, built for speed. Imagine rounding the corner on a trail to find yourself face to face with *that* creature!

California is by no means special in this regard. Wherever you live, an abundance of huge animals likely roamed in the not-too-distant past—a duration typically measured in decades or centuries rather than millennia. Indeed, for all but a few short geologic intervals during the past 250 million years (following mass extinction events), oversize carnivores have been present in most of Earth's ecosystems, both on land and in the oceans. Today we inhabit biological anomalies, impoverished shadow-realms in which large predators are rare, prowling the fringes of our world.

What happened to the wondrous ice age beasts of North America and elsewhere? The truth of the matter is that humans likely killed a large proportion of them. Following humanity's exodus from Africa beginning sometime between 60,000 and 100,000 years ago, we quickly extinguished most of the charismatic mega-fauna on every newfound landmass, whether island or continent. More recently, armed with boats and increasingly efficient hunting technologies, populations of whales and other sea-dwelling giants have been depleted more than 90 percent. I don't mean to imply that humans have never lived in harmony with their native ecosystems. They certainly have. But usually those ecosystems were first depleted of their big-bodied inhabitants.

Nature in its full glory is messy and dangerous, worthy not only of joy and awe, but fear and sometimes disgust. Maggot-filled carcasses and coyotes tearing apart week-old fawns are as much a part of the natural world as towering redwoods and soaring eagles. We humans came of age enmeshed in habitats at once awe-inspiring and danger-filled. In our sanitized Western societies, both kinds of experiences have progressively been lost, replaced by a utilitarian view of nature as raw materials.

Today, a growing movement seeks to reinstate that ancient sense of nature as divine, spiritual, sublime—a sacred ground of being with which to commune. But in our rush to romanticize nature, we forget the fear factor that is equally part of our wild heritage. What have we lost by rising to the top of the food chain and vanquishing the bulk of big beasts? In the words of zoologist G. E. Hutchinson:

> During nearly all the history of our species man has lived in association with larger, often terrifying, but always exciting mammals. Models of the survivors, toy elephants, giraffes, and pandas, are an integral part of contemporary childhood. If all

these animals became extinct, as is quite possible, are we sure
that some irreparable harm to our psychological development
would not be done?

Urban humanity now lives apart from all but a handful of the
persistent mammal survivors. What are we missing as a result?
More basic still is a question that would have been nonsensical
to our hunter-gatherer forebears . . .

Do We Need Nature?

A few years ago, I attended a fundraiser for an organization
seeking technological solutions to the world's big problems. I
struck up a conversation with one prominent attendee about the
ballooning human-nature gap. "I don't get it," the thoughtful
and clearly intelligent fellow replied. "Aren't we simply in the
middle of a long, inevitable transition from natural to manmade
environments? It seems to me that nature is pretty much a thing
of the past."

My initial reaction was shock. After all, every bit of those
innovative technologies is made of (often nonrenewable) ingredients derived from nature. And our supply of healthy air, water, and food ultimately depends on healthy natural ecosystems.
Besides, a large proportion of humanity still lives in a mostly
low-tech world where nature's effects, both positive and negative, are omnipresent—and worsening in many regions thanks
to rising global temperatures. Then there's the fact that we share
this planet with millions of other species, many of which are
even more dependent on diverse, healthy environments.

Yet heading home later that evening, I realized that this fellow held a common, even standard, view of the human-nature

relationship. Every major ecosystem on Earth has been impacted, most in fundamental ways, by our actions. Technological innovations over the past few centuries have leapfrogged us into a strange new, human-dominated world. Clothes, shoes, cars, buildings, heating and air-conditioning, packaged foods, gadgets—all separate us from nature, isolating our senses from surrounding landscapes. Vast numbers of us now go through our days with little thought to nature beyond the daily weather. ("Hmm . . . shall I wear the light jacket or the heavy jacket?") Even our worldview tends to marginalize nature. Cities were constructed on the notion that civilization's progress can be measured in terms of our separation from, and dominion over, nature. The unspoken message is that nature is something to be controlled and subdued.

It's an indisputable scientific fact that we are deeply connected with nature. For the most part, we simply fail to realize this connection. From the perspective of ecology, our bodies are made of all-natural stuff. Throughout our lives, we exist only as flow-through beings, constantly consuming and evacuating nature in order to maintain our physical selves. On and within you are trillions of bacteria, many of which are essential for your survival. From an evolutionary viewpoint, we evolved from nonhuman primates, which in turn were spawned by a multibillion-year cavalcade of mammals, amphibians, fish, worms, and bacteria. Greater than 95 percent of our tenure as humans has been spent living in intimate contact with the nonhuman world. Our bodies, minds, and emotions were fashioned by evolution in wild places where a deep sense of connection was essential for survival.

The key question, then, is this: Here in the twenty-first century, can we be healthy without meaningful experiences of nature? If the issue is exercise, certainly we (and our kids) can get fit in a gym or running around on well-groomed playing fields. Some may choose to hike, ride, paddle, or run in outdoor settings, but they could accomplish the same physical goals with indoor alternatives. As for mental fitness, aren't healthy human relations the key element rather than strolls in the park or mountain vistas? Perhaps, but before addressing this question further, we must address another, even more fundamental query . . .

What Is Nature?

When we think of nature today, too often the only images that come to mind are wild, expansive places like Yellowstone and the Grand Canyon, or even more remote wilderness like Alaska's Arctic National Wildlife Refuge. Viewed through the wildlands lens, nature is something you might visit at best a couple of times a year on vacation. Yet nature, even wild nature, is everywhere—in our backyards, schoolyards, city parks, and farmlands. Indeed, nature is quite literally everything, from stars and galaxies to planet Earth and the stuff in you. As Henry David Thoreau once claimed:

> It is in vain to dream of a wildness distant from ourselves. There is none such. It is the bog in our brains and bowels, the primitive vigor of Nature in us, that inspires that dream. I shall never find in the wilds of Labrador any greater wildness than in some recess of Concord.

If we're going to connect children (and ourselves) with nature, we must learn, as Thoreau did, to experience nearby nature often, and with our full suite of senses.

Environmentalists and like-minded others typically reserve

the word *nature* for the earthbound world exclusive of the human sphere, with the latter culled out as *culture*. For the most part, I shall follow this convention, though with some blurring of lines detailed below. Nevertheless, we must continually remind ourselves that humanity, although spectacular and unique in many of its expressions, is not outside and above the natural world, but embedded deeply within it.

We can divide the human experience of nature into three commonsense categories: wild, domestic, and technological. By *wild nature*, I refer to organisms and natural settings not substantially controlled by humans. This of course includes places we refer to as *wilderness*, among them national parks such as Yosemite and Yellowstone. Today, even in these places, humans increasingly dictate much of what goes on—for example, reintroducing wolves into Yellowstone National Park. Yet the day-to-day interactions of organisms occur largely on their own terms, in contrast to, say, livestock on an industrial farm. But wild nature is not limited to locales far from cities. That red-breasted robin singing in the backyard is wild and self-willed, as is the worm churning the garden soil, and the monarch butterfly passing through in summer.

By this reckoning, wild nature occurs in a diverse array of forms. At the wildest extreme are national parks and tracts of true wilderness like California's Ansel Adams Wilderness Area, encompassing greater than 230,000 acres of mountainous Sierra terrain and an altitudinal span of 7,000 to 14,000 feet. Near the other end are parks and nature preserves within city limits—places where plants and animals may be limited and heavily influenced by people, yet still function within semi-independent ecosystems. The Sims Bayou Urban Nature Center in Houston, Texas, is one example. With a diminutive footprint of just over an acre, this urban sanctuary features seasonal wetland trails and a pond with native plants. The aforementioned Marin Headlands in northern California, although a far cry from wilderness, would also qualify in this scheme as wild nature. At the more domestic end of the wild spectrum are urban settings with backyard birds, insects, and the many soil denizens; though their human-dominated environment may be tamed, these organisms exist as wild creatures.

The second category, *domestic nature*, refers to nature under human control. Here too we find a variety of expressions, from backyard gardens and green schoolyards to organic farms and urban parks—places where many organisms exist under direct human supervision. In this sense, your indoor potted plant and pet dog qualify as nature. Although many urban areas appear virtually devoid of anything nonhuman, the truth of the matter is that our cities are draped over ancient landscapes and watersheds that are still alive (if not entirely well), waiting for the opportunity to blossom. Most residents of Denver, Colorado, where I now reside, have no idea that they live on a short-grass prairie, one of the most endangered ecosystems on the continent. A central tenet of this book is that we must reconnect urban populations with nearby nature. Another is that we must re-nature—or better yet, *rewild*—our native places. The future of humans and countless other species may well depend on both.

Finally, *technological nature* denotes any human-produced facsimile of the natural world, from the cave paintings of Lascaux and the photographs of Ansel Adams to museum exhibitions and television documentaries. This category may seem counterintuitive, made up solely of culturally generated depictions of the natural world. However, as technological innovations speed us impulsively into an uncertain future, portrayals of nature are rapidly expanding in both variety and quality, allowing people to interact with stunning simulations, sometimes in high-definition 3D. So it's important to consider these virtual manifestations as well when contemplating how to connect people with nature.

Boundaries distinguishing the members of this trio are somewhat arbitrary. Whether one calls an urban park wild or domestic depends on a variety of subjective measures. Certainly many creatures living in these parks are wild and self-willed, living outside direct human control. Similarly, the boundary between domestic and artificial blurs when we think, for example, about experiencing nature through a window. Yet my concern for the moment is less with defining divisions and more about which of these broad categories we need most, and in what amount, to establish a meaningful connection with nature. This issue becomes all the more pressing as wild nature is rapidly replaced—both in actual abundance and human experience—by domestic and artificial nature.

Natural Benefits

Traditionally, psychologists have pretty much ignored the other-than-human world, rarely taking their studies of mind beyond the city limits. The implicit assumption has been that psychology is restricted to human social relations. A little reflection reveals the myopia of this view, given humanity's lengthy heritage in intimate contact with wild nature. In recent decades, several nascent fields within psychology have begun to explore the human-nature interface. For example, evolutionary psychologists now investigate the influence of biological evolution on the human mind. Meanwhile, ecopsychology and various other forms of psychological investigation examine the influence of present-day nature on us. Thanks to a bounty of recent research, nature's health benefits are now undeniable. Beyond the obvious cardiovascular pluses of outdoor walking, running, and biking, less well known are nature's other physiological and cognitive effects. Following are just a few highlights.

Simply being in the presence of natural landscapes tends to reduce stress and promote relaxation. Such experiences lower mental fatigue and boost mental clarity while enhancing both work performance and healing. One early study found that surgery patients recovered faster and required less pain medication if their hospital room had a window overlooking a natural setting. Another found similar effects in a prison population: prisoners with windows facing out toward rolling farmland and trees had 24 percent fewer sick call visits than their counterparts with views of an empty interior courtyard. Yet another investigator found that in contrast to urban outings, even a brief time spent in nature restores our ability to apply directed attention and working memory, both critical mental assets.

Since at least the 1980s, the Japanese have embraced a tradition called Shinrin-yoku, or "forest bathing," in which people take trips to a forest for relaxation and recreation. While there, they walk, breathe deeply, and open up all their senses, spending much of the time in silence. Cell phones and other electronics are actively discouraged. Recent research has provided scientific support for what the Japanese seem to have known all along. One study found that Shinrin-yoku practitioners experienced a drop of 16 percent or more in the stress hormone cortisol. In the forest, blood pressure tends to drop as well, while the immune system gets a major boost, increasing expression of white blood cells and anticancer proteins. At least a portion of these effects appears to be due to chemicals emitted by the plants.

Animals are another form of nonhuman nature with the capacity to promote health and well-being. From fish in aquariums to birds, cats, and dogs, a large number of studies have documented the measureable benefits of pets, including decreased levels of blood pressure, cholesterol, and stress. Various psychiatric conditions have been effectively treated with animal-facilitated therapy, and today many hospitals use dogs to promote patient healing. Research into so-called human-animal bonds indicates that positive effects are greatest for people with companion animals. No wonder, then, that Americans currently spend an astounding $50 billion per year on their pets.

Plants are good for you too. One researcher found that post-surgery patients with living greenery in their hospital rooms had significantly lower blood pressure, anxiety, heart rate, and pain level relative to patients in plant-free rooms. Numerous studies have documented the health benefits of gardening, or just being in a garden. "Horticultural therapy" has proven its mettle in promoting healing and reducing stress.

Even a few trees can make a real difference. A remarkable set of studies looked at the effects of trees on residents of two high-rise housing complexes in a low-income Chicago neighborhood. Compared with residents whose building was surrounded by barren ground, those living in a building with a view of stands of trees enjoyed substantially lower levels of aggression, violence, and reported crime, along with increased effectiveness managing life issues.

Over the past few years, increasing numbers of doctors have been writing "park prescriptions," encouraging children and adults to spend time outdoors in natural settings. This growing trend is driven in large part by the desire to get people more active and to lower obesity rates. The National Park Service has even gotten in on the act, encouraging doctors to write prescriptions for walking, biking, or kayaking in a nearby national park.

Most investigations of the natural world's impact on humans

have focused on domestic nature: plants, pets, and parks. Yet a growing body of research supports the notion that immersion in wilderness settings—places where humans are not in control, where nature is raw, untamed, maybe even dangerous—can have even stronger positive effects. Nighttime, starlit walks in wild places far from city lights are especially effective at awakening the senses and opening new windows of awareness. Such experiences tend to foster not only awe and wonder, but humility—a sense of something much deeper and perhaps even more meaningful than our human-centered obsessions. People returning from wilderness trips often report a strong sense of renewal and aliveness, as well as an awareness of connection with nature. No surprise, then, that wilderness has been prescribed as therapy for a spectrum of psychiatric ills, among them addiction disorders, posttraumatic stress, and various emotional disturbances. As I detail in Chapter 8, a long-lasting human-nature bond may just depend on periodic trips to truly wild places.

What are the effects of technological nature? My colleague and good friend Peter Kahn, a psychologist at the University of Washington, has spent years examining human interactions with the natural world, including technological nature. In one study, his team installed 50-inch plasma screens in windowless offices on the university campus to display real-time live feeds of local nature. Office occupants reported that these technological nature windows offered considerable satisfaction, and participants unanimously preferred this high-tech artificial nature to no nature at all. Yet they also found that the big screens paled in comparison to actually being outdoors experiencing real nature, or even experiencing it through a glass window.

These studies and many others appear to show that real nature—both domestic and wild—is far superior to technological nature when it comes to evoking emotional responses and connection in adults and children. Some may counter this claim by pointing out the blistering pace of technological innovation. Granted, one day innovative engineers may harness replicated matter, force fields, and tractor beams to generate hyperreal artificial environments akin to those of Star Trek's holodeck. Meanwhile, Peter Kahn's compelling argument is that technological nature experiences will continue to be impoverished relative to the real deal.

What about children? Do they enjoy the same nature benefits as adults? Apparently so, from reduced levels of stress and depression to improved concentration and problem-solving skills. Unsurprisingly, rejuvenated brains translate into improved learning abilities. Additional kid bonuses arising from nature interactions include greatly reduced symptoms of attention deficit hyperactivity disorder (ADHD), improved social interactions, a heightened ability to combat sickness, and a reduction or elimination of bullying.

As for truly wild nature, teens returning from one- to two-week wilderness excursions frequently report that these programs were among the most influential, worthwhile, and satisfying experiences of their lives. Most claim to have a stronger sense of confidence and better coping skills. And the vast majority express a heightened awareness, appreciation, and concern for natural environments. Critics point out that it's difficult to tease out the effects of wilderness experience from other factors such as the vacation-like quality of such trips, the achievement of difficult goals, and the group bonding that often occurs. Nevertheless, the positive effects of wild places seem clear.

Finally, children apparently mimic adults in their reactions to technological nature. Although human-made depictions of nature are considered enjoyable, their positive effects are substantially lower than experiences of domestic or wild nature. For example, Peter Kahn's team examined the reactions of preschool-age children to a robotic dog called AIBO. While the kids enjoyed AIBO, they were easily able to discern that it was not a living, breathing canine, and their strong preference was for the latter.

In short, although much research remains to be done, the emerging consensus is clear. On the whole, nature is good for us, both as children and adults, and real nature is superior to technological alternatives. Hey, even sharing space with a potted plant can boost your health! All of these benefits demonstrate nature's capacity to ameliorate "direct harms" to our physical and emotional well-being. Stressed out? Go for a forest walk. Heading to the hospital for surgery? Be sure to ask for a room with a view. Want to cut down on bullying? Get children playing in natural areas. Fair enough. But there's another, more insidious variety of harms even more deserving of our attention.

Impoverished Childhoods

Imagine a child growing up in a setting polluted with dangerous chemicals, unable to flourish because of the toxic load carried within her body. Although virtually impossible to see on a day-to-day basis, the long-term effects might include impaired development and lifelong impoverishment of body and mind, as well as premature death. Peter Kahn refers to such long-term negative health effects as "harms of unfulfilled nourishing." Avoiding such developmental harms, it seems to me, constitutes perhaps the strongest argument for connecting children with nature.

Today, many of us don't regard the natural world as an essential element of childhood. For evidence, look no further than the current trend to sequester children indoors, both at home and at school. In recent years, children-in-nature efforts notwithstanding, this indoor bias has only swelled. Recess is being eliminated from many school systems as administrators attempt to squeeze every last moment of classroom learning (that is, test preparation) out of the school day. Harried parents no longer find time to head outdoors with their children. Nor do Mom and Dad encourage the kids to play outside on their own. Instead, television and other gadgetry increasingly serve as high-tech babysitters. The negative consequences of this protective "house arrest" may be exponentially greater than generally appreciated.

Beyond the obesity, stress, and other negative effects of remaining indoors, recent research indicates that unstructured play in natural settings is essential for children's healthy growth. As any parent or early childhood educator will attest, play is an innate drive. It is also the primary vehicle for youngsters to experience and explore their surroundings. Compared to kids confined indoors, children who regularly play in nature show heightened motor control—including balance, coordination, and agility. They tend to engage more in imaginative and creative play, which in turn fosters language, abstract reasoning, and problem-solving skills, together with a sense of wonder. Nature play is superior at engendering a sense of self and a sense of place, allowing children to recognize both their independence and interdependence. Play in outdoor settings also exceeds indoor alternatives in fostering cognitive, emotional, and moral development. And individuals who spend abundant time playing outdoors as children are more likely to grow up with a strong attachment to place and an environmental ethic. When asked to identify the most significant environment of their childhoods, 96.5 percent of a large sample of adults named an outdoor environment.

In recent years, "forest kindergartens," also known as "nature preschools," have popped up in North America, though they have been around for twenty years or so in Germany and Scandinavia. The fortunate children attending these schools spend abundant time outside all year long, much of it immersed in play. Rain pants, boots, hats, and mittens are standard equipment, and daily discoveries of the damp, squishy, and dirty kind are celebrated. These schools embody the slogan, "There's no such thing as bad weather, only bad clothing." Studies show that kids in these schools experience fewer accidents and are more adept at assessing risk. They also tend to rate well above average academically, including in reading and math, and their teachers find them to be more curious and motivated.

Why is nature play so powerful? For one thing, it offers a multisensory smorgasbord of seeing, hearing, touching, and tasting, immersing children in a much grander world than can ever be captured indoors, even on a computer screen. For another, natural playspaces tend to be complex, with a far greater variety of unspecified props (rocks, sticks, mud, plants, etc.) than indoor counterparts. So they stimulate more creativity and imagination. Then there's that all-important sense of wildness engendered by birds, trees, insects, and various creepy-crawlies, along with the potential to create special places away from prying adult eyes.

We desperately need more research into the physiological, cognitive, and emotional effects of nature, especially the long-term impact of nature on childhood development. At present, it's impossible to state with any exactness the ideal mix of wild, domestic, and technological nature necessary to forge a lasting nature connection. Yet research insights and anecdotal reports rule out certain alternatives. For example, exposure to technological nature alone—from *The Lion King* to *Shark Week*—isn't going to foster emotional bonds with the nonhuman world. Similarly, domestic nature by itself likely won't cut it either, unless perhaps you grow up on a farm and develop close ties to the land. For most of us, deep nature connection will include regular contact with some sort of wild nature.

I'm not denying that domestic and technological nature can play an important role in fostering nature connection. They certainly can, as we shall see. Nevertheless, in contrast to these alternatives, wild nature seems to be an essential ingredient. When Louise Chawla of the University of Colorado asked a group of environmentalists to summarize the reasons behind their career choice, most identified two factors: "many hours spent outdoors in a keenly remembered wild or semi-wild place in childhood or adolescence, and an adult who taught respect for nature." Another study of 2,000 urban adults from across the United States, ranging in age from eighteen to ninety, similarly found that experiences playing in wild nature prior to age eleven were particularly critical in shaping both environmental behaviors and attitudes during adulthood. This does not mean that nature connection depends on outdoor experiences prior to age eleven, as we shall see, but those experiences certainly help.

The importance of wildness for falling in love with nature should come as no surprise. The human brain evolved over hundreds of thousands of years in intimate contact with wild nature. And let's face it—healthy relationships depend on recognizing and nurturing the autonomy of both partners. If we are to foster human-nature bonds, we must experience nature on its own terms, outside human control. On the flip side, daily, weekly, or monthly time spent in wilderness is neither practical nor necessary for forging a persistent nature connection. What's required is day-after-day, week-after-week exposure to wild or semi-wild nature.

"But hold on," I can almost hear you objecting, "what about the hundreds of millions of us who live in cities? Where are *we* going to find wild nature?" This question underscores a critical point. *Like beauty, wildness is in the eye of the beholder.* A child's perception of wildness changes with age and life experience. A backyard or empty lot with bushes, bugs, and an abundance of dirt, while ho-hum to most adults, can be plenty wild for a young child. Kids in early childhood instinctively focus on the immediate—flowers and earthworms rather than forests and mountain vistas. For children in middle childhood, a walk up a rocky creek flanked with trees is a wild adventure. Adolescents require more expansive natural places, including occasional wilderness excursions.

As we'll see, the geography of nature connection expands as children grow, but the foundation of a deep bond with the natural world will mostly likely be established close to home. Truly wild places are important elements, but they can be a minor part of the nature diet, particularly during early childhood. Kenny Ballentine, who heads up the Nature Kids Institute, describes this goal in his Nature Connection Pyramid, analogous to a food pyramid. This pyramid's broad base is composed of abundant, everyday experiences in nearby nature, and the narrow peak is composed of yearly visits to truly wild places. In between are weekly excursions to explore local nature and monthly visits to regional, state, and national parks.

We'll delve deeper into the shifting target of wildness in coming chapters. For the moment, let's simply define a key challenge. *Connecting children with nature demands that kids play freely and frequently in wild nature close to home.*

A Country of Naturalists

Indigenous peoples on this continent and every other have traditionally been expert naturalists who formed deep bonds with their local places. Native peoples continue to speak of this close attachment, and even co-identity, with their homelands. In the words of Luther Standing Bear, an Oglala Sioux:

> The American Indian is of the soil, whether it be the region of forests, plains, pueblos, or mesas. He fits into the landscape, for the hand that fashioned the continent also fashioned the man for his surroundings. He once grew as naturally as the wild sunflowers; he belongs just as the buffalo belonged . . .

Similarly, Marlowe Sam, a member of the Okanagan Indian band in British Columbia, states: "As Okanagan people, we are from the land; we are part of it."

European colonists, although certainly bearing more of a conqueror mindset, found that they too had to be students of nature to survive in the New World. In the bloody wake of indigenous decimation, new generations of naturalists set out to rediscover North America's wonders. The nineteenth century in particular witnessed an explosion of fascination in natural history. Nuttall, Bartram, Clark, Agassiz, and others steeped in the Linnaean tradition collected and classified legions of North American species. Birds, beetles, butterflies, seashells, and wildflowers were favorite targets, but Cope and Marsh expanded the scope to fossils, competing to see who could recover the greatest number of dinosaurs and other ancient monsters from the western territories.

As difficult as it might be to imagine today, even the White

House was occupied by a variety of naturalists. Early in the nineteenth century, Presidents Washington and Jefferson were both
ardent naturalists. Jefferson had a prehistoric giant ground sloth
named in his honor. A century later, Theodore Roosevelt proudly
brandished the naturalist label, translating his lifelong fascination with the outdoors into conservation of wilderness areas.

In the 1870s and 1880s, nature fever overtook the general
public, resulting in hundreds of small natural history associa-
tions from coast to coast. Membership in these societies surged
as people relocated from the countryside to towns and cities.
This public passion for nature translated into construction of
natural history museums, both in the United States and overseas,
to house and display growing nature collections. The Academy
of Natural Sciences in Philadelphia, the American Museum of
Natural History in New York, and the California Academy of
Sciences in San Francisco are all products of this period. By the
close of the 1900s, most Americans could describe themselves as
naturalists.

The nature craze continued early in the twentieth century
with more clubs, more museums, and more learning. Indeed,
an education was considered incomplete if one lacked a general knowledge of local plants and animals. The chief guide for
outdoor adventuring became Anna Botsford Comstock's *Handbook of Nature Study*. The Old and New Testaments may have
held sway on Sundays, but Comstock's *Handbook* revealed the
wonders of God's creations the remaining days of the week.
With abundant illustrations and vivid descriptions linking animals to habitats, she introduced a generation of schoolchildren
to fireflies, toads, dandelions, clouds, rocks, and robins. Comstock's firm belief was that experiential education in nature
should form the bedrock of education. And, while certainly not

all reached adulthood as naturalists, the practice of natural history was highly valued, both as an amateur pastime and a professional vocation.

But nature study took an abrupt and precipitous decline following World War II. Contributing factors included the mounting exodus from countryside to cityscape, further separating people from nature, and the reinvention of biology as a strictly empirical science focused on genes and molecules rather than whole organisms. Field observations, the bread and butter of natural historians, were replaced by replicable experiments conducted in sterile laboratories. By the time I began exploring that forest on Vancouver's west side in the mid-1960s, natural history had become a quaint hobby for amateurs. With landmark exceptions such as Harvard biologist E. O. Wilson, *naturalist* is now a label adopted only rarely by biologists.

Nevertheless, there's still much reason for hope. People still flock to museums, botanical gardens, aquariums, zoos, and science centers. They head to beaches, mountains, lakes, and parks on weekends, as well as to natural wonders on vacation. It's been only three generations, well within the lifetime of my mountain- and forest-loving mother, since the majority of people in this country shared a significant link with nature. Viewed in this way, our present mode of thinking can be considered a recent aberration set against a lengthy history of uniting people with their local environs. The capacity to fall in love with nature lies dormant within all of us, waiting to be reawakened. We're closer than you might think to rebuilding a country of naturalists.

How might we accomplish such a feat? By raising one wild child at a time. And, as we shall see in the following chapter, it turns out that the best place to begin is wherever you happen to be.

Secret #1 for Raising a Wild Child

A deep connection with nature doesn't arise only through peri-odic trips to national parks or other wilderness. While such trips can leave deep impressions, even more important are abundant experiences in wild or semi-wild places, typically close to home.

Nature Mentoring Tips

MAKE NEW HABITS

Changing behaviors is all about making new habits. So start a habit of getting the children in your life into nature more often. Take some time to discover the varieties of wild or semi-wild na-ture close to your home and explore these places with your chil-dren. For young children, it might be the local park, the school-yard, or your backyard. Even a few minutes a day is a great start. Chances are you and your kids will quickly discover that there's far more to see and do than you imagined. Most young chil-dren will have no problem engaging with their natural surround-ings. Their curious minds are built to do just that. Older children who've established a bias toward electronic screens may take a little more coaxing; this is where grown-ups need to exercise some imagination, and even foster a trickster mentality. Rather than telling children that they need to go out because it's good for them, think about encouraging them to play games like tag and kick the can. The key here is to establish nature as the fun and preferred option for playtime. And here's another habit to work on: the more you demonstrate the value of nature through your own actions, the more kids will tend to adopt the same value.

GET OUT ON WEEKENDS

In addition to giving kids a daily dose of nature, or "vitamin N," plan a few weekend outings for your family, or for groups of kids. Especially effective are those that encourage children to stretch their senses. Set up a short forest rope course and invite the kids to navigate it blindfolded. Or ask them to close their eyes and name every sound they can hear. Another easy yet impactful activity is to go for nighttime walks, preferably in a natural place like a park or beach. For a bounty of ideas, check out books like Joseph Cornell's *Sharing Nature With Children,* Jennifer Ward's *I Love Dirt!,* and Susan Sachs Lipman's *Fed Up with Frenzy.* Another easy and engaging way to connect kids with nature is to visit your local nature center. There you'll likely find guided trail experiences, naturalists who can offer guidance on what to look and listen for, and often exhibits as well. Nature centers are a terrific way to get started in nearby nature.

INVITE THE WILD INTO YOUR YARD

Bird feeders, birdhouses, and birdbaths are perhaps the easiest add-ons. Others include seeding native plants (which attract native insects) and adding a "bat box" (yes, to attract bats). If you're adventurous, relatively simple backyard makeovers—complete with rocks, logs, and pond—can turn some (or all) of your backyard into a natural wonderland, and cut down on grass-cutting! You'll be surprised by the numbers of cool creatures that will make an appearance if you only invite them! For a bevy of renaturing ideas, check out Douglas Tallamy's wonderful book, *Bringing Nature Home.*

MAKE THE SCHOOLYARD A CLASSROOM

If you're an educator, head outside with the kids often. Whether the topic is reading, math, science, or art, just being in a natural setting will have positive effects. Whenever possible, tie the lesson to what the children can see and feel around them. Make learning relevant to your local place. (More on that in the next chapter.) Note differences in behavior and attention span between indoors and outdoors. If your school doesn't have an outdoor classroom, think about creating one. This space could be as simple as some stumps in a circle, or as involved as a covered structure with bench seating. Once other teachers hear about how much fun your kids are having, they'll want to use it too! Organizations like The Nature Conservancy and the David Suzuki Foundation have lesson plans available online, with plenty of activities designed for schoolyards. In a later chapter, we'll explore naturalized schoolyards, which offer many more options for nature connection.

WILD INSPIRATIONS

Regular doses of nearby nature are absolutely essential for nurturing a deep connection with the natural world. Yet periodic escapes into wilderness offer another, entirely different, exceptionally powerful experience, a grand banquet of seeing, hearing, touching, even tasting that taps deeply into our emotions. No virtual simulation can compare to hiking a glacier-capped mountain, or a face-to-face encounter with a moose, fox, or coyote. Nature viewed on a screen is detached, almost imaginary. In contrast, a growing body of research suggests that immersion in wilderness not only awakens the senses and provokes deep thoughts and feelings. It also leads often to transcendent experiences that deepen the bond with nature. Does falling in love with nature require regular wilderness trips? No. Does such a connection require at least some wilderness time? Almost certainly. So make the effort to plan trips to wild places, whether for camping, hiking, fishing, or just hanging out.

2

The Power of Place

Discovering Nearby Nature

You can't know who you are until you know where
you are.

— WENDELL BERRY

TODAY, WE HUMANS—especially those of us in the urban developed world—exist largely without a meaningful connection to place. We are dis-placed.

I confess to being a shining example of such placelessness. After growing up in Vancouver, I spent seven years in Toronto, followed by six years in and around New York City, eight years in Salt Lake City, and another eight years in the San Francisco Bay area, before finally moving to Denver early in 2013. My story is hardly unique. In the high-tech twenty-first century, multiple long-distance moves, typically for work or love or both, are the norm. In my latest home of Denver, on the order of half of the residents are transplants like me.

Even for those of us who stay in our natal cities and towns, a meaningful sense of place is the all-too-rare exception. Each day, we travel paved pathways through neon mazes emblazoned with all-too-familiar corporate logos. Just as these corporations are generally based somewhere far away, so too the energy fueling our bodies, cars, and homes tends to come from distant locales. This fact applies equally to the information we consume and to most of the "stuff" that clutters our lives. Globalization has homogenized the industrialized world. Bolstering this detached state of affairs is the precipitous decline in firsthand experience with nature. Awash in a sea of sameness, we lack emotional attachments to the places we live. After all, if our lives are spent largely indoors, and if one place looks pretty much like any other, what difference does it make which of these we call home?

Perhaps all the difference in the world.

In stark contrast to our rampant placelessness, the overwhelming majority of humanity's tenure has occurred in the guise of hunter-gatherers intimately tied to their natal habitats. In addition to being steeped in local communities—cultures, foods, and social relations—people living in foraging societies have possessed detailed knowledge of local plants, animals, and landscapes. They have understood local rhythms—what month of the year a certain migrating bird arrives or a particular tuber can be harvested. Much of this knowledge has borne the mark of scientific investigation, involving careful observation, experimentation, and hypothesis testing. Terms like *traditional ecological knowledge* (TEK) are now used to refer to the detailed understanding of place that still characterizes numerous indigenous cultures.

Now, to make it clear at the outset, I have no intention of arguing for a return to "simpler" times, whether in the guise of nomadic hunter-gatherers or agrarian farmers. We are now a predominantly urban species, and any sustainable path into the future must embrace cities and technology. We must find a brand-new path into a more sustainable future. Nevertheless, if our goal is to reconnect with nonhuman nature, it seems reasonable that a good place to start is with cultures for which a deep nature connection is the norm. So let's spend a little time looking at older, more traditional lifeways in order to generate a new lens with which to gaze forward.

The Most Complex Structure in the Universe

As a bona fide member of *Homo sapiens*, you inherited a host of features that distinguish you from other mammals, including your close evolutionary cousins, the apes. One such feature is the oversize brain you are currently engaging to read these words. Believe it or not, that three-pound, Jell-O-like mass in your noggin is the most complex structure in the known universe, home to about 200 billion neurons interlinked by hundreds of trillions of synapses. Why are our brains so stunningly complex? To answer that, let's delve into a few other traits that make us uniquely human.

One such trait is our strong penchant for cooperation. Far more than other mammals, we humans collaborate in work, pool our resources, learn from each other, and rear children communally. And collaboration is a critical element of our success, enabling us to generate and accumulate knowledge well beyond that of Earth's other life forms. One individual may have an amazing idea — say, for creating a more effective tool — but it's only through collaboration that this idea can be fine-tuned, elaborated, and disseminated. Combining big brains with collaboration offers the potential of accumulating cultural knowledge across generations, far exceeding the capacities of any single person or community.

Another of your inheritances is an exceptionally prolonged childhood. Other species of upright primates (hominins) — from small-brained australopiths to big-brained neanderthals—grew up faster than humans, with a much smaller proportion of life devoted to childhood. Childhood is typically the most vulnerable time in any primate's life, with threats not only from predators but from older members of the same group. And stretching out childhood means delaying the onset of reproductive age, which would seem to run counter to evolutionary expectations.

So why do we prolong childhood? Why not push through that preadult phase as fast as possible, like most animals do? Historically, anthropologists argued that a lengthy childhood was necessary to allow our big brains to mature. Yet it turns out that human brains grow extremely fast, doubling in size in the first year of life and reaching almost adult size by five years of age (resulting in the characteristic "oversize" heads of toddlers). Clearly, then, there's more to the story.

One fascinating clue is the pattern of brain growth. In humans, the cortical brain—the wrinkly outer layer that enables higher brain function—develops rapidly after birth, so key aspects of brain development occur outside the womb, stimulated by talking, touching, smiling humans and a smorgasbord of additional sensory inputs from the surrounding world. In an effort to explain our remarkable pattern of brain growth, some researchers have focused on the importance of social factors, highlighting the extra time available for forming bonds with parents and other kin, and for building extended social networks. Other, more ecologically minded investigators have underlined the enhanced time devoted to learning survival skills. Perhaps they're both right. Perhaps the ultimate reason that we humans possess the trio of features cited above—big brains, collaboration, and long childhoods—is that they allowed for yet another hallmark of humanity: adaptability.

We humans are astoundingly adaptable, evidenced by our

unparalleled flexibility in homemaking. Whereas the vast majority of species on Earth tend to be adapted for life in a particular place—or at most a set of places—within well-defined environmental limits, we have the capacity to live virtually anywhere on the planet, from equatorial rainforests to Arctic tundra. From humble African beginnings, people dispersed around the globe. Current anthropological consensus is that our species, *Homo sapiens*, originated in Africa around 200,000 years ago and began migrating to other continents sometime around 75,000 years ago. The migration was rapid, beginning in the Near East and followed soon thereafter by South Asia, Australia, Europe, and East Asia. North and South America were finally added to the world tour around 13,000 years ago (though some investigators argue for a much earlier arrival). Among mammals, only the Norwegian rat even approaches the global range of humans, co-occurring with us on every continent except Antarctica (though, it must be added, rats accomplished this feat by hitching a ride on our ships).

Humanity's inexorable spread around the planet was accomplished entirely by hunter-gatherers, nomadic peoples who made a living gathering plants and hunting game. As noted at the outset of this chapter, hunter-gatherers invariably have a detailed understanding of their surroundings. Daily survival depends on knowing where to find food and water, how to avoid predators, and how to navigate the changing of the seasons. To give one example, here's what anthropologist Wade Davis has to say about hunting among the nomadic San peoples of southern Africa's Kalahari Desert:

> Hunting in teams, the San men watch for signs. Nothing escapes their notice: a bend in a blade of grass, the direction of the tug that snapped a twig, the depth, shape, and condition of

the track. Everything is written in the sand . . . From a single animal track, San hunters can discern direction, time, and rate of travel. Armed with ingenuity, and living in direct competition with serious predators such as leopards and lions, they manage to kill an astonishing array of creatures. With pits of poisoned snakes they lay traps for hippos. Risking their lives, they run upon the heels of elephants, hamstringing the enormous animals with the swift blow of an axe. Hovering near a lion kill, they wait until the animal is satiated, and then chase the sluggish cat from the carcass of the dead. Birds are snared on the fly with nets. Antelope are literally run to ground, often over a period of days. The San bows are short, with little power and an effective range of perhaps 25 metres. The arrows rarely penetrate the prey. They nick the skin, but generally this is enough, for the arrows are tipped in deadly toxin derived from the grubs of two species of beetles that feed on the leaves of a desert tree, *Commiphora africana*.

The kind of in-depth knowledge exhibited by the San hunters must be accumulated over a lifetime, beginning early in childhood. And of course, for such nomadic peoples, every place offers its own unique suite of challenges, requiring mastery of abundant local knowledge.

Our ancestors' ongoing need for place-specific understanding helps to explain the prolonged pattern of brain growth in humans. Baby brains are far more interconnected than adult brains. They're built for learning, imagination, and curiosity-driven exploration. Anyone who has watched a toddler explore a new setting—touching and tasting anything within reach—can attest to all three capacities. As we grow older and accumulate more experiences, our brains prune away weaker, less used pathways and reinforce those with the heaviest traffic. In short, whereas most animals tend to be hard-wired for survival in a specific setting, our brains are designed to help us thrive in whatever environment we find ourselves, adapting to local contingencies, both human and nonhuman. From a structural perspective, it's as if our brains start out looking like the myriad of narrow, interweaving streets of Paris, and end up resembling a bunch of broad, crisscrossing superhighways.

Just like every human in every previous generation, you were born with the capacity to live virtually anywhere on Earth, to become immersed in any culture, and to learn any language. This astounding adaptability, arguably humanity's defining hallmark, is due in large part to the trio of genetic endowments outlined here: large brains built for learning and imagination, a bias toward collaboration and information sharing, and prolonged childhoods allowing our brains to learn and conform to a bewildering array of settings. We owe our modern, high-tech world mostly to the evolutionary collision of these three features.

Topophilia: A Love of Place

A few years ago, I began to wonder if the hallmarks of humanity listed above might hint at yet another feature we all share: an inherited propensity to bond with nature. I was by no means the first to contemplate a built-in bias toward nature bonding. In 1984, famed biologist E. O. Wilson proposed that humans possess an inherited tendency to affiliate with other life forms, a penchant he called *biophilia* (literally, a "love of life"). A wide range of evidence has been put forth to support the biophilia hypothesis, from the health benefits of being outdoors and living with companion animals, to our apparent affinity for savannah-like environments, said to be left over from our lengthy evolutionary heritage in tropical Africa. Yet for the most part the scientific community has ignored biophilia (a rarity in Wilson's highly distinguished career), largely because the idea has been regarded as untestable.

In 1947, poet W. H. Auden coined a similar word, *topo-philia*—literally, a "love of place"—to refer to the affective bonds that people often form with the places they live. In the 1970s, geographer Yi-Fu Tuan popularized the notion of topo-philia in a cross-cultural examination of human bonding with both natural and cultural environments. I decided to borrow this neologism to put forth a new idea, the *topophilia hypoth-esis*, which proposes that we humans possess an innate bias to bond with local life and landscape, inherited from our foraging forebears. Let me explain.

Bonding is a powerful and oft-repeated theme in the animal world. Bonds between mother and infant promote infant sur-vival through improved access to, among other things, food and water, protection from predators, and heightened learning of essential behaviors. Bonding between adult males and females, particularly prevalent among birds and mammals, serves a simi-lar role, increasing the odds of infant survival by bolstering the father's input into childcare. The topophilia hypothesis posits that another form of bonding, this time between people and place, may have been similarly adaptive. An inherited penchant to form emotional bonds with one's native place would have helped humans acquire critical, place-specific knowledge.

Every generation of hunter-gatherers over the past tens of thousands of years has faced a daunting challenge—born with the physical and cognitive capacity to live virtually anyplace, yet required to learn to live in intimate relationship with a par-ticular place. Hunter-gatherer survival from the Pleistocene ice age to the present day may have depended on nurturing a built-in bias to bond with local place. Such bonds would have promoted place-specific learning passed on from generation to generation. The bond between mother and infant encourages mothers to devote more attention to their babies, boosting the odds of children's survival. Similarly, a bond between person and place would encourage individuals to affiliate more with their local environs and to be curious about nearby nature, enhancing survival through heightened observation skills and the accumulation of detailed, place-based knowledge. I've proposed that topophilia evolved to help humans adapt to a diverse range of settings, each with its own unique suite of life forms and landforms.

If correct, the topophilia hypothesis has broad implications for present-day society, from parenting and education, to architecture and city planning, to politics and the arts. For one thing, human bonding with nature is likely to be most effective when initiated early in childhood, during the critical phase of emotional development from the first year of life to six years of age. Another implication is that periodic exposure to nature in a diverse range of settings, from zoos to national parks, will likely be less effective in fostering bonds with nature than abundant time spent outdoors in a single, most likely local place. And bonding with nature will be most effective when aided by adult mentors. Most important of all, topophilia is at best an inherited bias, one that can be reinforced, dampened, or extinguished by cultural experiences.

Given that the blossoming of human-nature bonds is so tenuous, dependent upon specific kinds of experience and knowledge, we might be tempted to conclude that it is a weak phenomenon with minimal influence on mental and emotional health. However, if the human bond with nature has always been built upon cultural reinforcement beginning early in childhood, an absence of such reinforcement will invariably result in a lack of topophilia, regardless of its relative import for health and well-being. Just as mother-infant bonds are essential to the mental health of the infant (and the adult they will one day become), so too may children-nature bonds turn out to be critical for healthy development.

Whether or not we possess a genetic bias toward topophilia, it's clear that a deep passion for local place often develops, particularly among those living in oral, indigenous cultures. It's equally evident that the kinds of cultural reinforcement necessary for topophilia to bloom are intimately tied to a sense of place. The key lesson here is that childhood brains are literally shaped by experience, so we'd better be thoughtful about the kinds of experience we expose our children to.

Viewed in this light, nature connection isn't a philosophy or a religion or some new-age perspective. It's ergonomics, akin to fitting a chair to your particular body type so that you can perform at the highest level. Our body, mind, and senses are "designed" to connect with nature.

Experiential Learning

Having briefly explored humanity's roots, let's return to the central question posed in the first chapter: *How exactly do people form a meaningful, lifelong connection with nature?* Although the science of nature connection is in its infancy, a clear signal is emerging. As noted earlier, a meaningful connection with nature does not arise in a single, emotionally charged event, no matter how powerful. Rather, it emerges organically and gradually over many years, the result of a spiraling feedback loop interweaving emotions with understanding.

And a growing mountain of evidence suggests that *the best place to fall in love with nature is wherever you happen to be.*

After several years of poring over published studies—spanning anthropology, psychology, education, neuroscience, and biology—three themes have emerged for me as being most critical in promoting nature connection: experience, mentoring, and understanding. For the remainder of the book I use the shorthand EMU to refer to this trio. All three apply to every stage of childhood, though with different emphases, as we shall see. Indeed, we can think of experience, mentoring, and understanding as the three pathways through which nature connection occurs. Let's explore these themes briefly now and then return to them as necessary in later chapters.

First is experience. A meaningful connection with nature is forged first and foremost through firsthand, multisensory experiences, from abundant unstructured time in the backyard to weekends in the park and occasional visits to wilderness. Although nature connection experiences can occur indoors, we need intimate contact with the denizens and landscapes of our local places. Education too must be experiential, in and out of the classroom. Scientific ideas are far more memorable and meaningful when we perceive and reflect upon them directly with our full suite of senses. A deep understanding of nature must be absorbed through our eyes, ears, nose, and pores, as well as our minds.

Above all, we need to engage children in natural settings. Firsthand experience outdoors has the potential to stir our emotions deeply. As most of us know, smelling wildflowers, holding a slug, and beholding a full moon in an otherwise dark sky are all experiences that differ mightily from virtual alternatives. Chapter 3 explores the role of experience in more detail, though it will pop up repeatedly throughout the remainder of the book.

Second on the list is mentoring. In stark contrast to traditional teaching methods, the role of mentor is not that of the expert passing down information. Particularly for kids in early childhood, it turns out to be far more effective to engage in playful, side-by-side exploration. Accomplished mentors listen more than they talk. They model key behaviors. They observe closely, inspire curiosity, and "pull" stories from their mentees by asking questions that gently push the limits of awareness and knowledge. Being an effective mentor means becoming a coconspirator, a fellow explorer, a chaser of clues. It means allowing plenty of unstructured time, engaging kids in activities focused more on imaginative play than digesting information. We'll delve into the art of mentoring in Chapter 3.

Finally, the third component of EMU is understanding. Here I refer not so much to the accumulation of detailed facts (for example, the formal names of plants and animals), though they can certainly be a part of understanding. Instead, emphasis should be on understanding a few big ideas. How does the sun's energy flow through your local ecosystem? How does matter cycle around it in loops, moving from plants to animals and back to the soil? What's the story of your place? Where does your food and water come from, and where do your wastes go? Much evidence demonstrates that learning can be more powerful, and longer lasting, if you start with a few big ideas and then flesh them out through the addition of facts. In Chapters 4 and 5, we'll dive into the notion of understanding.

Relearning to See and Hear

Arriving at our backyard "sit spot," Jade and I didn't have to wait long before the familiar chickadee duo appeared in a nearby thicket and began chirping happily. A male robin patrolling his territory wasn't far behind, his pulsing crimson breast pumping out a gorgeous melody. Next to emerge, seemingly out of thin air, was a pair of song sparrows, who began a staccato of *seep-seep* calls. "I'm here." "Yes, I'm here too."

Suddenly, like a lightning strike, the calm morning was upended. The chickadees flew to a higher branch. All the birds switched to high-pitched alarm calls, echoed by other birds previously unseen. A host of avian eyes peered downward, searching. Somewhere in the underbrush, a predator had arrived . . .

When I began work on this book, I had a certain sense of self-satisfaction, convinced that a lifetime of outdoor play, hiking, and camping—including, cumulatively, years spent living in tents in remote places while digging dinosaur fossils—had forged within me a deep bond with nature. But researching this book destroyed that perception. Instead, I found that, like most of us, I was oblivious to most of the natural goings-on around me. Indeed I often impacted these events in negative ways.

My insights came in part from reading about "bird language," the acquired skill of understanding the meaning of local animals' calls and movements. Bird language offers a powerful tool to heighten our awareness of, and connection with, nature. Hunter-gatherers tend to be fluent in the local dialects of bird language because it can be a matter of life and death. A bird's call might lead you to your next meal, or prevent you from becoming some other animal's meal.

I decided it was time to learn bird language, and my daughter Jade, then ten years old, gladly joined in on the fun. Our guide for the journey was Jon Young's inspiring 2012 book, *What the Robin Knows*. By the end of the first month of regular visits to our backyard sit spot, Jade and I were beginning to see the neighborhood differently. For one thing, those nameless little feathered creatures chirping in the trees were transforming into distinct species, and even distinct individuals, each with a unique voice and character. Our journals soon included such entries as, "Pair of chickadees singing in thicket to west," and "Four European starlings sitting in Monterey pine to the south." Through diligent awareness (aided by a pair of binoculars and a birding app on my iPhone), we were beginning to see and hear more.

Although birds are nearly ubiquitous outdoors, rarely do we stop and consider what they're doing, or why they're doing it in that spot and not another. Because we've forgotten what it's like to hunt or be hunted, our implicit assumption is that birds move about almost randomly. But for most animals, predator and prey, random behavior is the fast track to premature death. If you're a North American songbird, predators come in various shapes and sizes, and threaten from every direction. Foxes and cats prowl the ground. Raccoons and ravens raid nests in trees. Hawks and owls attack from the air. Most feared of all, it seems, are *Accipiters* like the Cooper's hawk, a common but rarely seen aerial assassin befitting the title "Death from Above." Cooper's hawks are experts at killing birds on the wing, diving fearlessly into trees and thickets.

No surprise, then, that most songbirds have small territories that they know intimately, and tend to follow the same paths through these spaces. Along with understanding local geography, those robins, wrens, and ravens are fluent in bird language. Always vigilant, they listen continually for alarm calls, and not just from their own kind. A robin will react to the alarm of a song sparrow and vice versa. For the same reason, squirrels and rabbits know bird language too. The end result is a vast web of awareness that generates a local, ever-shifting "mood." If the mood is relaxed, "baseline" behaviors such as feeding and song dominate. If things turn tense, alarms will sound, silence may ensue, and animals often flee. Although we tend to ignore our avian neighbors, it turns out that the birds know us, and our pets. Why? Because it's a matter of life and death. Local birds even react in predictable ways to our behaviors. We simply fail to notice.

But Jade and I were starting to take note. We learned that the way we walk to our sit spot—slow and relaxed instead of hurried—can greatly reduce the time it takes for the birds to resume their baseline behavior. The biggest challenge in becoming adept at bird language, we found, is getting to know this baseline for a variety of local birds. Each species uses several different vocalizations, from melodious songs and subtle companion calls to boisterous territorial squawking and, in the case of hungry babies, impatient screams. Only by gaining firsthand understanding of this background behavior can one begin to detect disturbances that might indicate a predator's presence.

Yet even with just a few weeks' practice under our belts, Jade and I found our awareness expanding, and with it our sense of appreciation and even empathy. When familiar birds were absent during our sit-spot sessions, we wondered what they were up to. And we found ourselves slowing down more often as we entered and exited the house, listening for signs of the neighborhood mood. Wildness just outside the front door was helping us deepen our bond with nature.

Such interactions, I have come to realize, are essential to nature connection. If we are going to foster in our children (and ourselves) that all-important sense of internal wildness, we must first have abundant experience of external wildness. In the end, to be connected to nature is to expand one's awareness and become native to place.

The Great Triad

The mysterious power of the number three has a long and distinguished history. There's the Holy Trinity (Father, Son, Holy Spirit) and the trinity of self (body, mind, soul). Among the classical Greeks, Plato suggested that truth, beauty, and goodness are the primordial values against which all things can be judged. His student Aristotle, speaking on rhetoric, argued for three essential modes of persuasion: logos, pathos, and ethos—that is, appeals to logic, emotions, and the character of the speaker, respectively.

Combining the latter two trios results in what I like to think of as the *Great Triad*, embodying different kinds of knowing. All of us have had the experience of understanding something intellectually that has minimal impact on our emotions (street names or geometry, for example). Conversely, knowing may be purely rooted in emotions, fostering deeply held beliefs with little to no basis in reason (feelings of sexual attraction, a sense of connection to a particular place). A third kind of knowing is grounded in values and morals—a sense of what seems right or wrong.

Perhaps the most potent form of knowledge—the sort most likely to change behavior—arises from the union of all three. I refer here to instances in which intellectual understanding is bolstered by an emotional connection so as to affect values and, ultimately, behavior. For example, individuals who act on behalf of the environment, a political party, or some other cause typically do so because of a blended kind of knowing that includes head and heart.

Western societies today focus overwhelmingly on intellect and scientific truth, giving little credence to the role of emotions. We live too much in our heads, not enough in our hearts. This centuries-old bias often misleads us into decisions devoid of beauty. Any remedy, then, will include approaches to learning that inspire the heart as well as the head. Lacking a sense of what is beautiful, let alone sacred, knowledge is sterile, typically unable to influence worldviews and behavior (or doing so in dangerous ways).

Whether explicit or implicit, beauty, truth, and goodness are all essential aspects of learning and education. Value-free education is impossible. Simply by focusing on one set of things and not another, children gain a vivid sense of what grown-ups value, and typically come to value the same things. No wonder, then, that the great majority of children grow up to embrace the views and political leanings of their parents.

If adult caregivers keep children indoors and show no interest in nature, the unspoken value message is still loud and clear: the natural world doesn't matter. Conversely, when grown-ups exhibit a passion for nature, kids are far more likely to grow up with a similar passion. (To this day my daughter Jade still gravitates toward dead animals when we're at the beach, simply because I passed this bias on to her. My wife Toni is not entirely happy about this shared penchant for seaside carcasses, but she tolerates it.) So beauty, truth, and goodness deserve to be essential aspects of learning and education, and we must be thoughtful about how and where we direct the attentions of youngsters.

The lesson of the Great Triad is this: knowledge is at its best when it passes through our heads *and* our hearts. A strong sense of place rooted in emotional connection reveals the beauty of the natural world, the truth of our embeddedness within nature, and the goodness inherent in caring for one's home ground. Of the three essential elements embodied in EMU, experience may be linked most closely with beauty, understanding with truth, and mentoring with goodness.

Adult values are molded by a lifetime of experiences. Children and adolescents continually modify and hone their sense of what is beautiful, true, and good. How, then, might we engage the Great Triad to inspire a love of nature? In subsequent chapters, we'll explore what may be the most effective tool of all: experiential learning.

For now, I invite you to think about beauty, truth, and goodness as threads in a blanket, one that each of us creates and wears throughout our lives. You cannot weave this blanket for another, not even your own offspring. Instead, your role is to ensure that the child possesses the needed inspiration, skills, and raw materials (experience, heart, and understanding) necessary to make her own unique, vibrant cloth with a balance of all three threads. Oh, and there's one other essential ingredient: freedom. The wild child longs to be free, taking risks and pushing edges. Effective nature mentors, then, may start close, but the gap between them and the children in their lives continually widens, allowing space for sunlight to spur healthy growth.

Let's turn now to the art of nature mentoring.

Secret #2 for Raising a Wild Child

Children will tend to value what you value, so start noticing nature yourself, taking a few minutes each day to become more aware of the other-than-human world around you.

Nature Mentoring Tips

START NOTICING NATURE

As noted at the close of this chapter, a first big step in deepening children's connection with nature is for you to start noticing it. If you don't pay any attention to the natural world, it's doubtful that your children will. So when you step outside in the morning, instead of rushing to the car, pause for a moment. Feel and smell the air. Check out the clouds and the trees. Listen to the birds; how many different kinds of song can you hear? What kinds of birds are they? When possible, take time to enjoy sunsets, freshly bloomed flowers, budding trees, and the smell of newly fallen leaves. The goal is simply to become more aware of the natural wonders around you. Forming a nature habit won't take much time, and it will pay big dividends for you and your kids.

EXPLORE LOCAL NATURE

Take some time to discover the varieties of wild nature close to your home and explore these places with your children. For young children, it might be the local park, the schoolyard, or even your backyard. Once again, the key is simply to take notice. For older kids (six to eleven years), venture slightly farther afield; something as simple as walking up a creek can be a grand adventure. Or head to the local nature preserve. Where possible (and legal), get off the beaten path and do some exploring. Encourage children to notice nature with you. Most kids need little enticement. Make a game out of counting bird varieties that you can see or hear. Invite them to figure out which flowers smell the best. You don't need to be an expert. You don't even have to talk. Simply sitting down with them to enjoy some quiet time in natural surroundings, even in your backyard, can be a powerful experience for you both, especially as your senses awaken to the surrounding life. And remember that kids connect best with nature by physically engaging with it. So let 'em get dirty. Even encourage it!

VISIT YOUR LOCAL NATURE INSTITUTIONS

Although firsthand experience outdoors is essential for fostering a love of nature, experience alone isn't enough. Learning is also critical. Understanding can transform the familiar into something wondrous. Gazing up at a starry night sky is awe-inspiring, if we take the time to really take it in. But knowing that you're made of "star stuff" (and why) vastly heightens that experience. Fortunately, virtually every major city today is home to over a dozen institutions invested in reconnecting people with nature. Examples include natural history museums, zoos, aquariums, planetariums, botanical gardens, and nature centers. These places offer the potential for powerful experiences augmented by hands-on learning—the E and the U of EMU. Scientists and educators can assist you (and your kids) in shifting perspective so that you come to see the everyday world with new eyes. So, whether you're a parent or a teacher, take advantage of your local nature learning institutions. Support them with your attendance, use them as a resource, and think about volunteering. Amazing experiences await you.

SEEK OUT NATURE-RELATED MEDIA

From books to websites to movies, nature-related media offers powerful tools to promote nature connection. The experts recommend minimal or no screen time for very young children, but there are plenty of engaging, educational, web-based offerings for somewhat older kids. Books are arguably even better, because they encourage imagination. For many years, my wife Toni and I read to Jade every night. One multivolume series we devoured focused on owls. The books were filled with details about natural history, and to this day owls remain Jade's favorite group of birds. Stories are the key here. Engaging narratives that feature nature tend to make a deep and lasting impression.

GETTING STARTED

Here's a simple activity to get nature connection started. Take one or more kids outdoors into the backyard, schoolyard, or park, and guide them to find some bit of nature they're interested in. It could be a flower, leaf, tree, rock, cloud, or whatever. (Birds and bugs are great too, but sometimes don't stick around long enough.) Once they've selected their subject of interest, invite them to observe it very, very closely for just a couple of minutes—looking at details, touching, smelling, and (if appropriate) listening and tasting. Next, hand the children pencils and paper (best if anchored to a clipboard) and ask them to spend a few minutes drawing their chosen subject. Whatever they produce, be sure not to comment on the quality of the illustration, good or bad; doing so makes it about the art rather than the exercise. Focus instead on the details they've observed. For school-age children, the next step is to have them write something about their flower or rock—perhaps listing a few features, creating a poem, or generating a line or two about why they chose that particular item. Finally, have them share out loud what they learned or found surprising.

This activity works best with small groups of kids (or adults!), who are often fascinated by the choices and insights of others. The drawing is key because it engages a different part of the brain and enhances memory. One of the most important aspects of this exercise is entirely unspoken: having an adult mentor display interest in nature and in the children's observations. That's it. Observe, draw, write, and share. For more nature journaling inspiration, I recommend Clare Walker Leslie and Charles Roth's beautiful book, *Keeping a Nature Journal*.

Part II

ESSENTIAL ELEMENTS

3

The Way of Coyote

Nature Mentoring Basics

Hands-on experience at the critical time, not systematic
knowledge, is what counts in the making of a naturalist.
Better to be an untutored savage for a while, not to
know the names or anatomical details. Better to spend
long stretches of time just searching and dreaming.

— E. O. WILSON

"I'VE GOT TRACKS!" The excited yell came from off to my left, through the forest. I bushwhacked my way over to find ten-year-old Sebastian (a.k.a. Bash) with Jade, both faces pressed close to a dirt road. Other grown-ups emerged from the forest, responding to the call. "They're deer tracks," said Sebastian, standing with obvious pride. And sure enough, a series of two-toed footprints made by an adult deer headed away from us, up the hill, captured in the dust of a shallow tire rut.

Jade, who had migrated to the opposite side of the road, looked up suddenly and announced, "I think there's bobcat tracks here." A few of us hopped over, careful not to disturb the soft surface in the adjoining tire rut. It took a few moments to see the tracks in the sun-dappled shadows. But there they were: four toes tipped with claws and a large heel pad behind.

We broke small sticks into even smaller pieces, each about four inches long, and began placing them upright along the trackway—one for each footprint—to better visualize the discovery. As our search image improved, more and more cat tracks appeared, headed in the same direction as the deer.

I moved a few meters downhill in search of more predator tracks, but they disappeared. In their place, however, were much smaller, two-toed footprints—a fawn, likely traveling with its mother. The prints, much shallower than those of the adult, were difficult to discern. But slowly the trackway lengthened. More vertical sticks, and a deepening mystery.

About that time, Sam, the twenty-something leader of our Coho Salmon Clan, arrived. After a brief survey, he began asking questions, aimed mostly at the kids. "How many toes does the cat have?"

"Four," the kids replied in unison.

"What direction do you think the animals were heading?" Bash and Jade both smiled, pointing up the hill.

"Were they walking or running?" A brief pause, then both agreed that given the short spacing of the tracks, the animals must have been walking.

After a few more of these, Sam upped the ante. "When were the tracks made?"

Hmm. This one was a little tougher, but Bash quickly surmised that the tracks must be recent because they were on top of the tire tracks, and hadn't been disturbed by rain. Smart kid.

Then Sam dropped the question bomb. "Those cat tracks look pretty big for a bobcat. Can you think of any other animal that might have made them? Jade and Bash thought for a moment, and then both sets of eyes widened as they said, "Mountain lion!"

"Could be," replied Sam, still looking down, perched on his bare feet. But his nonchalance did not prevent a shiver from cascading down Jade's spine. A bobcat was like an oversize tabby. A mountain lion could be a real threat.

"So do you think the mountain lion was hunting the deer?" This last question from Sam hung in the air, causing all of our minds to race.

Several of us set to work sketching the tracks and writing notes in journals. We talked through the series of clues, trying to determine if the deer or the lion had passed by first or last. Eventually, the team surmised that a mother and fawn had traveled up the road within the past day or two. Later, a young mountain lion, likely a yearling, climbed out of a gully beside the road (leaving claw marks on the bank) and headed off in the same direction. Was the lion after the deer, even targeting the young fawn? Perhaps. We'll never know for certain.

Just as we were packing up after lunch, still pondering the trackways, a pickup truck roared up the road. The ball cap–wearing driver ignored our protestations and cruised past, flattening the sticks and demolishing the predator-prey mystery. An unexpected lesson in the transience of things.

Nevertheless, the rest of our nature scavenger hunt went well. After the trackway (✔) we caught newts down in a nearby pond (✔) and looked them in the eye (✔). We also found a feather (✔), a medicinal plant (✔), and later added the shed body casing from a cicada (✔)—all on the list. We did not manage to find any huckleberries or a yellow jacket nest, but no matter. The group headed back to camp late in the afternoon, satisfied with the day's adventure.

If you want to learn the art of nature mentoring, you'd be hard-pressed to find a better teacher than Jon Young. Mid-fifties with a slim build, piercing eyes, and a face etched by countless days spent outdoors, Jon is a world-renowned tracker, naturalist, and mentor. He's written several books, including *What the Robin Knows*, introduced in the previous chapter. He also co-

founded the 8 Shields Institute, which offers a range of products—among them books, recordings, workshops, and support
networks—aimed at helping people gain a deeper connection
with nature, and becoming nature mentors themselves.

I had first met Jon a couple of years earlier when Jade and I
attended one of his bird language workshops in beautiful Point
Reyes National Seashore, north of San Francisco. It was there
that I received my first real glimpse into deep nature connection. Jon was talking to the assembled group about the various
kinds of calls birds make when he paused and asked, "What do
you hear in the trees behind me?" We all listened. Nothing but
silence. "And what was going on in there a few minutes ago?"

"Lots of birds singing," someone offered.

"So what happened to all the birds?" Jon probed.

"Maybe they went somewhere else," another suggested.

Jon smiled and shook his head slowly. He proposed that the
birds were still there but had gone silent, likely because a predator had arrived. And the most likely culprit, he added, was that
aerial assassin known as a Cooper's hawk.

The scientist in me was skeptical. *How could he possibly
know this?* I thought. Birds don't sing continuously, and they're
certainly not present in all places all the time. But a few minutes
later another participant pointed out a Cooper's hawk flying out
of the thicket. Almost immediately the birds began sounding off
again. *Wow,* I thought, *this guy is good. I need to learn more of
this stuff.*

So here I was, once again with Jade at my side, joining about
200 other participants in a weeklong "Art of Mentoring" intensive in California's Santa Cruz Mountains, about an hour
southwest of San Jose. The group, ranging from newborns to
seniors, had a strong air of California bohemian. Clothing was
predominantly handmade or consisted of secondhand shirts,

shawls, and cutoff shorts in an array of earth tones. Most were running around either in flip-flops or barefoot. I felt a little out of place in my high-tech, multizippered REI gear. Jade, meanwhile, seemed right at home, quickly abandoning her shoes and running off to join the other kids.

At registration, we were divided into clans with names like California Garter Snakes, Acorn Woodpeckers, and Coho Salmons. The youths were further split into subgroups by age. Jade spent most of her days during the week hanging out with the nine- to twelve-year-olds, engaging in games and other activities such as hiking, tracking, soaking under waterfalls, and learning "primitive" skills such as fire making (that is, without matches). Most of us adults, meanwhile, engaged in a mixture of lectures and hands-on experiences aimed at deepening our understanding of nature mentoring.

The Nature Mentor

The word *mentor* comes from Homer's ancient Greek epic, *The Odyssey*. In the story, Mentor is a man charged with caring for Telemachus, son of Odysseus, and serving as his advisor. Athena, the goddess of wisdom, adopts the guise of old Mentor to teach the young prince to stand up for himself, and eventually guides him out to sea to find his father, the King. Telemachus emerges from this experience having ignited his own inner wisdom and strength. So we can think of a mentor not only as a trusted advisor, but as something of a trickster who helps another awaken to their full potential.

Okay, so what about nature mentors? Well, first of all, picking up where we left off in the previous chapter, nature mentors value the natural world and demonstrate it as much through actions as words. They regularly marvel at nature's wonders, seek to deepen their own awareness and connection, and probe mysteries that catch their interest. Yes, I'm afraid this is going to mean spending regular time immersed in outdoor settings. Don't worry. You'll enjoy it. You may even find the experiences transformative. Ideally, you'll also practice some of the core routines outlined below so that you can share stories with your child afterward. Your dedication will help motivate the child to push through those inevitable times when interest temporarily wanes.

When all is said and done, if you don't value nature, it's highly unlikely that your children will get it. Conversely, if you model this behavior, the kids in your life are likely to follow, and to see value in nature as well.

Second, mentors also pay close attention to their mentees. How does your child learn best? Through stories or hands-on activities? Alone or with other children? What is she most interested in outdoors? What topics and games capture her imagination? What are her greatest strengths, and how can these be brought to bear in connecting with nature? Where are the edges of her understanding and experience, and what are the most effective ways to stretch those edges? Being able to answer questions like these is essential. By watching closely over time, you'll gain essential insights into your child's passions and be able to use these to leverage curiosity and inspiration, key ingredients in deepening nature connection.

Third, nature mentors are active listeners and questioners, encouraging children to tell stories of their nature encounters and being fully present to hear them. We all need this kind of witnessing, and offering it to children will accelerate the nature connection process. Of course, youngsters often need a bit of prodding, and this is where the questions come in. "How did you feel when that happened?" "What else was going on when the rabbit ran by?" The right question at the right moment can help pull an engaging, memorable narrative out of what might otherwise be a few lackluster statements.

It's also important to point out what nature mentors are not. They are not the people with all the answers. To begin, you may have no answers at all, yet this won't prevent you from being an effective mentor. Even those with plenty of nature knowledge should share it only in judicious tidbits, allowing the child to discover answers on his or her own, often through direct experience. Mentoring is far more about asking questions than providing answers.

Nature mentors are also not the ones typically in the lead. When many people think about helping children to connect with nature, they imagine themselves striding purposefully out into the wild, child in tow, to teach the youngster how to chop wood or use a GPS or go fishing or whatever. Certainly some elements of mentoring entail exactly this kind of one-on-one instruction. But the vast majority of the time, it's best to follow the child's lead.

Kids of every age have innate longings that manifest themselves outdoors. Your job is to determine what those longings are and feed them. So, difficult though it may be, the better option most of the time is to push gently from behind rather than to pull from in front. Take your cue from the original Mentor, guiding from the back of the boat. Your reward will be watching the child's eyes light up with curiosity, propelling him to the next mystery.

In the end, nature mentors take on three distinct roles. First is the Teacher, the person who conveys information. Second is the Questioner, the one always seeking to ask that next query to pique curiosity and engagement. Third is the Trickster, the clever Coyote who hides in plain sight, able to leverage a child's longings to stretch edges. The most effective mentors limit their role as Teacher, focusing instead on embodying both Questioner and Trickster. The great news here is that you don't need to be an expert. The bad news is that you'll often need to stifle the urge to offer answers and think instead about how you can extend the learning experience with a provocative question.

But here's the most important thing. Nothing, *absolutely nothing*, will spark your child's passion for nature more than your own embodied passion for the natural world.

Okay, so what kinds of activities are best for connecting kids with nature? In *Coyote's Guide to Connecting with Nature,* coauthors Jon Young, Ellen Haas, and Evan McGown cite thirteen "core routines," among them mapping, tracking, journaling, and bird language. However, they emphasize that two of these routines are more "core" than the rest. Both are consistent with the latest research, as well as the EMU approach advocated in this book. Let's take a closer look at this dynamic duo.

Sit, Wander, Play—It's All About the Experience

The first core routine is the most obvious and the most important. It's also one we've already emphasized—regular time out in nature. Daily outings are best. Particularly for children, the minimum goal should be three to five days per week. Without such ongoing experiences, the process of nature connection will be limited. For young children, this outside time might consist almost entirely of play. From middle childhood on up, other powerful tools can be brought to bear, like wanders and sit spotting.

A *wander*, or walkabout, consists of moving through a natural landscape without any specific agenda or purpose. The wanderer's attitude is one of open curiosity. Ideal places are those where you can head off-trail whenever the urge strikes. The pace is usually slow, because rapid movement makes it difficult to engage all the senses and broaden awareness. A wander can be conducted solo or as part of a small group. It can be done with children of virtually any age, though the younger the child, the more you will need to pay attention to their needs. A sense of timelessness is important. So tuck away watches and other time-pieces.

Be honest. When was the last time you went out wandering, with no place to go and nothing in particular to do? In our overly scheduled world, with time seemingly in short supply, the notion of aimless wandering may seem frivolous, even a little wacky. But the beauty of the wander is exactly its lack of goals. Just being out on the land with open awareness fosters connection in ways otherwise impossible. And you never know what you might find out there—perhaps even yourself!

As a child and a teen, I had plenty of timeless wandering and bushwhacking. In retrospect, it should come as no surprise that I chose a profession, paleontology, grounded in wandering. On many occasions I've heard paleontologists talk about the importance of softening their awareness and opening their senses while out fossil hunting. If you search too hard, the fossils stay hidden. But if you develop the habit of moving slowly, easily, in the rhythm of the landscape and following your curiosity, the ancient remains of animals and plants seem to appear more often.

During my Art of Mentoring week, adults of the Coho Salmon Clan went on a daylong wander. I confess. At first it seemed rather odd for a group of men and women to set off into the forest with no set goals or destination. (Even I was used to devoting my wanders to a specific purpose—fossil collecting.) But we soon embraced the proper spirit and opened to the adventure. The rapid result was discovery of multiple mini-mysteries. Why were the California quails, notoriously poor fliers, expending so much energy moving to branches high in the trees as we passed by, especially when plenty of lower branches were available well beyond human reach? What conditions prompt two tree species, a redwood and a Douglas fir, to grow into a V-shape from a single united base? Other finds included a delicate, dome-shaped spider web, the hauntingly beautiful song of a lone hermit thrush, and a wood rat nest littered with acorn husks, debris from countless meals. We didn't have all the answers, or even all the questions, but pondering these discoveries certainly triggered interesting discussions. Late in the day I headed off on my own and reveled in the luxury of solo timelessness in a coast redwood forest. That night, we all returned to the campfire with stories to tell.

Sit spot is another activity, one with perhaps even greater potential to deepen nature connection. The aim here is to find a place where you can sit quietly most days and simply observe, using your full suite of senses. As with the wander, the best approach is to open up those awareness channels and stretch your senses. What's the most distant sound you can hear? Which direction is the breeze coming from? How does the air feel, and the soil? How many different kinds of bird song and other noises can you discern? There's something about sitting still in the same place, day after day, that enables an even deeper level of connection.

Sit spot allows you to get to know one little place in intimate detail. What kinds of plants and animals live here? When are you mostly likely to see and hear the various critters? How does this place change over the course of the day, and through the seasons? Eventually, your sit spot becomes an intimate friend you look forward to being with. And that friend has potential to be your greatest mentor in deepening nature connection. Guided by your sit spot, you'll develop a quiet mind and learn how to open your senses, both critical to being an adept mentor. You'll also learn the secret language of birds and deepen your connection with nearby nature.

Where should your sit spot be? Here's the rule. The best sit spot is the one you use. By definition, then, it will be close to someplace you spend time daily, usually home. For this reason, the front porch, the backyard, or even the window by the bird feeder make excellent sit spots. Although you may have an idyllic vision of the perfect sit spot, perhaps on the beach or beside a gurgling mountain stream, unless you live in such a place, you'll need to dial back expectations so that the perfect does not become the enemy of the good. Besides, you'll quickly learn that nature is ubiquitous, and that almost any place, including one in the middle of a city, has much to teach us.

One of the essential elements of sit spotting is stillness. Cultivating the habit of being still has multiple benefits. First of these is quieting the mind. As meditators have long known, there's something about sitting still that enables us to observe our frenzied thoughts and slow them down. Second, a quiet mind and body make it easier to open your senses and become aware of your environment. Third, when you embody stillness, the animals are more likely to make an appearance and go about their daily routines. Most of the time we have no clue what impacts we're having on the nature that surrounds us. To give a prime example, you'll soon find that it takes about fifteen minutes after you arrive for the birds to return to their baseline behaviors.

Most kids are able to initiate a sit spot practice during middle childhood. To start, you might want to join them and sit together or a little ways apart. Jade and I have enjoyed sitting together, and extending each other's senses by noting faint sounds at the edge of awareness. Many people like to take brief notes while sit spotting. Journaling can be a powerful tool to document and deepen your awareness and understanding. Rest assured that when you begin to visit your sit spot, many things will be happening that you will fail to see, hear, or feel. However, particularly with good mentoring, previously hidden elements and mysteries will reveal themselves, and amazing stories will begin to unfold.

Story of the Day

Second of the core routines featured in *Coyote's Guide* is "story of the day." For the nature mentor, this simply means encouraging children to tell stories about their daily outdoor adventures. With Jade I often start by asking, "What happened out there today?" or, "What was the coolest thing you discovered?" The goal is to get the ball rolling and then artfully pull the story out with further questions.

Granted, particularly at the start, most kids are reluctant storytellers. Your challenge, then, is to ask questions that encourage the child to go deeper and make unseen connections. Often the best strategy is to play on a youngster's passions. "Did you play kick the can today? You did? Cool. Where'd you hide? Did you get to kick the can?" For older children with some nature connection under their belts, you might kick off with, "Hey, did you see or hear anything new when you were out today?" Eventually, after some practice, the story-dredging typically becomes easier. The key is to make it fun. If, after a few probing questions, the storytelling is still a struggle, it's probably best to let it go that day. If you push too hard, story of the day will feel more like the Spanish Inquisition, and no one will be happy.

Storytelling can and should take on multiple forms. Most obvious is the verbal narrative, but other modes include journaling and art. Especially with young children, art can be a terrific entry point to tell stories. The child might draw a tree or a butterfly, or whatever captured her attention. With older kids, sketching and writing in a journal can be a powerful combination, bringing out all kinds of narratives. Poems are an especially good tool to encourage children to focus their storytelling. Whatever the chosen activity, it should not take long, a few minutes at best for younger children. And it definitely shouldn't feel like an assignment. As kids grow up, they'll love going back and looking at their nature journal to see how their observation, writing, and drawing skills have improved. The journal also offers a lasting record of advances in understanding, and of deepening connection. For an in-depth look at nature journaling, I recommend *Keeping a Nature Journal*, by Clare Walker Leslie and Charles Roth.

Another option is photography, sometimes included as part of journaling. These days, digital cameras are all but ubiquitous and of course kids love them. So you might ask children to go outside, take as many photos as they want, and then pick three favorites (or even just one) to tell stories about. Video is another option, but one that should be used judiciously and with extra care, because children often focus almost all their attention on the video rather than nature. Here is an opportunity for you, the mentor, to step in and model behaviors. You might start by walking outdoors with the child, observing things closely and stopping only once in a while to take a photo or video. Afterward, you could share images and take turns telling your stories.

One last storytelling tool worthy of mention is the nature table. Consider putting aside a table for kids to bring in their latest discoveries. Rocks, sticks, pinecones, and bones are all

fair game. You might even encourage the collection of live critters—bugs and lizards, for example—to be kept temporarily in
clear containers (with air holes added, of course) before being
released. A further step, if your comfort level allows, is a ter-
rarium, often made from a recycled aquarium with a lid added.
Terrariums allow kids to care for animals and watch them for
extended periods. At least a portion of the objects in this mini-
zoo can be changed out on an ongoing basis, as new finds arrive.
The beauty of a nature table is that it can be something your
child is proud to curate. Jade's nature table has been a great font
of stories, giving her the opportunity to retell key events to family and friends.

Story of the day can be done solo—through art, journaling,
or photography, for example—one-on-one, or in groups. Many
families have a storytelling tradition, often played out around
the dinner table. If your family doesn't have such a tradition,
think about creating one. Stories provide a wonderful way for
family members to connect with one another, often aided by
emotion-filled laughter and tears. Getting groups of kids to share
their nature stories can be equally potent. At the Art of Mentoring, group leaders use various techniques to entice youngsters to
share their tales. Sitting in circles and passing a talking stick are
effective strategies to focus attention and ensure that the storyteller has the needed time to tell her tale.

Perhaps most important, watching other children tell stories
may be the greatest inspiration for those who tend toward being
shy, withdrawn, and soft-spoken. Over time, reluctant storytellers often emerge bold and powerful, looking you in the eye as
they convey the excitement of their outdoor moments. Group
storytelling also has the added benefit of sharing knowledge.
Individuals learn from one another, and their own stories gain
deeper meaning as new insights are sparked. If you're a teacher,

consider instituting schoolyard nature excursions multiple times a week and circling up afterward. Kids might share their stories verbally, or with the aid of drawings or writings.

Done well, story of the day can transform a brief outing or a cold, muddy slog into a lasting memory brimming with meaning. But bringing that story to the surface often demands some mentoring in the form of questions. By tugging on various threads, you can help create not only the story, but the storyteller. What kinds of questions are best? Well, I'm glad you asked.

The Questioner

One day while Jade and I were out walking near our home in California, she spotted a tall bird sitting perfectly motionless in a clearing adjacent to the creek. "What kind of bird is it?" she queried. My strong inclination was to blurt out the answer, particularly since it was one of my favorites, a great blue heron. Instead, I turned it back to her. "What kind of bird do you think it is?" She thought for a moment and came back with, "Maybe a heron. I'm not sure."

"Great idea," was my response. "Let's sit here and watch it for a while."

And so we did. "Why do they have those long beaks?" I asked.

"For catching critters," was Jade's quick reply.

"So what do you think it's doing now?"

"Maybe hunting," came her response.

"What do you think it's hunting for?"

"I dunno. Probably rodents."

Sure enough, within a couple of minutes, the heron performed its classic slow-motion head bow, as if in solemn prayer, followed by a lightning-strike jab at the ground. When it rose up again, it held some kind of small mammal firmly in its beak.

"I was right. It's got a rodent!"

We watched as the giant bird skillfully maneuvered its prey within the jaws and then swallowed it whole, the neck contorting as the animal passed down the gullet. Fascinated, we stayed long enough to watch two repeat performances, as the heron depleted the clearing of its rodent population. When we got home, Jade immediately grabbed one of the bird books and paged through it until she found the correct entry. "Look, Daddy, that bird *was* a heron. A great blue heron!"

When a child asks a question and you know the answer, it's natural to want to share it. Providing the answer makes us feel good and we presume that kids really want to know. But this inclination can lead us astray. Oftentimes, our response ends the interaction by cutting off curiosity. Counterintuitively, children are often looking for our engagement more than our answers, hoping that the focus of their attention will become ours too.

By turning the question back on them, we crack open a learning opportunity, a chance for them to actively participate in solving a mystery. If I had followed my first inclination and named the heron when asked, chances are good that we would have kept walking, and that Jade would not have remembered the name later. A missed opportunity. Instead, to this day, Jade fondly talks about the hunting heron. (Rest assured, I've blown this same kind of opportunity many times by giving the answer instead of asking a question.)

Questions from mentors come in three flavors: easy, medium, and hard. Easy questions fall well within the wheelhouse of a child's understanding. Often asked in rapid succession, the aim is to build confidence and keep enthusiasm high. Medium questions, in contrast, are intended to stretch the edges of knowledge, pushing a child to build on what he already knows to reach a novel conclusion. Such edge questions are best offered only after a succession of easy ones. Finally, hard questions go just beyond the limits of a kid's knowledge. These are the mystery-makers, the queries that set up a search for clues that may last minutes, days, or years.

Coyote's Guide recommends the following balance of the three types: 70 percent easy, 25 percent medium, 5 percent hard. In short, the majority of your questions should be straight-up confidence boosters, with occasional edge-stretchers and very rare edge-busters. Most of the time, the asking sequence should begin with easy before venturing to medium and hard. Why? Because difficult questions often have the same effect as answers, killing curiosity rather than bolstering it.

Think back to the tracking story at the beginning of this chapter. Sam demonstrated his adeptness as a mentor by starting with a series of easy questions, like, "How many toes does the cat have?" and "What direction do you think the animals were heading?" Then he moved on to a couple of medium questions, asking when the footprints were likely made, and whether the cat tracks might belong to a larger feline. Finally, he ended with a mystery. Was the mountain lion hunting the deer? By the time this last query arrived, the hook had been set. Kids and adults alike were fired up, enthusiastic to search for more clues.

"Hold on," you might be thinking. "Surely there are times to provide answers as well as questions." Absolutely. Teaching is one of the primary roles of a mentor, and it's essential to share information. The key is knowing *when* to share. If it feels like a group really needs an answer, and you happen to have it, by all means pass it along. But first try to make sure that curiosity levels are high. Look at the faces of your mentees to see if they're truly engaged.

Mentoring is akin to gardening. Questions are like fertilizer; they help prepare the soil for learning to occur. After all, if the soil isn't rich with nutrients, plants can't grow, or at best they won't be able to thrive. Answers, in contrast, are more like trowels. They are sharp tools for increasing leverage and creating spaces for seeds or young plants. So, before you go into teacher mode, ask yourself if the soil is ready. Is your response likely to decrease or increase curiosity? If the latter, you're on the right track. There's no way to learn this skill except through trial and error. So get out there and plant a learning garden. Before long, it'll be overflowing with greenery!

Artful questioning removes the mentor from the role of expert and places the learner in charge. Our goal is not merely to talk about gardening, but to empower children to become gardeners themselves. From a mentoring perspective, it can be hard to break the Teacher habit (trust me—I know this from direct, repeated experience). But doing so will reap amazing results. A handy saying to remember is, go from being the sage on the stage to the guide beside.

So, as an exercise to build your Questioner muscles, try this experiment next time you're outdoors with children. Watch closely to see what they're interested in and start there. Ask plenty of easy questions and a few medium ones, refraining from offering any answers. If the children ask you something, deflect with more questions aimed at raising curiosity. Odds are excellent that you'll be surprised by the positive response generated by this approach. And if you're feeling a bit bummed that you aren't the one providing clever answers, console yourself with the knowledge that you have begun morphing into the Coyote.

There you have it. Three core mentoring routines: nature experience, story of the day, and questioning. These routines encompass the main elements of nature connection: experience, mentoring, and understanding (EMU). According to Jon Young, "The antidote to Nature Deficit Disorder may be this simple: get people to spend time in nature, and when they return, be there to ask good questions and catch their stories."

Going Coyote

Many North American indigenous cultures have stories about the trickster Coyote. In some of these tales, Coyote is the creator. In others, he plays the fool or the clown. Most often, he has the magical powers of a transformer, able to shape-shift into other creatures and hide in plain sight.

By now I hope you're getting a sense of the Coyote role played by nature mentors. Effective mentors are almost invisible. They deepen connection and learning in their mentees without even appearing to be teachers. They start by using the longings of youngsters as both bait and distraction. For young children, those longings likely revolve around free play. For kids in middle childhood, passions might be directed toward playing a game or showing competency of some sort, so you might ask them to head out to gather berries or apples. For teens, longings revolve more around pushing personal limits in the company of peers. As mentor, your role might be to organize an outing that meets these goals—perhaps ziplining or backpacking.

Particularly when established as habit, wanders and sit spots are powerful tools for opening senses, expanding awareness, and deepening nature connection. Rather than setting these activities as tasks, Coyote mentors build excitement by modeling the right attitude and engaging in the same activities. Afterward they exchange stories and ask questions that build confidence and probe the edges of understanding. Nature mentors are also active, unconditional listeners, watching body language and facial expressions to determine where interests lie, and when to insert a provocative factoid or another confidence-boosting question.

Returning to the great triad of beauty, truth, and goodness, these values are best conveyed not through teaching, but through modeling. It's not what you say, it's what you do. Henry David Thoreau once said, "You cannot perceive beauty but with a serene mind." Mentors, then, need to model a serene mind, taking time outdoors just to sit quietly and notice. Children will see this and soon follow, particularly if invited. Given that understanding is nurtured far more through active participation than passive consumption, good nature mentors model an insatiable curiosity. They ask leading questions and engage wholeheartedly in nature explorations.

As for goodness, the Coyote approach is simply to model caring and empathy for nature. Invite children to close their eyes and imagine being a giant tree. What does it feel like to have roots penetrating the earth, a trunk pulling water up from the soil, and thousands of green leaves soaking up sunlight? Or how about a four-legged mule deer, casually munching on plants and then stopping suddenly to stand upright and listen, turning those giant ears toward an unfamiliar sound? Through an invitation to experience the world like another animal or a plant, the child builds a sense of place brimming with "others," each with its own inclination and role specific to that place. Through this style of mentoring, beauty is revealed, truth is discovered, and goodness builds from within.

What about Coyote's role as fool and clown? There's definitely a place for that too. Imitating a raven's call or walking like a bear might be just the prompting that children need to make meaning from a nature experience. Acting things out—even if your imitations bear only a mild resemblance to the original—engages different parts of the mind, making an experience more memorable. And if things are feeling too serious, try reinvigorating the group's energy by hiding in the bushes and popping out as the kids go by. (My father did this on multiple occasions when we were kids, and always got a great response.) Nature connection has to be fun. Without this essential ingredient, children will quickly lose interest. So stretch your own edges and work on being the human embodiment of the trickster Coyote!

We'll delve further into Coyote tricks in subsequent chapters. Right now, with some new mentoring tools in your tool belt, it's time to turn to the power of big ideas, starting with the notion that everything is interconnected with everything else.

Secret #3 for Raising a Wild Child

Pay close attention to children's interactions with nature and follow their lead. Tailoring experiences and questions to kids' specific interests is the best path toward inspiring passion for the natural world.

Nature Mentoring Tips

HEAD OUT ON A WANDER

Get some kids and head out into nature. For at least a portion of the time, invite them to go ninja-style, moving slowly and quietly to see what they can see, hear, and smell. Remind them that the animals will run away if they're too loud. See what kinds of mysteries you (and they) can find while in this stealth mode—things that capture their interest. Then ask some questions about them. (What does it feel like? Does it have a distinct smell? How many colors can you see? Why do you think it's shaped like that?) Correct answers aren't important. The goal is to use your nature mentoring skills to stretch senses and fuel curiosity. Make sure you display your own passion for the discoveries that you find most intriguing. Consider making a list of the coolest things you see, or perhaps take photos of them. Afterward, go over the list or photos with the children and see if you can extend youngsters' engagement by playing with the edges of their understanding. If the child is really seeking answers, feel free to get on the computer to find them. Most important, have a lot of fun out there!

START SIT SPOTTING

Find a place in or adjacent to a natural (or seminatural) setting where you can sit and observe. Pick a place that's close—for example, in the backyard, courtyard, or neighborhood park—so that it's easy to get to. Remember, the best sit spot is the one you use! Visit your sit spot regularly, preferably daily or at least several times a week, and sit quietly there, observing with all your senses. If possible, stay for thirty to forty minutes, but even five minutes is far better than nothing. Listen for birds and other animals, tracking your observations with notes and pictures in a nature journal. If the kids in your life are seven or older, encourage them to do the same. Vary the time of day, enjoying morning, noon, and night, to see how your sit spot changes. Eventually, you'll come to know this little corner of the universe better than anyone else. With a little patience, anyone can learn the local "bird language," the acquired skill of understanding the meaning of local animal calls and movements. I have done sit spot off and on for years, and I find that I'm a much happier, more relaxed person when I make the time for it. In general, middle childhood is the best time to initiate a sit spot for kids, starting with just a few minutes at a time and building slowly from there. For adolescents and adults, there may be no better way to deepen nature connection. And you'll quickly find that this activity changes the way you and the youngsters in your life experience where you live. For more information, check out a pair of books by Jon Young: *What the Robin Knows* and *Coyote's Guide to Connecting with Nature,* Second Edition.

OPEN SENSES AND EXPAND AWARENESS

Whether wandering, sit spotting, or just hanging out in nature, it's important to fully open your senses and expand your awareness to everything around you. Encourage the children you're with to do the same. To begin, play with Deer Ears and Owl Eyes. Deer have amazing hearing, thanks in part to their very large ears, which capture the faintest of sounds. Try having children (or adults) cup their hands behind their ears and notice the difference in the sounds they can pick up. Ask them to figure out the most distant sound they can hear, and the total number of different sounds they can identify. Similarly, owls have amazing eyesight (and hearing). In this case, invite kids to soften their vision so that they can see as much as possible in multiple directions. Ask them to look straight ahead and move their outstretched hands forward from behind their heads to find the point where their hands first come into view. What is the most distant thing they can see? Then, on subsequent visits outdoors, pause once in a while to remind kids to use their Deer Ears and Owl Eyes. The mentor's role is to continually push the boundaries of the child's sensory sphere, helping her to see, hear, feel, touch, and smell the everyday nature that surrounds us.

BECOME A SNEAKER

One of the best ways to open your senses is to try moving with utter silence. Some call this "sneaking." Kids love sneaking games like kick the can. While attending the Art of Mentoring weeklong workshop, I learned another one called "firekeeper." Have a group of kids (or adults) stand in a circle. One person takes the role of firekeeper and sits in the circle's center, blindfolded. In front of him is a hat into which some jangly keys are placed. The activity leader then points to two or three individuals at a time, who attempt to sneak into the circle and steal the keys from the hat without being heard. If the firekeeper hears the "sneaker" and successfully points to her, that person returns to the edge of the circle to wait for another turn. However, the firekeeper must point to a specific place (rather than waving toward a general area), and you might allow them only seven to ten "empty" pointing attempts to ensure that the person is truly focusing on sounds. To up the ante, move from a grassy area to a place with more sticks and dry leaves. This shift in venue forces the sneakers to "fox walk," carefully placing each foot before putting weight on it.

QUESTIONING

One of the most essential nature mentor roles is being the Questioner. After kids spend time outdoors, ask them what happened. What did they see, hear, and feel? What was their story of the day? Make sure the bulk of your questions are easy to answer, particularly at the start, so as to build confidence. Then try a few tougher questions that cause the children to really think and stretch the boundaries of their knowledge and experience. If you happened to notice that a particular bird was singing, ask the children if they noticed it. Once in a while, if you think the children are really hooked, drop in a mystery—something you may not have the answer to that's just beyond the kids' edges. Then return to that mystery once in a while to see if they've made any progress on it. Or think about seeking the answer together. This activity need not take much time; a few minutes will usually do it.

Another strategy is to start with a living thing, like a tree, and ask questions that work backward through all the steps and ingredients that had to happen for that tree to grow in that place. So, for example, your questions might entice children to reveal the role of clouds (for water) and soil (for nutrients). Afterward, consider encouraging an attitude of gratitude, thanking the many partners that helped that tree to grow, among them sun, rain, soil, and previous generations of trees. You can go through the same process with any food item. The most important thing here is to get into the habit of asking questions. In addition to the lessons learned, being the Questioner shows how you value both nature and the children's experience.

4

Hitched to Everything

Place-Based Learning

*When we try to pick out anything by itself, we find it
hitched to everything else in the Universe.*

— JOHN MUIR

IT'S BECOME COMMONPLACE to speak of the "web of life,"
the notion that all the living things within any given place are interconnected by flows of solar energy and recycling matter. The
oak tree captures sunlight; the beetle eats the oak leaf; the robin
eats the beetle; the hawk eats the robin; and the remains of all
are eventually decomposed by a bevy of critters, replenishing the
soil and fostering birth of subsequent generations of oak trees.
In any given place, this sort of "circle of life" is interwoven with
numerous others, creating the web that sustains us and all other
creatures. Taking this notion to a planetary scale (and thanks in
part to the popularization of climate change science), we now
conceive of Earth's biosphere as a single entity—a single web.
Greenhouse gas emissions in the Amazon rainforest of equatorial Brazil can have major impacts on sea ice and polar bears in
the Arctic.

The web of life is a powerful metaphor. Yet it has its limita-
tions. In particular, web thinking allows us to perpetuate the

myth that nature is out there somewhere, doing what it did before people showed up (albeit perhaps with fewer species now than in prehuman times). Following this view, we humans are separate, ensconced in our technological cities, with nature banished to the outskirts and beyond.

One of the most cherished and deeply ingrained notions in the Western mindset is the separateness of our skin-encapsulated selves—the belief that we can be likened to isolated, static machines. Having externalized the world outside our bodies, we tend to be consumed with thoughts of furthering our own ends and protecting ourselves. Yet this deeply rooted notion of isolation is pure illusion, as evidenced by our constant exchanges with the "outside" world.

At what point did your last breath of air, sip of water, or bite of food cease to be part of the outside world and become you? Precisely when did your exhalations and wastes cease being you? Our skin is as much permeable membrane as barrier, so much so that, like a whirlpool, it's difficult to discern where "you" end and the remainder of the world begins. Energized by sunlight, life converts inanimate rock into nutrients, which then pass through plants, herbivores, and carnivores before being decomposed and returned to the inanimate earth, beginning the cycle anew. Our internal metabolisms are intimately interwoven with this earthly metabolism, constantly replacing cells with matter ingested from the outside world.

You might counter with something like, "Okay, sure, everything changes over time. But *at any given moment*, I can still separate myself from all other life."

Not quite. It turns out that "you" are not one life form—that is, one self—but many. Your mouth alone contains more than 700 distinct *kinds* of bacteria. Your skin and eyelashes are equally laden with microbes, and your gut houses a similar bevy of bacterial sidekicks. Although this still leaves several bacteria-free regions in a healthy body—for example, brain, spinal cord, and bloodstream—current estimates indicate that your physical self possesses about 10 trillion human cells and about 100 trillion bacterial cells. In other words, *at any given moment*, your body is about 90 percent nonhuman, home to many more life forms than the number of people presently living on Earth; more, even, than the number of stars in the Milky Way galaxy! As you fight the urge to head for a long, hot shower, remember that we are utterly dependent on this ever-changing bacterial parade for all kinds of "services," from keeping intruders at bay to converting food into usable nutrients.

So if we continually exchange matter with the outside world and if each of us is a walking colony of *trillions* of largely symbiotic life forms, exactly what is this self that we view as separate? You're more bipedal colony or superorganism than isolated being. Metaphorically, to follow current bias and think of your body as a machine is not only inaccurate but destructive. Each of us is far more akin to a whirlpool, a brief, ever-shifting concentration of energy in a vast river that's been flowing for billions of years. You're not merely *connected* to nature through the web of life. You're *interwoven* with it, living in constant exchange with the natural world through your skin, your breath, your food, and the countless microbes on and in your body.

Nature connection is about connecting people with nature through mind and body. Too often, environmental educators and others engaged in connecting people with nature focus overwhelmingly on the sharing of ideas and information, emphasizing the names of plants and creatures. But, as we've seen, true nature connection thrives only when there is a strong experiential component as well. Just as falling in love with a person usually requires shared time in the presence of that individual, so too falling in love with nature is based on felt encounters.

Having said that, ideas are also essential to nature connection and should not be overlooked. Big ideas, in particular, have potential to create a frame or scaffold onto which smaller ideas can be attached. This whole-to-parts approach—beginning with the big idea and filling in missing pieces—has proven far more successful at generating meaning and understanding than the traditional parts-to-whole method that continues to dominate education.

So what are the big ideas? I'd like to argue for two, each of which highlights a different kind of connection. First is the notion that at any given moment, everything is interwoven with everything else. This is ecology writ large, the web of life, and it's the topic of the present chapter. Second is the idea of connection through time—evolution, for lack of a better word—which we'll delve into in the next chapter.

If children are given plenty of nature experience as youngsters, they're likely to intuit deep connections with nature. My early childhood pollywog encounter, described in the Introduction, is one example. Yet such understanding is fleeting if not supported by the adult world. What happens, then, as kids grow up? Why do children tend to lose this sense of connection, even to the point of severing their ties with nature? For at least part of the answer, we must turn to one of the most problematic institutions of Western civilization: schooling. Done right, formal education can progressively deepen our intellectual understanding of and emotional connection with nature, nurturing the wild child within each of us. Yet the dominant forms of education today tend to do just the opposite, alienating us from the other-than-human world.

Taming of the Child

Science is the human endeavor aimed at unraveling nature's secrets. Yet, ironically, during my school years I failed to equate nature with science. For me, nature was more verb than noun, more joyous bushwhacking than static learning. Science class, meanwhile, was a sedentary, indoor affair punctuated by regular tests and assignments subdivided into sections like Introduction, Methods, and Conclusion. How many times did I learn the water cycle without once setting foot outside to stand immersed in that omnipresent Northwest coast drizzle?

Although I was blessed with a smattering of standout teachers (thank you, Mrs. Smith and Mr. Duncan), for the most part science was mind-numbingly boring and surgically cut off from the real world. Suffice it to say, then, that my early childhood passion for nature survived public school in spite of, rather than because of, my classroom experiences. I shudder to think how my life would be different if my parents hadn't fueled my interest in nature. Certainly I would not be a scientist or an educator today.

My experience is hardly unique. Our present education system, far from nurturing the wild child within, tends to be highly efficient at stomping out such feral tendencies.

Consider this thought experiment. If you were tasked with designing the ideal learning environment for children, do you think you would ultimately opt for four-walled rooms where students are required to sit quietly for long periods, ingest streams of facts in one-hour gulps, and endure incessant testing in hopes of receiving good grades? Whatever your answer, I'm quite certain that few kids would vote for such a system.

So why do we force our children to endure such a dysfunctional mode of education, generation after generation? Dissecting the history and present-day circumstances of our public education system is well beyond the scope of this book. Besides, many authors have written on this topic far more ably than I ever could. Nonetheless, a few points may help to provide perspective.

The origins of the American education system can be traced back to its Puritan colonial roots. For colonial Calvinists in New England, school was intended to inculcate moral and religious values. In the Calvinist worldview, humans were born into original sin, which in turn was embodied by the untamed natural world. In the words of environmentalist Paul Shepard, "Nothing so clearly identifies the West as the distrust of the powers of the earth focused at last upon the undomesticatable wildness within."

Horace Mann, often touted as the father of the American education system, lived during the time of the Industrial Revolution. Although he saw schooling as a means to protect democratic rather than Puritan values, his focus remained on control rather than freedom, on taming rather than wildness. In an 1849 article, Mann wrote, "Those whose minds and hearts have been trained and disciplined by education, have control over their passions." The Massachusetts school system that Mann helped to create became the national model.

But hasn't institutionalized education in the United States transformed fundamentally since then? Well, it's certainly fair to say that education has not been static. "Education reform" has long been a ubiquitous phrase in American cultural and political circles. Yet the roots of our system have persisted relatively intact, and any outsider could easily conclude—correctly, I'm afraid—that we have yet to get education right.

In short, the origins of our education system have had persistent consequences; its original DNA has been passed on generation after generation, seemingly with little notice. At the risk of sounding overly harsh, public education in North America today is still geared toward control, obedience, and self-restraint much more than engagement, inspiration, and empowerment.

John Gatto, twice chosen New York State's teacher of the year, describes it this way:

> The secret of American schooling is that it doesn't teach the way children learn, and it isn't supposed to. School was engineered to serve a concealed command economy and an increasingly layered social order; it wasn't made for the benefit of kids and families as those people would define their own needs . . . Initiating, creating, doing, reflecting, freely associating, enjoying privacy—these are precisely what the structures of schooling are set up to prevent.

Today, the lion's share of effort in public schools is devoted to teaching math and reading, with science, social studies, and other topics receiving short shrift. Yet we struggle mightily even in our priority areas. According to the "Nation's Report Card" for 2013, 59 percent of American fourth-grade students and 66 percent of eighth-grade students scored below proficient in math. For reading, those numbers are 66 percent below proficient for both fourth and eighth graders. These days we hear a lot about STEM (science, technology, engineering, and mathematics), but STEM advocates have largely ignored important research findings related to nature-focused, outdoor learning (see below), focusing instead on indoor pursuits more closely tied to engineering, technology, and the physical sciences.

As was the case for most of the twentieth century, careerism is currently the lens through which we see and evaluate education reform, preparing students to successfully enter consumer society—that is, to be "upwardly mobile." Although we're well aware of the environmental calamity facing us today, and the fundamental role that "consumers" play in accelerating our pace toward disaster, education (K–16) is still organized as if no such specter sits out there on the horizon.

Recent education reform has targeted teaching performance, shifting blame toward the educators. With rare exceptions, the public school educators I've met yearn to make a difference in the lives of kids, to engage them in creative explorations and to inspire them to greatness. Yes, we need many more great teachers in our schools, but teachers are trapped in the current system every bit as much as students, typically forced to teach to the test or find another career. With minimal time available for creative approaches to learning, let alone providing individual attention to students, learning becomes focused on passive storage rather than active engagement.

We might consider following the lead of Finland, which, famously, continues to rate at or near the top in global assessments of education. The Finns have transformed teaching into a high-status, well-paid profession akin to medicine. With greatly increased salaries and much higher standards, the very best teachers are recruited and offered appropriate kinds of training before and after receiving their education certificates. Finland's education system differs in other fundamental ways. In particular, from early childhood onward, strong emphasis is placed on experiential education, much of it occurring outdoors. More on that shortly.

Beyond teaching and testing, however, perhaps the greatest problem with our current education system is its irrelevance to everyday life. The curriculum taught daily in the vast majority of classrooms in San Francisco and Houston could be freely interchanged with those in New York, Toledo, or New Orleans. Beyond the self-serving (and often distant) hope of one day earning enough money for "the good life," most of what students learn in school has little or nothing to do with their lives outside the school walls. When classroom learning is disconnected from the real, lived world, should we be surprised when students disengage or even drop out?

Of course, I speak here in gross generalities. Today, many thousands of outstanding teachers across the United States and throughout the world are engaging students and inspiring them to pursue their dreams. Similarly, thousands of schools are embracing radically different, often "wilder" approaches to learning, with numerous lessons for nature mentors. It's high time we studied these successful models and made transformational changes to our education system, including shifting away from the relentless emphasis on testing so as to free up teachers to explore other learning modes.

Learning in Place

Let's step back for a moment and imagine some of the qualities we might want to see in a reinvented, truly student-centered learning environment. Such a setting would celebrate students' autonomy and individuality, building on strengths and interests to drive curiosity. It would foster (rather than choke) inspiration and engagement through plenty of active, real-world experiences, many of them beyond the classroom walls. Emphasis would be on character development grounded in fundamental values, like beauty, truth, and goodness. And, if truly successful, this system would engender a deep-seated, resilient sense of wonder that, in turn, would translate into a lifelong love of learning.

Remarkably, a robust movement has recently emerged within education that embodies all of these qualities. So far the various factions of this movement are only disparately connected and known by a variety of names, including place-based education, experiential education, environmental education, education for sustainability, and expeditionary learning. Schools in the traditions of Steiner (Waldorf) and Montessori have long been at the forefront of this movement. While the various approaches listed above don't always align completely (for example, some experiential education schools do not focus on local nature), such differences are overwhelmed by commonalities, including experiential, inquiry-driven, hands-on, project-based, often outdoor learning, with built-in time for reflection. In part because words like *environment* and *sustainability* carry such a high connotation load, I prefer the more neutral term, *place-based education*.

At its best, place-based education uses the local community—encompassing nearby nature and culture—as the foundation for the entire curriculum. Whether the subject is math, language arts, science, or social studies, emphasis is on real-world experiences and integrative projects for which the surrounding community is the entry point. These projects often entail in-depth study that transcends traditional disciplinary boundaries, integrating, say, science, math, art, and language. Starting with the local turns out to be an effective way not only to communicate ideas, but to deepen the meaning of education. Community service is a common feature, with students engaging in such activities as growing gardens and reclaiming streams, planting trees and launching recycling programs. Another important element is that teachers and students typically assume some control over the curriculum, co-creating content based upon shared interests and collaborative efforts.

Far from being parochial, place-based learning uses direct

experiences in local landscapes to inform larger-scale explorations. Much better to understand and intimately experience one's local oak or fir forest before diving into books and videos about the disappearing Amazon rainforest. Even if the topic relates to historical events in some far-off place (say, the Vietnam War), it's often possible to begin in one's own community (for example, by interviewing Vietnam vets). The philosophy is that active learning requires firsthand experience, which of course is typically limited to the local region.

In contrast to the careerism ("learn to earn") model of schooling currently dominant, place-based education is grounded in values such as community, sustainability, and beauty—promoting exactly the kind of radical shift required if we are to renew the human-nature bond and preserve a viable planetary ecology and economy. Innovative educators have shown again and again that local surroundings provide an engaging context to communicate virtually any topic, from history and math to reading and science.

American schools, which rank about twentieth in the world, are leaning toward more and more classroom hours, accumulated through a longer school day and less time devoted to lunch and recess. In contrast, back in high-ranking Finland, educators are opting for shorter school hours and more playtime. Much of this play occurs outdoors in natural settings, even in the chilly Scandinavian winter months. In fact, alongside their regular recess, kids often get fifteen minutes of outdoor play between lessons! The Finns also give their teachers much greater independence to teach the curriculum.

The emphasis on outdoor learning and play is also being pioneered for younger children through "forest kindergartens," which originated in Europe and are now popping up around North America and elsewhere. Even in relatively nature-poor, densely populated cities, these forest schools are gaining a foothold. Aimed mostly at three- to six-year-olds, these institutions encourage play and learning in outdoor settings year-round. Rather than commercial toys, play objects consist mostly of natural, readily available "loose parts." If you're imagining miserable kids shivering in the cold or standing around in the muck, think again. By all reports, the children thrive outdoors. The setting also tends to boost immune systems while improving such physical traits as balance and agility. Counterintuitively, kids at forest schools have a lower incidence of accidents, in part because they learn to assess risks and gain confidence by moving through a range of settings.

Education's traditional emphasis on the "3 Rs"—reading, 'riting, and 'rithmetic—has provided students with essential tools useful in a range of situations. Yet if children are isolated from local nature by four-walled classrooms and homes, they miss the meaning and beauty of changing seasons, of birdsong and rainstorms. They ignore the ugliness of the built environment, and remain blind to deteriorating habitats.

David Orr, professor of environmental studies at Oberlin College, has written, "All education is environmental education . . . By what is included or excluded, students are taught that they are part of, or apart from, the natural world." Orr's critical point is that failing to include the environment as a part of schooling sends an unspoken, yet crystal clear message: the environment doesn't matter. By rooting learning in the local, students come to understand how their place came to be, how it works today, and what it needs to thrive in the future.

The notion of experiential, place-based learning is by no means a recent innovation. Famed philosopher and psychologist John Dewey advocated for this approach in his landmark 1938 book, *Experience and Education*. More recently, David Sobel and other experiential learning proponents have made strong arguments in support of place-based education. And multiple studies now demonstrate that this approach, along with fostering community engagement and a lasting sense of nature connection, boosts academic performance across the board. One nine-year survey of place-based education—encompassing thousands of surveys and interviews of teachers and students across 100 urban, suburban, and rural schools in twelve states—concluded that,

> The findings are clear: place-based education fosters students' connection to place and creates vibrant partnerships between schools and communities. It boosts student achievement and improves environmental, social, and economic vitality. In short, place-based education helps students learn to take care of the world by understanding where they live and taking action in their own backyards and communities.

One of Sobel's mantras is "No tragedies before fourth grade." Too often we teach young children about climate change, species extinctions, and vanishing habitats before they've even had a chance to connect with the natural world. Rather than engagement, the result is often alienation, with children feeling a great sense of loss and pessimism about the future. So, before we burden kids with the crises of our time, let them establish a bond with nature. Once they care, protection will follow. Of course, in this age of ever-flowing, media-driven information, most young children will hear about climate change and other environmental crises. We might compare this situation with media frenzies that surround school shootings, where our role is to honestly explain the situation without fostering fear.

Place-based learning is a powerful education approach

whose time has come. And it isn't just for schoolteachers. To fully take root, parents, caregivers, and informal educators must embrace this revolutionary approach (along with other nature mentors). Educators exposed to place-based learning typically acknowledge its value and potential. Yet several obstacles—including lack of awareness, minimal background in both science and local nature, the inertia of test-driven learning, class sizes, and a shortage of resources for professional development—have inhibited its widespread adoption.

Due to the entrenched nature of the American education system, with local control administered through school districts, a complete overhaul of schooling will take many years. Nevertheless, a vital first step could be taken by bumping up the amount of learning and free play outdoors, and by embracing the schoolyard as a learning environment. If you're a parent, consider working through the PTA or another avenue to ask for more place-based elements in the curriculum, more outdoor time for kids on the school grounds, and more experiential-learning field trips in natural settings. In the end, lasting change to our education system will occur when we demonstrate conclusively, through numerous examples in diverse settings, that this mode of learning outstrips more traditional schooling in promoting overall academic performance and healthy growth of children.

Finally, it's also worth noting that it isn't just the kids who benefit from taking the learning outdoors. Teachers are the winners as well. A study conducted by King's College London in the United Kingdom revealed that teaching outdoors builds the confidence and enthusiasm of educators, and fosters more innovative teaching strategies as well. In addition, teaching can be a highly stressful profession, so anything that ameliorates this stress during the school day can only be a net positive.

Natural settings, even a tree or schoolyard garden, can have calming physiological effects that result in higher levels of engagement for both teacher and student. And speaking of school gardens . . .

Food As Nature

Ten years ago, lunchtime at Berkeley's John Muir Elementary School was typical of most schools nationwide, dominated by processed, packaged, nondescript, greasy, well-traveled foodstuffs loaded with calories. In 2005, after becoming a pilot school for the Berkeley School Lunch Initiative, all that changed. Children in every grade now get regular hands-on time in the garden, and they all learn how to cook. Food wastes are placed into one of three bins: green for compost, gray for recycle, and galvanized for landfill. (Only a small fraction of wastes ends up in the landfill compared to pregarden days.) Lunch is no longer just something to eat. It's part of the curriculum.

School gardens are an amazing and rapidly growing phenomenon, with vegetable gardens being the most popular. Experiential learning includes preparing the soil, planting seeds, caring for plants, harvesting vegetables, and composting wastes to begin the cycle anew. Kids learn about the power and results of teamwork. Students at schools like John Muir explore the wonders of cooking and enjoy eating seasonal dishes. If your kids don't eat their peppers and cucumbers, get them into gardening. Children who grow their own vegetables are much more likely to eat them than those who don't. And establishing healthy eating habits early in children's lives is one of the most effective ways to stem the rising tide of obesity.

Gardens also offer up fonts of opportunity for adopting a place-based, science-as-wholes approach, underlining the inter-relationships of everything. There's nothing quite like watching seeds that you've planted burst from the soil and transform under your care into delicious foodstuffs. Every garden is a mini-habitat unto itself, replete with plant producers, plant munchers (like slugs and herbivorous insects), various predators (like spiders and birds), and all those creepy-crawly decomposers (worms and other soil critters). So they offer powerful, firsthand insights into the flowing, cycling web of life. You can talk all day long about the recycling work of decomposing organisms and not come close to the impact of a two-second hand plunge into the steaming heart of a compost pile!

For most of us, the notion of food as nature seems alien. No wonder, given that our experience collecting food has been reduced to purchasing packaged items at a grocery store. Gardens are almost magical in their capacity to lift the curtain on our alienation from nature. Placed into appropriate context, they allow us to take the larger, systems view of nature, with humans as an integrated and integral part. It's also a straightforward leap from gardens to a variety of related topics, among them environmental health, water conservation, genetically modified organisms, and the industrial food system.

Equally impressive are the pathways that creative educators have invented to teach the full range of subjects in school gardens. Students learn math by calculating the number and spacing of seeds within a given plot, or by determining the amount of fertilizer needed. They delve into social studies by investigating the kinds of plants that native peoples planted prior to the arrival of Europeans. The ever-changing garden landscape provides abundant fodder for writing language arts reports, short stories, poems, and blogs. And students explore new forms of creative arts, like printmaking and time-lapse photography. Some elementary school teachers have grounded the entire year's curriculum in a schoolyard garden.

Revolutionary farm-to-school programs are tapping into school gardens for nutritious food, and bringing additional locally farmed food into school cafeterias. In 2001, six of these programs existed in the United States. Today, they exist in all 50 states, integrating over 9,000 schools into vibrant ecological webs of relationships. Nature mentors can make great use of local foodstuffs to help connect kids with nearby nature. Raising awareness about the plants and animals we consume underscores the deep interconnections shared with other creatures and sheds light on the impacts of our daily decisions. Formal investigation of initiatives like Berkeley School Lunch shows that garden-based programs like these also increase students' nutrition knowledge and preference for healthy foods.

Green Schools

What if schoolyards were transformed even further, into ecologically diverse landscapes? That's the dream, and the compelling argument, of San Francisco–based Sharon Danks. Danks traveled much of the world, visiting 150 green schools and focusing in particular on what they did with the land around the school buildings. Afterward she wrote a book—*Asphalt to Ecosystems: Design Ideas for Schoolyard Transformation*—in which she presents a dizzying array of ideas.

We all have a pretty good idea of traditional schoolyards: mostly asphalt with some dirt or grassy fields and maybe a few trees and shrubs. If it's a preschool or elementary school, there might be a metal climbing structure tossed in for good measure.

Now imagine these old-style school grounds, based on 1940s thinking, replaced by a diversity of greenery, including plenty of native trees and bushes. Rain captured in downspouts flows onto the grounds, nurturing the plants. Children welcome migrating birds in spring with nesting boxes and frolic in the autumn leaves amidst lengthening shadows. In addition to a vegetable garden, there's a butterfly garden, another just for hummingbirds, and even habitat for bees, which produce delicious honey. The nearby pond and wetland supports dragonflies, frogs, and water striders, though the kids are particularly fond of lying down on the bridge to get a closer look at the brightly colored fish.

In addition to nurturing wildlife, this sort of space is healthy for children, providing natural places to run and play, nestled corners of solitude, and shade to escape the midday sun. Green, natural terrain schoolyards tend to reduce stress and uncivil behavior while promoting greater focus in the classroom. They also nurture minds, making connections to the surrounding world. Solar energy drives the pond pump system. The wetland filters and cleans gray water from the school, using it to support the diversity of plant life. And the many tendrils pulling in local wildlife help the kids understand how their local place works, and how they can have a role in nurturing that place.

Underlining these connections and making them visible, the teachers embrace a place-based, hands-on curriculum, teaching many of the classes in the outdoor classroom. The re-natured landscape becomes fodder for science and art, music and mathematics. In many cases, students, teachers, administrators, and parents all have a say in the initial design and take part in the actual construction. And unlike traditional school grounds, the green variety is a vibrant, living thing, constantly changing in response to the seasons, as well as through ongoing inputs from the students.

So you choose. Or better yet, think about what children would want: the drab 1940s schoolyard or the green twenty-first-century schoolyard?

Together with a handful of similar, forward-thinking individuals, Danks cofounded the International School Grounds Alliance (ISGA). After an initial Alliance meeting, thirty-four international leaders signed the Westerbeke Declaration on School Grounds, which states, "[The ISGA invites] organizations, institutions and individuals around the world to join an international movement to support and promote the development of school grounds that are good for students, good for learning, good for schools and good for the relationship between humans and the natural world."

Even more recently, Danks branched out from her business designing and installing green schoolyards to found a new nonprofit, Green Schoolyards America, which aims to be a resource hub and primary support for the movement here in the United States. She aims to spark a dialogue and empower Americans to lead the charge to transform school grounds around the country into thriving habitats. Sounds like a great plan to me!

A World of Wholes

One of the most prevalent ideas in science is that nature consists of objects. The very practice of science is grounded in "objectivity." We objectify nature to measure it, test it, and study it, with the ultimate goal of revealing its secrets. Most of the time, this process entails reducing natural phenomena to their component parts. Science subdivides nature into chunks or "-ologies": geology is the study of rocks, entomology the study of insects, and so forth. Within each discipline, scientists further dissect their object of study into an ever-smaller array of parts. Zoologists, for example, think of animals in terms of species, organisms, cells, genes, and the like. Yet this centuries-old bias of parts over wholes limits our ability to understand nature as subjects.

When Jade was five years old, she named a local red-tailed hawk Reddy and regularly called me over to witness Reddy's soaring spirals and raspy, piercing calls. (It was never clear to me how she could distinguish this particular red-tail, but she remained confident in her identification abilities.) This exquisite predatory bird prompted Jade to wonder how it must feel to fly, and she sometimes worried about Reddy finding his next rodent meal.

Youngsters like Jade often see animals as individuals with their own wills and inclinations. But her science classes tend to portray these creatures more as objects: *Buteo jamaicensis*, a large avian raptor of broad geographic distribution with rounded wings and a pronounced, broad tail.

Ironically, our scientific understanding of the world doesn't support such an object-focused myopia. For example, arguably the greatest lesson from biology is that all life on Earth, including us, belongs to a single, multibillion-year-old family. To date, however, this insight of the mind has yet to penetrate our hearts. Even those of us who fully embrace the notion of organic evolution tend to regard nature as resources to be exploited rather than relatives worthy of our respect.

Now, picture yourself strolling through a forest on a beautiful spring day. A companion asks you to describe what you see.

You'd likely start by listing some plants and animals: maybe an evergreen tree, squirrel, crow, butterfly, whatever. You might comment on the babbling stream nearby, or the play of light and shadow. The thing is, nature's answer to this same question would be completely different.

If we could put on Mother Nature's goggles, the revealed world would be a kaleidoscope of flowing relationships. A fir tree soaking up solar energy while siphoning water from the soil below. A beetle chewing on an oak leaf, gorging itself on green sunlight. A butterfly dancing atop a flower, finding food while helping the flower make more flowers. A spider wrapping up some winged creature for a later meal. A rotting log giving sustenance to a bevy of decomposing critters. Whereas we are conditioned to focus our attention solely on parts, Mother Nature sees relationships interwoven into dynamic, interacting wholes—flowing energy and recycling matter.

If we are to see ourselves as embedded within nature (rather than outside and above it), we'll need an alternative perspective closer to that of Mother Nature—a view that reanimates the living world. For this mind shift to occur, we'll need to embrace the idea of nature as subjects. After all, subjects have relationships; objects don't. This perspective is by no means a new one. Indigenous peoples around the globe tend to view themselves as embedded in animate landscapes replete with relatives. In our quest to raise healthy children and find a thriving, sustainable path into the future, we have much to learn from this ancient wisdom.

To subjectify is to interiorize, so that the exterior world interpenetrates our interior world. Whereas the relationships we share with subjects often tap into our hearts, objects are dead to our emotions. Finding ourselves in a relationship, the boundaries of self can become permeable and blurred. Many of us have experienced such transcendent feelings during interactions with nonhuman nature, from pets to forests.

But how might we undertake such a grand subjectification of nature? After all, worldviews are deeply ingrained, so much so that they become like the air we breathe—essential but ignored.

Part of the answer will likely be found in the practice of science itself. The reductionist Western tradition of science has concentrated overwhelmingly on the nature of substance, asking "What is it made of?" Yet a parallel approach—also operating for centuries, though often in the background—has investigated the science of pattern and form. Generally tied to Leonardo da Vinci, the latter method has sought to explore relationships, which can be notoriously difficult to quantify and must instead be mapped. The science of patterns has seen a recent resurgence, with abundant attention directed toward such fields as ecology and earth systems. Yet we've only scratched the surface, and much more integrative work remains to be done that could help us understand relationships.

More to the point for our present discussion, the shift to thinking of nature as subjects could be driven by science education. If we are to raise our children to see the world with such new eyes, we'll need to nurture (rather than extinguish) the innate inclinations of youngsters to see nature in terms of animate beings. While the practice of science, the actual *doing* of scientific research, must be done as objectively as possible—with the eye of an unbiased external observer—the *communication* and *experience* of science could embrace both objective and subjective lenses.

Imagine if the bulk of science learning took place outdoors, in direct, multisensory contact with the natural world. Imagine if students were encouraged to develop a meaningful sense of place through an understanding of the deep history and ecological workings of that place. And imagine if mentors and educators put less emphasis on the identification and functioning of species names and body parts (say, of flowers or insects), and concentrated instead on the notion that all organisms (including us) are sensate beings in intimate relationship with each other. What if students were asked to spend more time learning about how a particular plant or animal experiences its world? In contrast to the science-of-parts approach that currently dominates classroom teaching, this science-of-wholes would invite students to see themselves in deep relationship to the natural world.

Here's one avenue, then, for educators and nature mentors to bridge the chasm between humans and nature. Ultimately, science education, in concert with other areas of learning, could go a long way toward achieving the "Great Work" described by cultural historian Thomas Berry—transforming the perceived world from a "collection of objects" to a "communion of subjects."

Nature writer Barry Lopez came to the same conclusion about nature mentoring. This is his beautiful synopsis:

> The quickest door to open in the woods for a child is the one that leads to the smallest room, by knowing the name each thing is called. The door that leads to the cathedral is marked by a hesitancy to speak at all, rather to encourage by example a sharpness of the senses. If one speaks it should only be to say, as well as one can, how wonderfully all this fits together, to indicate what a long, fierce peace can derive from this knowledge.

Secret #4 for Raising a Wild Child

Begin with the big idea that everything (including us) is interwoven with everything else. Then seek out regular opportunities to feed the flame of wonder with this insight. We are part of nature, and nature is part of us!

Nature Mentoring Tips

VENTURE INTO THE BUBBLE

An essential ingredient of nature connection is learning to see animals, plants, and other life forms as subjects rather than objects. One of the best ways I know to establish and maintain this kind of attitude, great for both parents and educators, is the "soap bubble technique," invented by German biologist Jakob von Uexküll. Head outside and picture every plant and animal surrounded by a soap bubble that represents its own individual sensory world. Now imagine being able to step inside the bubble of your choice—say, of a robin, earthworm, butterfly, or pine tree. No matter what your selection, your world becomes transformed. Because all creatures have highly specialized senses, the experience of colors, smells, tastes, and sounds is very different in your chosen bubble world, as are your motivations.

Encourage kids to find their favorite animal, enter the imaginary bubble, and experience this alternate world. To spur thoughts in the right direction, you might ask questions like, "Do slugs see?" and "Why do you think that bird is singing?" Ideally, these questions will lead into mysteries that inspire more curiosity. Of course, the soap bubble technique is aided by some knowledge of the sensory world of the creature in question, but such understanding isn't necessary. It's the imagination that counts most. Best of all, by adding on new layers of knowledge, this approach can be used effectively with preschoolers all the way up to "university graduate schoolers," offering an amazing outdoor educational tool.

TAKE THE LEARNING OUTDOORS

Make nearby nature—whether in the backyard, park, or school-yard—one of the primary places for children's learning. The education focus need not always be on the natural world. Thanks to its many physiological benefits, nature is a great place for just about any kind of learning. If you're a parent, think about having kids do their homework outdoors some of the time. Reading can be done while sitting under a tree, and math is more fun when done with a stick in the dirt or sand.

If you're a teacher, no matter what the topic, try taking your lessons into the schoolyard. For those unfamiliar with place-based strategies, think about partnering with other teachers for support. Heading outdoors with a class of students may be unnerving at first, but chances are you'll find that it adds an entirely new dimension to your teaching, including more engaged kids, and even a more engaged you! Just by being out in nature, even merely sitting under a tree, you are demonstrating the value of nature. To help you get there, you will find a number of terrific teachers' guides online.

One easy nature-related activity for any nature mentor is to ask children to find as many examples of nature's interrelationships as they can. You might start out by naming an obvious one, like an oak tree getting its energy from the sun. The challenge here is to think about the role played by a given organism:

solar energy grabber, plant eater, animal eater, or decomposer. All of these roles are defined by interactions with other parts of nature. Some relationships, like those between predator and prey, are competitive. Others are collaborative, like bees pollinating flowers. A bird perching in a tree becomes a plant-animal relationship, and a worm pushing through the soil is an earth-animal pairing. If a particular relationship isn't clear, no worries. Put it aside and move on to the next one.

Think of nature's subjects as actors in a long-running, off-Broadway drama being played out daily all around us in backyards, schoolyards, and parks. Together, you and the children can become coconspirators seeking to discover the underlying story. Chances are there are plenty of local resources to help you along the journey. You'll be surprised how this approach gives you and your kids new eyes with which to see the world.

DON'T FORGET THE CORE WORKOUTS

As a nature mentor, remember to engage your core—core routines, that is, such as wander, sit spot, story of the day, and questioning. Use these routines to help deepen awareness of the big picture, the web of life that thrives in your local place. Start by listening to a child talk about her experience outdoors and then find a mystery that will help pull her to the next level of awareness. If she talks about a bluebird, ask her to keep an eye out for what that bluebird is doing. Sometimes, as she heads outside, give her a question to ponder, like, "What kinds of creatures do you think take care of the recycling around here?" It doesn't matter if you have no idea what the answer is. You're merely the catalyst, the co-explorer who's anxious to hear about the child's discoveries, and fascinated to find out more. The point here is to remind children that there is a big picture, an invisible set of threads that ties everything together. Their challenge (and yours) is to learn to become aware of some of those threads.

FOOD IS NATURE!

Most of us tend to think of nature as something wild, something found only rarely in and around urban settings. But nature is everywhere—in the air above us, in the ground below us, and in the spaces all around us. Nature is within us too. Every breath of air, sip of water, and bite of food that enters our bodies is nature. One of the most powerful ways to connect kids with nature is to raise their awareness about food. Grow a garden with children's help and watch them begin to love eating their veggies. If you can afford the extra expense, turn your family into a pack of locavores, eating predominantly local and organic foods purchased from places like farmers' markets. Each evening before dinner, take a moment with your family to give thanks to the plants and animals that are about to sustain your bodies. In our fast-paced lives, we rush through meals, rarely pausing to consider the source, or even the taste, of foods we consume. Nature connection begins with awareness, and healthy food is a wondrous place to start.

VISIT A LOCAL FARM

Take the kids out to a nearby working farm so that they can see plants, pigs, chickens, and cows being raised for food. Increasingly, farmers are hosting regular tours, proud to show off their practices. More and more of these farms are moving toward a sustainable approach, avoiding hazardous pesticides for plants and nontherapeutic antibiotics for animals. In many instances, agriculture and livestock are thoughtfully integrated with the surrounding ecosystem. Animals eat feed grown on the property, and animal wastes are used as a nitrogen source to help sustain crops. In this way, sustainable farms protect biodiversity and foster healthy ecosystems. Many farms now offer opportunities to volunteer for a few hours or a day, or for visitors to harvest their own fruits and vegetables, giving children and adults first-hand experience in something that most people knew intimately just a century ago.

Once you've visited a local farm, regularly bring home food produced there and remind kids where that food comes from. The memory of their visit will change the way they think about food, and make that predinner expression of gratitude even more powerful.

5

Mothers All the Way Down

Unearthing a Sense of Story

> A human being is part of a whole, called by us the
> "Universe," a part limited in time and space. He experi-
> ences himself, his thoughts and feelings, as something
> separated from the rest—a kind of optical delusion of
> his consciousness. This delusion is a kind of prison for
> us, restricting us to our personal desires and to affec-
> tion for a few persons nearest us. Our task must be to
> free ourselves from this prison by widening our circles of
> compassion to embrace all living creatures and the whole
> of nature in its beauty.
>
> — ALBERT EINSTEIN

GLORIOUS VERTIGO! Moments earlier, the seaside hilltop had
afforded unshakeable support. But now, as the last sliver of sun
slipped beneath the horizon, the landscape suddenly heaved and
tilted skyward. Gravity's tether, it seemed, had been severed,
leaving me perched precariously on a rolling behemoth. I braced
myself with one hand, trying to hold on to the dizzying sensation
as one might a lucid dream. Glancing at Jade, I was thrilled to
see that she too was giddy and wild-eyed, sharing the moment.

We all learn that our planet, Earth, revolves around a star, the
sun, which is part of a multitudinous assemblage of stars in our
galaxy, the Milky Way. Yet despite such pretensions to knowledge, *at heart* we're all flat-earthers, little different from the vast
bulk of humanity that preceded Hubble, Galileo, and Coperni-

cus. Why else would we continue to speak of sunrise and sunset, and actually feel these events when we experience them? Such persistent misperceptions are unsurprising, given our lengthy heritage as big-brained, upright apes whose senses—including proprioception, the awareness of bodily position—have been attuned by millions of years of evolution on terra firma. More to the point, great scientific insights tend to be nonintuitive. It's not easy grappling with the notion that you live on the side of a giant, spherical rock hurtling around a star at 67,000 miles per hour!

Yet, just as Jade and I did, it's possible to evoke a wondrous experience of this reality. Simply head to a place where the "sunset" will be visible, preferably amidst an expansive horizon. A clear day is best. After quieting your mind, remind yourself that the sun, although small in appearance, is a million times larger than Earth. Next, contemplate Earth as third in a gaggle of planets wheeling around in the same flattened plane, all anchored by the titanic pull of our central star. Finally, just as the sun's disk begins to disappear, picture yourself sitting on the side of an immense, spherical world spinning away from its stellar neighbor. *Wham!* Perhaps for the first time, you too will experience what it feels like to be an earthling living within a community of planets. Try returning to this awareness when the canopy of stars has unfurled, and you're likely to experience a vivid sense of moving, even falling, through the cosmos.

The rocky knoll that minutes earlier had been lurching, threatening to toss Jade and me into the ocean, was once again securely anchored to the North American coast. Far off to the south, San Francisco began to glow. Much farther still, starlit pinpoints poked through the darkening dome overhead, hundreds of suns replacing our nearby solar neighbor. Jade and I watched a clan of turkey vultures execute spiraling descents before settling for the night in a eucalyptus tree. Finally, we stood and began our own descent toward home. Still steeped in the effects of cosmic reverie, it seemed as good a time as any to tell her the biggest story of them all.

The Power of Story

At their best, stories are priceless word-jewels with the power to create, sustain, and transform worlds. Why do hundreds of millions of people each day read fiction, watch television, and line up to sit in darkened movie theaters? Stories. Carefully crafted tales enliven our senses. Full of wonder and mystery, they transport us to far-flung places and remote times, allowing us to see through the eyes of another. That featured Other may be human or animal, real or fantasy. Stories are all but ubiquitous in our lives, invading our minds throughout much of the night, while dreaming, and the day as well, while daydreaming. Author Jonathan Gottschall argues that stories are one of the defining, and least understood, characteristics of humans, "the storytelling animal."

In Chapter 3, we addressed the importance of pulling nature stories from children as a way of heightening meaning and learning. Now it's time to flip things around to think about you, the nature mentor, as storyteller. Done well, storytelling offers mentored experiences that boost understanding, embracing all three elements of EMU.

In our digital world deluged with isolated bits of information, it's easily forgotten that as a species, we were raised on stories. For all but the past few thousand years, an eyeblink of humanity's tenure, oral storytelling was the primary means of sharing not only information, but meaning, values, and a sense of place in the cosmos. For our oral ancestors, stories were lyrical encyclopedias, repositories of practical knowledge and wisdom accumulated over centuries, even millennia. Passed from generation to generation, myths and tales offered instructions on how to live in a given place: when, where, what, and how much to hunt; how to express gratitude for a successful hunt; which plants to seek and which to avoid; where to find water in times of persistent drought.

Traditionally, stories were told outdoors, offering a multisensory experience. Elders were given special status as storytellers. Scientist-author Jared Diamond notes that "Under hunter-gatherer conditions, the knowledge possessed by even one person over the age of seventy could spell the difference between survival and starvation for a whole clan." Oral stories were the cultural equivalent of genes, keepers of information necessary for perpetuating the group. It should come as no surprise, then, that spoken stories have an almost magical effect on us. And whereas cyberspace is placeless, seemingly everywhere and nowhere, oral culture is inherently local.

The best stories help us not only to live, but to dwell, both in place and time. Through storytellers we learn of our kinship with other creatures and with Earth itself. We see how the ripples of our actions have cascading effects far into the future. For oral cultures, stories are also a primary means of connecting with the land. Local plants and animals become protagonists and antagonists. Virtually every creature and place on the landscape—a chirping bird, gurgling stream, or gentle breeze—becomes sensate and is given voice. Once a story is learned, chance encounters with animal neighbors, or merely walking by a local landmark, bring to mind the associated narrative and its practical lessons. In this way, stories can breathe life into our unique surroundings and give them deep meaning.

Conversely, if the storytellers become silent, the land becomes mute as well, and its meaning dissipates. In the words of author David Abram:

> When oral culture degrades, then the literate mind loses its bearings, forgetting its ongoing debt to the body and the breathing earth. When stories are no longer being told in the woods or along the banks of rivers—when the land is no longer being honored, ALOUD!, as an animate, expressive power—then the human senses lose their attunement to the surrounding terrain. We no longer feel the particular pulse of our place—we no longer hear, or respond to, the many-voiced eloquence of the land. Increasingly blind and deaf, increasingly impervious to the sensuous world, the technological mind begins to lay waste to the earth.

Of course, children are still captivated by stories, from Snow White to Harry Potter. Although these tales typically take place far from our homes, many occur in nature and include wild animals—some real, some mythical. Beyond their enchanting allure, these stories help children understand and appreciate the natural world, and people's role within it. At least they used to. A recent review of seven decades of award-winning children's picture books revealed a steep and steady decline in illustrations of natural places and wild animals, as well as human interactions with both. It appears that even the literature of modern culture is no longer connecting kids with nature as it once did. More and more children's stories are becoming places where the wild things aren't. Perhaps it's time to restore the natural world, beginning with the places we call home.

• • •

Turning to Jade, I began with a flourish. "Once upon a time, billions of years ago, the universe was born in a gigantic explosion called the Big Bang. The universe started off super-hot—*trillions* of degrees—and was crammed into a tiny space, way smaller than a speck of dust." (For effect, I revealed a grain of sand held in my palm.) "The universe cooled as it grew bigger, beginning as a simple place with no stars, no planets, and no life.

"Stars came first, born from huge clouds of hydrogen gas. Gravity's pull caused parts of these clouds to collapse into giant balls. As they shrank smaller and smaller, these balls of hydrogen got hotter and hotter until, suddenly, they ignited on the inside and began to burn incredibly bright. What had once been a simple cloud of gas now held thousands of glowing suns. These were newborn stars, and they gathered with others in vast, spiraling cities of stars called galaxies. Our home galaxy, the Milky Way, looks to us like a thin veil of light crossing the night sky. But point a telescope at that veil and you'll find that it's jam-packed with stars.

"Although stars are pretty simple—just enormous balls of hot gas—they share a lot in common with people. They're born, they have lifetimes, and they die. They come in different sizes and, like you, they go through many changes as they age. A major difference between stars and people, though, is how they die. Truly gigantic stars go out with a bang in monstrous explosions called supernovas. A single supernova can outshine all the other billions of stars in its home galaxy!"

Embracing the Storyteller Within

Why tell nature stories? Because they feed children's longings to be protagonists in their own tales. As a nature mentor, a trickster Coyote, your verbal imagery can help kids walk their edges and imagine venturing beyond them—say, being quick enough to catch a lizard, or sneaky enough to touch a deer. Equally tricksterlike is the capacity of narratives to convey information in meaningful, memorable ways without so much as a hint that any teaching has occurred. Without doubt, stories are one of the most powerful ways to engage young minds and deepen their nature connection.

Ever since Jade was very little, she has relished hearing tales of my outdoor adventures, asking me to retell select favorites again and again. Some of these stories take place in far-off lands: a close encounter with a hyena in Kenya, and another with a crocodile in India. Others come from my childhood: a bear sauntering through our campsite in British Columbia, and a bison stampede bearing down on me in Alberta. Still others are much more mundane: a spectacular sunset on an evening walk, or catching a lizard and having it relax in response to some belly-stroking.

The range of tales is important. If all the narratives occur in distant places, or feature only heroic feats, a child will likely conclude that these are the kinds of things that happen to other people. So be sure to include a lively mixture of grand adventures and everyday encounters, with a healthy dollop of edge-stretching tales thrown in for good measure.

Where can you find engaging nature stories? All over. Start by plumbing the depths of your own experience. Did you play outside as a kid? If so, there must have been occasions when you stayed out at night, looked a wild animal in the eye, got lost in some natural landscape, or felt the adrenalin rush of hiding in bushes. Did your family ever go hiking, camping, or fishing? All make excellent fodder for narratives. Personal stories are powerful because they're authentic and they come from *you*, the storyteller.

Another terrific source is traditional nature-based myths and tales. Having been raised in Canada, I am particularly fond of stories from North American indigenous peoples. One of my favorites is the Haida myth in which the Raven, the Trickster, creates the world. But these stories can be Amazonian, Polish, Japanese, Celtic, or from some other place. Virtually all traditions tell tales that embody nature connection. Think about searching your own ancestry for stories.

There's also plenty of inspiration to be found in the vast and growing collection of adult-aimed nature writings. Some offerings, like those of Wallace Stegner and John Steinbeck, are fictional. Others were written by naturalists such as Henry David Thoreau, Edward Abbey, Farley Mowat, Terry Tempest Williams, Barry Lopez, Scott Russell Sanders, and Peter Matthiessen.

Finally, look to nature herself for inspiration. Plenty of story-worthy events are occurring every day just beyond your front door: birds nesting, flowers blooming, ants colonizing. Beyond that, keep your eyes open for interesting tidbits in books, documentaries, and news flashes. It might be something about the intelligence of scrub jays, or the volcanic history of Yellowstone, or the feeding habits of octopus. Every day the Internet highlights new discoveries that shed light on some thread of nature. All of these are opportunities to play with your storytelling.

It might seem odd to think of yourself as a storyteller, but I'll bet you tell plenty of stories. We all tell stories. Your narratives may be modest most of the time—perhaps reading the occasional fairy tale aloud or acting out a movie scene for friends—but you likely venture into grander scales on occasion. If telling stories to your child or to a circle of children seems daunting, remember, you were made to do this. Humans have been sharing stories since the beginning. Best of all, children (and adults) find stories enchanting, so your efforts are likely to be rewarded with appreciation and passionate requests for more.

There are a few tricks to storytelling. Some you likely know already. If you're making up a story from scratch, begin by setting the stage. What did the place look, smell, sound, and feel like? What time of day was it? Was it a forest, beach, or mountaintop? Details matter. The more vivid a picture you paint with your words, the more likely the image will be a "sticky" one, recalled weeks or months later when you least expect it.

Push your own edges. Adept storytellers are shape-shifters (there's that Coyote again), able to morph into different characters. Chances are, the more you let yourself go, becoming free and loose, the more effective you'll be. So throw your body into the story with movements and gestures. Walk like a beaver, or mimic the quaking leaves of an aspen tree. The more vivid and animated, the better.

If all that sounds waaaay outside your comfort zone, start by playing with the inflection in your voice—fast and loud during the exciting bits, quiet and slow when things get suspenseful. For tales with multiple characters, give each of them a different voice. And remember, silent pauses are your friends. Use them to grab attention if your audience is losing focus, or just before making a key point. Humor is also essential, for both kids and adults. A laughing audience is an engaged audience. Find your own style and work it. Pretty soon, if you stay observant, you'll see exactly what captures attention and launches imagination.

I stooped to pick up a hunk of sandstone, handed it to Jade, and continued.

"Deep inside those very first stars, all that burning transformed hydrogen into heavier and heavier bits of stuff, like helium, carbon, oxygen, and iron. When giant stars exploded as supernovas, all this heavy matter was blown out into surrounding space, creating more clouds of gas and dust. Eventually, all those rumbling shock waves from supernovas triggered the collapse of more wispy clouds into new stars.

"The leftover heavy stuff swirling around newborn suns became families of planets. Our sun was one of those later stars. It was born with eight circling planets—from little, rocky worlds like Earth and Mars to gas giants like Jupiter and Saturn. Billions of other planets in billions of other solar systems are traveling around billions of other stars in the Milky Way and other galaxies. So the stars gave birth to the planets. And all the stuff that makes up planets—from that rock in your hand to the entire Earth—was created inside burning stars!"

Jade's eyes widened as she handled the chunk of stardust gingerly, as if it might still be hot.

"When Earth was born," I continued, "it was red-hot, bubbling with molten lava. There wasn't any life back then. Not even any land or oceans. Over millions of years, the surface cooled and formed a thin crust. Think of a hot apple pie, and you'll get the idea. Earth's rocky crust split up into enormous chunks that moved around, bumping into each other. You and I are standing on rocks that formed underwater during the Age of Dinosaurs. And this particular chunk of Earth's crust, including that rock you're holding, started way down south near the equator. Over millions of years, the land crawled slowly northward, traveling about the same speed as your fingernails grow. Eventually, it crunched into North America down near Mexico and was shoved northward. It set off lots of earthquakes as it inched its way up to where we are today, near San Francisco Bay."

Jade grasped the rock tightly and whispered, "Coooool."

The Immense Story

Most powerful of all stories are cosmologies, cultural narratives that explain the origin and ordering of the world. Throughout human history, virtually all cultures have been rooted to their native places by such narratives—from Raven bringing forth the light in Haida culture to the Genesis story of Christianity. Although the lives of present-day indigenous peoples and most followers of religious traditions are imbued by one cosmology or another, most of us living in Western societies today represent an historical anomaly, existing largely without one. This lack of an origin story contributes to the dearth of greater meaning and purpose experienced by many of us, feeding the dysfunctional human-nature relationship at the heart of the sustainability crisis.

Yet an astonishing and staggeringly beautiful account of our deep time history has emerged within science over the past several decades. Variously called the Universe Story, the Epic of Evolution, the Great Story, the New Story, or Big History, this grand narrative has potential to unite humanity and root us in both local places and deep time. From this broader perspective, evolution is much more than Darwin, natural selection, and a changing parade of species. It is no less than the cosmic story, from that primordial flaring forth to this very moment. Far from leading to the desolate view that the universe is a colossal expanse of dead space, this saga paints a picture of a dynamic, emerging unity, a creative cosmos in which we are deeply embedded. The Epic of Evolution, informed by virtually all scientific disciplines, is perhaps science's greatest contribution, offering a direct glimpse into where we come from and what it all means.

Although certainly a creation story, the evolutionary epic is not a true cultural cosmology. Instead, this science-based saga offers a framework to be molded into a spectrum of cosmologies, each one informed by specific historical, cultural, spiritual, and ecological contexts. Indeed, the Immense Story allows for an endless medley of interpretations and beliefs, with and without God(s). Theologian John Haught put it this way:

> Darwin has gifted us with an account of life whose depth, beauty, and pathos—when seen in the context of the larger cosmic Epic of Evolution—exposes us afresh to the raw reality of the sacred and to a resoundingly meaningful universe.

Thomas Berry and Brian Swimme have argued persuasively that this story must become a central element in redefining the human-nature relationship. Yet decades later, the Immense Story remains all but absent from Western culture, ignored by scientists, philosophers, educators, environmentalists, and spiritual practitioners alike. How can it be that we, who have access to by far the most rigorous and comprehensive story of the cosmos, do not use it to inform the arc of our lives?

Those distant stars that brilliantly adorn the night sky are our long-lost cousins, they and we birthed from the wombs of earlier stellar generations. The myriad organisms with which we share this blue-green world—from redwoods to dung beetles—are even closer relatives, the lot of us descended from microbial forebears. And, together with the water, air, and rock, life on Earth seamlessly coevolved into a single, ever-changing entity that many now refer to as Gaia. The most recent chapter of this narrative traces all seven billion humans alive today to a small band of Africans whose descendants blanketed the globe during the past 70,000 years. The Age of Science began as humanity grappled with a bewildering notion: Earth is not the center of the universe. In our present moment, it's time that we embraced another nonintuitive scientific idea, though one congruent with many wisdom traditions. We are offspring of an immensely ancient and creative universe.

Carl Sagan had it right. We are star-stuff, made of matter forged within stellar furnaces. But the real story—the Immense Story—goes much deeper. We're also Earth-stuff, composed of matter from the planet's crust. And we're life-stuff too, every one of our human cells the product of ancient bacterial mergers. You and all other animals exist today because of a deep time cascade of ever more complex mergings, each one dependent on its predecessor: atoms combining to form heavier elements; heavy elements bonding to make chemical compounds; compounds meshing to create bacterial cells; cells lacking nuclei coalescing into nucleated cells; and nucleated cells uniting into multicellular life. This repetitive pattern of unification and diversification, of merging and proliferating, has been essential to the universe's creativity. Sea stars could not have preceded bacteria. Water would have been impossible prior to oxygen. All of these innovative partnerships and many more still coexist in our bodies. We are, in a sense, cosmic mongrels.

"The universe is made of stories, not of atoms," wrote poet Muriel Rukeyser, underlining the power of narrative. Why does the Epic of Evolution merit a central place in education, and in our culture generally? Because this grand saga encapsulates our best understanding of the evolving universe; because internalizing the notion of our shared ancestry helps us reconnect with nature and the places we call home; and because this story offers a compass to orient humanity at a pivotal moment in deep time. Only when the evolutionary epic is finally expressed throughout our culture—not just in science, but in poetry, song, sculpture, and dance—will we begin to truly understand what it means to be part of a single, evolving universe. Only then will we begin to conceive of nature not as resources for our exploitation, but as relatives deserving of our compassion and empathy. As a nature mentor, you can do your part simply by telling the story.

Cosmologist Brian Swimme summarizes the entire multibillion-year narrative in a single sentence: "You take hydrogen gas, and you leave it alone, and it turns into rosebushes, giraffes, and humans."

Upon reaching the beach, Jade and I trod barefoot into the surf, the icy vestiges of waves dancing across our legs and feet. Stooping to gather a cupped handful of seawater, I said, "How many living things do you think I'm holding?"

"Millions," she guessed.

"Hundreds of millions," I replied slowly. "The oceans are overflowing with tiny microbes."

Jade scooped up her own watery sample, staring intently in hopes of glimpsing the bacterial bounty.

"Life got started here in the sea," I continued, "made from stuff in Earth's crust. The earliest kinds of life were all bacteria, each one made of a single cell. And believe it or not, for most of the past four billion years, all life on Earth remained one-celled and microscopic. But those early bacteria were amazing. They figured out how to do things like breathe oxygen and grab energy from the sun."

From among the flotsam and jetsam, I grabbed something long and whiplike.

"Hundreds of millions of years later, some of the sunlight-eating bacteria began to merge with each other, becoming creatures with many cells. Their descendants gave rise to seaweed like this bull kelp, and also to land plants."

We continued down the beach, Jade clutching her rock in one hand and dragging the bull kelp with the other. After crossing Redwood Creek, we paused to visit some familiar seaside neighbors. Unable to discern much in the gathering darkness, I encouraged Jade to gently feel the bounty of rock-clinging critters: thickly ridged shells of blue mussels, granular arms of ochre sea stars, leathery "necks" of goose barnacles, and tiny swirls of checkered periwinkles. The squishy stickiness of a giant green anemone elicited a delighted scream. Amidst the din of breaking waves we could hear the scurryings of rock crabs.

"Along with the sunlight catchers, other kinds of life learned to feed on the sun's energy by eating each other. These were ancient ancestors that would one day give birth to animals, including the sea stars, mussels, and barnacles on these rocks. Fishes eventually appeared too, becoming top predators in the seas. The great white sharks out at the Farallon Islands, and the coho salmon that fight their way up Redwood Creek every year, are direct descendants of those primitive fishes. After millions of years, a few of those ancient fishes found their way onto the land, transforming first into amphibians and much later into reptiles. Some of those scaly reptiles became dinosaurs that stomped around right here on the coast of North America. And a few of those dinosaurs sprouted feathers, and then wings. Today we call their living descendants 'birds.' So when you and I are sitting in the backyard learning bird language, we're really learning a dinosaur language invented millions of years ago!"

The Second Big Idea

In the previous chapter, we looked at the importance of ecology—the interconnectedness of everything—as one big idea in nature connection. The second big idea is evolution—the notion that "it's all relatives." It seems to me that meaning, purpose, and belonging have less to do with where we are at any given moment than where we've been and where we're going. Perhaps, then, the core of nature learning needs to spin on a pair of axes, a duo of big ideas: ecology and evolution. Alongside the horizontal connections viewed through the temporal snapshot of ecology, evolution offers us vertical, transformational roots in deep time. Whereas ecology addresses *how nature works* at any given moment, evolution focuses on *how nature came to be*.

These big ideas, and indeed most abstract insights in science, are far more memorable and meaningful when we perceive and reflect upon them directly with multiple senses. A deep understanding of nature must be absorbed through our eyes, ears, nose, and pores, as well as our minds. As Maria Montessori, Rudolf Steiner, John Dewey, and other early twentieth-century educational pioneers knew all too well, meaning must be actively constructed, with learners participating directly rather than being treated as information receptacles. Stories can be amazing allies in this effort.

But if ecology and evolution are the big ideas at the heart of nature connection, how are we to weave the Immense Story—populated by billions of galaxies, stars, and planets—together with the delicate web of streams, rocks, spiders, and trees in our local places? After all, the former deals with the grandest scales of time and space, whereas the latter is concerned with the very intimate nearby.

Oddly enough, this question makes sense only to Westerners. For most indigenous peoples the world over, no dividing line exists between the cosmic and the local; all are part of the same community, the same story. Their cosmological sagas feature a variety of local denizens—the trickster raven, the wise mountain, the changeling butterfly. We would do well to emulate this approach.

Fortunately, potential protagonists abound. A local mountain, desert, or slab of limestone makes an exceptional entry point into the story of Earth and the solar system. A stately oak or vegetable garden might help convey the saga of bacteria harnessing solar energy. And an arrowhead or cell phone would make an ideal trigger for sharing the human chapter of the evolutionary epic. The Immense Story can be told outdoors around a campfire, as indigenous storytellers have done for millennia. Or a simple walk down a hillside might suffice.

The key is that all major innovations of the cosmic evolutionary epic—stars, planets, bacteria, plants, animals, and human culture—are still present in one form or another in every place. Each telling of the Immense Story, or parts of it, can be tailored not only to local nature, but to the age and knowledge base of the audience. Indeed, anyone can construct their own version of the story, choosing local characters and themes most meaningful to them.

The story of everything can be told anywhere.

Whether or not you decide to tell the Immense Story, look for stories to tell children that help them see their interconnections in both space and time. You might decide to look back only 1,400 years or 140 years, instead of 14 billion years. Either way, seek out the magic of narrative to share information about how your place works, and how it came to be. And remember that storyteller is one of the most important roles you will play as a nature mentor. Go ahead. Embrace it.

I settled myself on a chunk of driftwood and Jade immediately clambered onto my lap. We were nearing home, and the story's end.

"When people first arrived here around 13,000 years ago, the place looked like the Serengeti of Africa today, with lots of huge herbivores. Mammoth, mastodon, giant ground sloth, horses, camels, and bison all roamed along this coast. There were plenty of big carnivores too: lions, wolves, saber-toothed cats, and giant bears. It was the ice age. It was so cold back then that a lot of Earth's water froze into ice, causing the level of the sea to drop. Back then, there was a grassy plain between where we're sitting and the Farallon Islands more than twenty miles away. And that grassy plain was jam-packed with animals. Imagine walking from here to the Farallons, and having to keep an eye out for elephants and saber-toothed cats!

"Sometime after those big mammals went extinct and the oceans grew bigger again, the Coast Miwok people arrived. They lived here for thousands of years, sharing the oak forests and grasslands with wolves, grizzly bear, and condors. The Miwok hunted mule deer, fished for salmon, ground up acorns, and made woven baskets. In the 1800s, people from Portugal settled in this beautiful spot; they also caught salmon and they farmed the land too. Today, you and I are fortunate to share this place with bobcats, skunks, and red-tailed hawks. Many others will come after us.

"The secret of this story is that the universe's journey is *your* journey. Your mom wasn't the only one responsible for your birth. It was your grandmother, and, before that, your great-grandmother and great-great-grandmother. Long before that, it was the long, unbroken chain of mammal mothers, reptile mothers, and amphibian mothers. We also owe deep thanks to our fish mothers and the countless other sea creatures and bacteria that gave rise to them even further back in time. Earth Mother gave birth to the first life, and the Great Cosmic Mother birthed the first stars. You can think about it as a huge family tree, with each branch being a different ancestor. And on this cosmic family tree, from the tips of the topmost branches to the deepest roots, it's mothers all the way down! Without them, you and I wouldn't be here, and neither would all the other wondrous creatures on this planet.

"Most important of all, the journey is far from over. Every plant and animal alive today, including us, is part of this journey, and nobody can say for sure how things are going to turn out. So *you* can make a big difference in the future of the universe. Pretty amazing, huh?"

Jade nodded slowly, paused, and then broke into a wide smile. "C'mon, Daddy," she blurted out, now leaping up and tugging me toward home, still gripping rock and kelp. "We've *got* to tell Momma!"

Secret #5 for Raising a Wild Child

Everything around us is interconnected not just through the ecological flow of energy and matter, but also the flow of relationships through time. We're surrounded by relatives, all of us intertwined in a grand, unfinished story. Understanding and experiencing this story can help foster deep nature connection.

Nature Mentoring Tips

NATURE STORY TIME

Although nature may be slowly disappearing from children's books, you can still find numerous titles that feature nonhuman characters (see appended list at the end of this book). Your local library is bound to have plenty of examples appropriate to any age. One of the greatest predictors of children's reading abilities is whether or not their parents read to them daily. So fill their imaginations with fairy tales and other stories full of amazing landscapes and magical creatures. For young children, remember Albert Einstein's injunction: "If you want your children to be intelligent, read them fairy tales. If you want them to be more intelligent, read them more fairy tales." Animal stories are terrific for fostering a sense of empathy for other creatures. For children in elementary school, try looking for books that have been awarded the Caldecott Medal or placed on the Caldecott honor list. I love *The Other Way to Listen* and similar books by Byrd Baylor. Teen nature titles are fewer, but an Internet search will still uncover many options.

INDIGENOUS TALES

Seek out stories from the lore of indigenous peoples native to where you live. These tales are frequently grounded in local nature: plants, animals, and landforms. They often convey memorable narratives of how particular animals got their names, of plants used for medicinal purposes, and of places held sacred. And they typically embody a spirit of deep nature connection, with humans fully embedded in the web of life. One example is *North American Indian Tales*, by W. T. Larned. Think about using stories like these as an entry point to understanding the native peoples that lived in your region prior to the arrival of Europeans.

CREATE YOUR OWN STORIES!

Once in a while, put aside the storybooks and renew the sensuous art of storytelling grounded in local nature. Use your whole body and voice to answer questions such as where did those fir trees come from, and why are they so tall? Who lives in our local pond, and how long have they been there? Why did coyotes and rabbits survive the last ice age while mammoths and saber-toothed cats disappeared? Your local library, natural history museum, or nature center will be happy to provide the necessary fodder. The goal here is to animate nearby nature, to bring it alive through narratives. This is exactly what indigenous peoples have done for thousands of years, wherever they lived. If you tell stories like these even once in a while, you and the children will start to understand, and experience, your local place very differently.

GO COSMIC

Learn the basics of the Immense Story, and tell it to the children in your life. Around a campfire is best, but anyplace will do. ("A very long, long, long, long time ago . . .") Several great kids' books have been written on this topic, including a wonderful four-part series by Jennifer Morgan. Bring the Immense Story alive by rooting it in the natural history of local characters—for example, plants, animals, streams, and hills. Even a garden can serve as the foundation for telling this mind-boggling narrative. If the whole story seems too daunting, break it up into shorter narratives. A crow or robin serves as a great entry point for telling the story of dinosaurs to birds. And that croaking frog in the early evening is a modern-day reminder of our water-to-land legacy. The most important thing is to link our present-day world with the ancient narrative of how we got here. With time, children will begin to understand that the story of everything is really *their* story, and that they have a role to play in determining how it ends.

MAKE NATURE LEARNING EXPERIENTIAL

Think about how you might combine stories and outdoor experience to convey various aspects of science and nature, transforming abstract insights into felt encounters. For example, head outside under a starry night sky to share the secret that all animals, including us, are made of stardust. Try the sunset activity outlined at the beginning of this chapter. For teens, head to a forest and tell them why they share about a quarter of their genes with the trees (answer: we share a distant common ancestor with the trees). If you're a science teacher, think about getting out of the classroom to convey key concepts in the real world. Water, earth, insects, clouds, birds, rocks—they are all there waiting to become part of your next lesson. Consider hosting a "Council of All Beings," in which each participant takes on the role of a different character from nature. This exercise, which transforms objects into subjects, can be a powerful tool for building emotional connections with local place.

Part III

LIFE STAGES

6

The Playful Scientist

Mentoring Young Children

There are no seven wonders of the world in the eyes of a
child. There are seven million.

— WALT STREIGHTIFF

MORE THAN A half-century of future has slipped into past since
Rachel Carson's world-changing book, *Silent Spring*, made its
debut. Unfortunately, Carson did not live to see the ensuing
revolution, with cascading consequences that included the environmental movement, the Environmental Protection Agency,
banning of various pesticides, and Earth Day. No surprise, then,
that for most people, the name Rachel Carson brings to mind
the ardent activist bravely confronting chemical companies in
defense of human and environmental health.

Yet this humble woman also excelled as a nature writer — one
of the best in the English language, according to Carson's biographer, Linda Lear — with a deep passion for fostering wonder
in children. If you're a lover of oceans, and you haven't read
The Sea Around Us or *The Edge of the Sea*, you're missing out.
But my favorite piece of Carson prose resides in a wonderful
little 1956 essay called "Help Your Child to Wonder." Here she

articulates a clear vision for fostering a deep connection with nature in children. Rachel's recipe is simple: *abundant outdoor experiences in wild places in the company of at least one adult mentor.*

Public response to this essay was so positive that Carson decided to write a "wonder book." Yet her dream was to remain unfulfilled. First, the quest to produce *Silent Spring* got in the way. And shortly thereafter, breast cancer brought a premature end to her life. Nevertheless, Carson's wonder essay remains a profound, lyrical testament to the raw power of nature connection, highlighted by experiences shared with her young nephew Roger.

Her thesis is embodied in the very first, image-rich paragraph:

> One stormy autumn night when my nephew Roger was about twenty months old I wrapped him in a blanket and carried him down to the beach in the rainy darkness. Out there, just at the edge of where-we-couldn't-see, big waves were thundering in, dimly seen white shapes that boomed and shouted and threw great handfuls of froth at us. Together we laughed for pure joy—he a baby meeting for the first time the wild tumult of Oceanus, I with the salt of half a lifetime of sea love in me. But I think we felt the same spine-tingling response to the vast, roaring ocean and the wild night around us.

This paragraph answers one question that may have crossed your mind. At what age should nature connection, and thus nature mentoring, begin? The answer: at birth. Or even before that. As an adult, my mother told me that while I was still in the womb, our family went camping at what would one day become perhaps my favorite place in the world—Long Beach, near Tofino on the west coast of Vancouver Island, British Columbia. Maybe that pounding Pacific surf made a strong impression on me even then.

Judy Swamp, a Mohawk elder, once shared with Jon Young that mothers in her culture commonly take crying babies outside and whisper to them, pointing at something in the distance. Being outdoors in a natural setting seems to break the spell of upset and calm the infant. Independently, I've found that this strategy works well with older children too.

In this chapter, we'll explore nature connection during the early childhood years, with a focus on ages two to six. Rachel Carson cautions that mentors must fight the urge to teach, striving instead to be co-adventurers. Things work out best if the grown-up adopts the child's perspective. In this way, the child becomes teacher, enabling the adult to witness a world of wonder through youthful eyes. Carson further underlines the importance of emotions over understanding. In her words, "If facts are the seeds that later produce knowledge and wisdom, then the emotions and the impressions of the senses are the fertile soil in which the seeds must grow."

The dual emphasis on experience and mentoring captures the E and the M of EMU. A deep and lasting sense of wonder typically emerges through abundant experience, much of it outdoors in the company of a compassionate adult.

Nevertheless, we must not overlook the third EMU element—understanding. Here I'm not speaking of facts, like animal names or flower parts. If the young child seeks such information, as many do, that's great; feel free to provide some. Or better yet, ask questions and seek out answers together. But don't let facts hinder the experience, because it's in the experience that young children are likely to find the greatest understanding, and in ways we are only now beginning to comprehend. Recent discoveries have given us an unprecedented glimpse inside the minds of young children, and some of the results are, to say the least, surprising.

The Playful Scientist

We tend to think of children as miniature, inept, highly dependent versions of ourselves in need of growth and maturing. Until recently, this view was the norm for the general public and professional psychologists alike. Famed developmental psychologist Jean Piaget, for example, considered preschooler thinking to be irrational and illogical, the very opposite of scientific thinking. Not surprisingly, this "adults-in-training" perspective has had large and cascading effects on parenting, education, and policy.

But is it accurate? Research over the past two decades paints a very different picture, suggesting that we've grossly underestimated the talents of toddlers.

Psychologist Alison Gopnik is among those at the forefront of this new perspective. Recall from Chapter 2 that kids' brains are far more interconnected than the brains of adults. All that extra networking enables young children to make novel connections at a blinding pace, an ability heightened by the way they think and experience the world.

Gopnik's work shows that babies and young children tend to display a broad and diffuse kind of attention, resulting in what she refers to as "lantern consciousness." This kind of unfocused attention makes sense if your greatest need is to explore and absorb as much of your worldly experiences as possible. Think of a crawling infant who flits from a stuffed animal to a piece of fluff on the floor to the leg of a table, seemingly with the attention span of a gnat.

The attention of adults, in contrast, tends to be far more narrowly directed. This "spotlight consciousness" is the mental state you would expect to have when, say, reading a book. Whereas spotlight thinking tends to be purpose driven, with the beam tightly focused on a particular subject, lantern thinking illuminates broadly, shedding light on a wide range of subjects.

In a very real sense, then, kids don't have short attention spans. They just focus their attention more widely. If you're still having trouble imagining the lantern consciousness of a young child, Gopnik offers this description: "It's like being in love in Paris for the first time after you've had three double espressos."

"Children aren't just defective adults," she says, "primitive grown-ups gradually attaining our perfection and complexity. Instead, children and adults are different forms of *Homo sapiens*." She compares humans to butterflies, with very different growth stages, each highly successful in its own right. In our case, however, it's the youngsters who are the butterflies, flitting about from thing to thing, whereas we grown-ups fill the caterpillar role, steadfastly moving through our focused tasks.

Despite its diffuse nature, much of youngsters' thinking turns out to be surprisingly scientific. Preschoolers learn from statistics and make accurate inferences about cause and effect. They construct theories of the world around them. And they readily generate hypotheses and test them by conducting experiments. No, really.

Fei Xu and Vashti Garcia conducted an ingenious experiment with an unlikely goal: to determine whether or not eight-month-old babies had a sense of probability statistics. Since their study subjects couldn't talk, the psychologists measured "looking time," based on the finding that infants gaze longer at unexpected events. First, the adult experimenter showed infants a box of red and white balls. In one set of trials, the box consisted mostly of red balls and just a few white balls. In another set, the opposite was true—the box was dominated by white balls.

Next, the adult closed her eyes and withdrew a sample of balls from the box. If the sample were random, we'd expect the balls to represent the distribution in the box (for example, more red balls pulled from a red-dominated box). But in some trials the adult performed a sleight of hand, retrieving mostly white balls from the red-dominated box. The infants were able to see that the sample either matched or did not match the expected distribution, and they tended to gaze longer at the nonmatching sample. In other words, they were surprised by the low probability result. Yes, even babies have a sense of probability statistics!

Gopnik's "baby lab" at the University of California–Berkeley conducts similarly clever studies aimed at revealing the thinking capacities of babies and young children. A key aspect of science is learning from the ideas and findings of other scientists. So the baby lab group decided to test the observational learning abilities of preschoolers. They undertook a study in which four-year-olds watched an experimenter manipulate a blue ball with rubbery protuberances. The grown-up began by telling the child that the toy made music, but that she wasn't sure how. The experimenter then tried such actions as rolling, shaking, and knocking on the ball. Some of these actions activated music (controlled remotely by the experimenter) and some did not. When the youngsters finally got their hands on the toy, they frequently demonstrated their observational learning skills by mimicking only those actions that activated the toy.

Another experiment features a game called "blickets," in which young children play with a collection of variously shaped blocks. They're told that some blocks are blickets, but most are not, and that you can't tell which ones are blickets simply by looking. Instead, "blicketness" is assessed by placing a block on the "blicket detector." If the detector plays music, you've got a blicket. If not, no blicket. In truth, of course, there's no such thing as "blicketness." The adult running the experiment simply flips a switch under the table to turn the machine on.

In one trial, the grown-up put one block, say, a cube, on the machine. No response. The cube was then replaced by a cylinder, which caused the machine to light up and play music. Finally, the cylinder was removed and both the square and cylinder were placed atop the machine. Music and lights once again ensued, and the experimenter invited the child to make the music stop. Children as young as two years old were relatively adept at assessing cause and effect, inferring that the cylinder is the blicket and that removing it turns the machine off.

A pretty neat finding, given the age of the kids, but hardly earthshattering. As adults, we use the same kind of this-*or*-that reasoning on a daily basis.

In a different trial, however, Gopnik and her colleagues changed things up, invoking this-*and*-that reasoning. A blicket now revealed its blicketness only when placed on the machine with another blicket, and it lit up the box even if a third, non-blicket object was added. Here the four- and five-year-olds consistently outperformed UC Berkeley undergraduate students in their ability to infer causal relationships. And the youngsters had great fun, effortlessly spinning off new hypotheses and testing them by adding and subtracting blocks. Adults, it appears, are biased toward this-or-that reasoning, whereas children, lacking such proclivities, are more flexible and open-minded in their learning capacities.

You've seen it dozens of times—a child fiddling endlessly

with some object, maybe a ballpoint pen or a rock, manipulating it to test its properties. Experimental observations might include scratching, rubbing, hitting, kicking, throwing, and licking. In the same vein, making a sand castle is a grand experiment in physics. How high can you make a sand tower before it collapses? What happens if you make the walls thicker or thinner, or add more or less water to the sand? Children observe closely, make adjustments, innovate, and learn from others around them. We are natural-born scientists, it seems, generating observations and experimenting with the world to better understand it.

And how do children carry out their investigations into the nature of the world? Through play, of course! Play is the signature of childhood, its *raison d'être*. Kids are literally *driven* to play. But why? Why are youngsters compelled to learn about the world through play? Here we move into the realm of speculation, but my bias follows that of a growing cadre of scientists.

As discussed in Chapter 2, we far exceed other animals in our capacity to exhibit flexibility and creativity. This in turn has led to our unparalleled ability to adapt and change. Empowered by our big brains, we seek to understand our environment, imagine alternatives, and transform those imagined worlds into reality. Neuroscientists use the term *plasticity* to refer to our exceptional ability to change in the light of experience.

And this is where small, playful scientists enter the story. Childhood is the time of life when our brains conform to wherever we happen to find ourselves. It is the time when we explore diverse possibilities with our imaginations, and not just the useful ones. The great bulk of this exploration occurs through play. As the ever-quotable Albert Einstein once said, "Play is the highest form of research." In short, childhood is about experiencing, learning, and imagining the world through play. Adulthood is the time to put all that experience, knowledge, and imagination to use. Gopnik summarizes this age-based division of labor as follows:

> There's a kind of evolutionary division of labor between children and adults. Children are the R&D department of the human species—the blue-sky guys, the brainstormers. Adults are production and marketing. They make the discoveries, we implement them. They think up the million new ideas, mostly useless, and we take the three or four good ones and make them real.

If this view has merit, the evolution of prolonged childhoods (described in Chapter 2), with their playful, butterfly-like explorations, enabled our human ancestors to adapt to whatever circumstances they found themselves in. And if so, we owe a great debt of thanks to earlier generations of children (as well as adults) for our unrivaled success as a species. In a very real sense, play made us human.

What Is Play, and Is It Really Important?

Most of us have long forgotten what play really feels like. I refer here to *free* play, the real McCoy, the kind initiated and driven by kids and frequently occurring outdoors. Damming streams, building makeshift forts and dens, holding back the tide with walls made of sand, creating miniature houses or cities, being a fireman one minute and Tarzan the next, quickly followed by Superman—these are the kinds of things that happen during real play. Psychologists tell us that real play is spontaneous, freely chosen by children, and kid-directed. And play activities are intrinsically motivated, with no external goal or reward.

If you're over thirty-five or forty years of age, chances are your childhood was filled with such unstructured, exuberant play. And not just on weekends. Odds are equally good that you look back fondly on those play-filled years.

Nevertheless, today we tend to regard play as trivial, an outlet for kids to "burn off energy." From this perspective, schoolyards contain playing fields and climbing equipment for children to rid themselves of excess exuberance so that learning can take place. Learning, according to this view, is the important stuff that happens in classrooms, typically when adults share information with students. No surprise, then, that demands for more rigorous academics have resulted in recess and gym class being cut back or eliminated from many schools.

Yet recent research, including the studies summarized above, confirms that this view is wrong-headed. If you're a kid, play is serious stuff, and *young children actually learn best through play*. Some child psychologists go so far as to equate the two: play equals learning.

And the benefits of play, it turns out, extend far beyond learning. Another growing body of research points to the importance of play in children's emotional, spiritual, and social development. Near the top of the list of benefits are enhanced creativity and imagination, both of which blossom under the influence of unstructured play. Children are experts at exploring imaginative possibilities, conjuring up alternatives and trying to make them reality.

Then there are all the bodily benefits linked to growing bones, muscles, senses, and brains. Movement and balance are enhanced through walking on logs and climbing trees. Sensory skills are developed, particularly outdoors, by the kaleidoscope of sights, sounds, smells, textures, and tastes. Motor skills are fine-tuned through manipulating toys, constructing makeshift forts, and skipping stones on the water. Brains enlarge and form complex neural pathways in response to playful experiences. The American Academy of Pediatrics recommends sixty minutes of unstructured free play per day to support children's physical, mental, and emotional health.

Finally, we mustn't forget the all-important social benefits of play. Next time you're at a playground, keep an eye out for young kids meeting each other for the first time. You'll quickly see that names don't matter (though, interestingly, ages do. "I'm four. How old are you?"). Youngsters who've known each other for mere minutes will naturally start to play, often in imaginative games with flexible rules. Through play children learn how to socialize—make friends, collaborate, resolve conflicts, and bounce back from failure.

We now know that childhood experiences have a direct and lasting influence on brain chemistry and brain growth. So it is not hyperbole to say that adults literally guide the growth of children's brains by exposing them to different experiences. All the more reason, then, to choose those experiences carefully—to know which are likely to be harmful and which beneficial.

One of the most profound and disturbing discoveries in neuroscience has been the direct link between infant brain chemistry and adult psychology. It turns out that adult success is not genetically determined. Rather, it depends largely on those first few years of life, when the brain is rapidly growing and transforming. Toxic stress—for example, physical or emotional abuse—turns out to be a far better predictor of success (or the lack thereof) later in life than IQ.

Okay, we know what children don't need. So what *do* they need to grow up to be healthy adults? Of course, they need adults to feed them, clothe them, and protect them. They need an abundance of love and nurturing that forges a strong bond with at least one parent. They need plenty of time around one or more grown-ups speaking and reading to them. But equally so, kids in early childhood need daily doses of unstructured playtime where they can use their imaginations and explore the world around them. Especially during early childhood, then, understanding—the U in EMU—will follow naturally if children get appropriate experience and mentoring (the E and the M).

Nature Play

A few years ago *Wired* magazine published an article called "The 5 Best Toys of All Time." Particularly given the source, readers were surprised to learn that rather than high-tech games, the list consisted of (1) stick, (2) box, (3) string, (4) cardboard tube, and (5) dirt. What do all of these toys have in common? All of them qualify as "loose parts," things with no designated role. In other words, such toys can be adapted to an almost infinite range of purposes, limited only by children's imaginations.

Take the top toy on this list—the stick, inducted into the National Toy Hall of Fame in 2008. Sticks come in an amazing array of sizes, shapes, colors, textures, and heft. Indeed, no two are exactly alike. You can use a stick to make interesting patterns in sand, snow, or dirt. You can balance a stick on your hand, or lean on it as you walk. Sticks can easily be transformed into wands, scepters, telescopes, fishing rods, shovels, and, yes, swords (or the higher-tech version, light sabers). A bunch of sticks—or better yet, logs—make terrific building materials, with construction possibilities spanning towers, chairs, houses, and hideouts. Big sticks offer kids opportunities to test their strength. I fondly remember dragging mega-sized branches along trails as a kid. (Mom: "Scott, put that thing down!" Dad: "Oh June, let the boy have some fun.")

If the thought of your young child playing with sticks triggers blaring internal alarms, a few simple rules may suffice, such as no touching of people with sticks and no hitting of anything.

Now, compare the multipurpose stick with the standard array of stuffed animals, dolls, action figures, and toy cars. When kids are playing, a stuffed dog, lion, or sea otter will typically exhibit behaviors appropriate to its species. Likewise, dolls and action figures tend to act like humans (albeit with the occasional supernatural abilities), whereas cars and trains perform as the vehicles. I don't mean to imply that such traditional toy favorites are bad, only that they can and should be augmented by more open-ended loose parts.

Loose parts are far more abundant and varied outdoors than in. String, boxes, and cardboard tubes typify the smattering of human-made loose parts commonly available indoors. Sticks and dirt, in contrast, are accompanied outside by a rich spectrum of open-ended, readily available objects. Rocks range from boulders to stones to pebbles, with limitless roles in play. Plant parts are also varied. Alongside sticks may be leaves, bark, pinecones, flowers, fruits, seeds, and acorns. Then there's the highly varied outdoor terrain, typically with natural elements such as trees, grass, and water, together with uneven topography interrupted by roots, rocks, hills, and bushes. Add to this the presence of birds, insects, earthworms, and other critters, together with their byproducts—shells, nests, tracks, and the like—and you have a truly engaging playspace that's tough to beat.

Why is nature play with loose parts important? Because it provides fuel for growing brains and bodies. Rates of childhood obesity in the United States have almost tripled since 1980, now hovering around 17 percent. The Centers for Disease Control (CDC) regards outdoor play as an essential strategy to combat this disturbing trend. Gross motor skills benefit from manipulating big objects such as rocks, whereas play involving irregular small objects enhances fine motor skills. Nature play strengthens muscles and bones. Being outdoors offers kids regular doses of vitamin D, which many urban children today are deficient in. Recent studies demonstrate that because outdoor play demands shifting one's gaze between near and far, it greatly decreases the odds that children will develop nearsightedness later in life. It encourages liberal use of creativity and imagination. It fosters both sensory awareness and collaboration. Those loose parts generate unlimited opportunities for children to name, sort, and arrange things. Not surprisingly, play in natural settings also ups the odds of children growing into adults who are passionate about environmental conservation.

Learning, too, is enhanced through such open-ended nature play. Without even knowing it, kids are working on their math and science skills as they construct things. Those loose parts are often counted, or even used as currency. Playful scientists glean important lessons in physics by tossing stones in the water or rolling rocks down a plank (for example, understanding that the speed of a rolling rock increases with the angle of the plank). Kids also tune their aesthetic sensibilities by decorating and arranging with natural objects. So what may at first glance appear to be frivolous play is often engagement in a hyper-rich learning environment.

Here's a simple experiment. Try giving kids a bucket of rocks of varying sizes, shapes, and colors. Chances are you'll quickly find that the possible activities are endless. Children will roll, stack, arrange, bury, wash, hide, and sort rocks. They'll drop them into water and mud. They'll transform them into trucks or castles or dinosaurs. If encouraged, they will happily paint rocks or use them to make pieces of art. Far more than Barbie dolls or Tonka trucks, those rocks are likely to inspire a wondrous variety of imaginative play. This kind of hands-on experience—the E in EMU—is essential to nature connection.

At this point, you may be thinking, "Yeah, all that sounds great. But my kids would rather hang out indoors and play video games." Perhaps you've even had the frustrating experience of taking your children outside, excited to get them "into nature," only to find that they claim to be bored and ask to head back in the house where the TVs and iPads are. While I've found that this response is rare among preschoolers, it's much more common for kids of middle childhood age, particularly those who've had plenty of screen time and minimal experience playing outside. In such instances, you may have to get creative and Coyote-like to begin with, coming up with activities to get things kicked off. These activities might be quiet, such as drawing, or more active—for example, games like hide-and-seek. With some engaging nature time under their belts, most children will choose to be running around outside immersed in imaginative play. Without a doubt I preferred to be outdoors as a kid, and my guess is that you did too.

Dirt Is Good

"But wait," I can already hear the next objection. "If we let our toddlers play outside, they're gonna get dirty *all over* and probably taste some of those loose parts along the way." Fearing filth, falling, choking, "germs," or some other hazardous outcome, our natural tendency is to intervene immediately. But learn to hold yourself back. Unless there's true risk to life and limb, let children explore. Let them explore on some occasion even when there is some risk. And be careful of your expressions and body language. Kids tend to mirror your internal state, whether it's fearful or calm. So if you're worried or afraid, they will be too.

As for the dirt and germs, it appears that kids are merely following a natural and healthy inclination. You've likely heard of the hygiene hypothesis, the idea that children raised in super-sanitized settings tend to have more allergy and asthma problems than kids who grow up with regular exposure to soil microbes and other invisible critters. This idea has received big-time support in recent years, much of it summed up in Mary Ruebush's book, *Why Dirt Is Good: 5 Ways to Make Germs Your Friends*. According to Ruebush, the child who eats the most dirt wins because his immune system becomes so robust. Our immune systems are set up during the first year of life. So early exposure to a bevy of potential allergens is one of the surest pathways to a healthier life thereafter. Ruebush also cites evidence that playing in dirt lowers stress levels, together with the odds of getting irritable bowel and gut-based disease, while upping focus and attention spans.

The dirtier the better, suggests another recent study. Ilkka Hanski and colleagues at the University of Helsinki conducted an intriguing investigation of allergies, comparing adolescents living in neighborhoods surrounded by natural areas with those in neighborhoods landscaped in concrete and neatly trimmed lawns. They found that people immersed in more natural settings, places home to greater varieties of native plants, were themselves covered with a wider range of microbes and were far less likely to exhibit allergies than folks in the more sanitized settings. So let 'em get out there and get dirty!

Remember, too, that nature connection is a contact sport. Sitting on the manicured sidelines looking out at the field of green pales in comparison with actually getting out there and getting muddy. Whenever possible, give kids the full experience. And let them entice you to get into the game yourself!

Natural Playgrounds

Adam Bienenstock is a passionate nature play advocate with a big personality. Leading with his bald head and ever-present smile, he exudes a unique blend of intensity and joviality—a Buddha with a cause.

Through his company, Bienenstock Playgrounds, in Dundas, Ontario, Bienenstock is on a mission. His bold aim is to replace traditional play areas of monkey bars, swings, and slides with playspaces of logs, boulders, trees, paths, and rolling hills, all rooted in local nature. Sourcing the bulk of his materials from within 100 miles, he sees playgrounds as one of the best ways to connect communities with nearby nature. I agree.

As a test, Bienenstock once asked the mayor of Toronto to give him the worst park in the city, the one everyone had given up on, and let it be transformed into a natural playground. The mayor complied, offering up a corner parkette frequented more by IV drug users than surrounding neighbors. Bienenstock's group removed the tired play apparatus and pretty much took the space back to bare ground. They then installed a variety of natural elements, including groves of trees, logs to walk on, musical instruments made of wood, pathways punctuated by comfortable benches, and boulders of various sizes. The response was immediate. With the park revitalized, the neighbors returned, and the negative elements effectively disappeared. Within a year, housing prices in the immediate vicinity spiked 20 percent. The day we visited, mothers were chatting comfortably on one of the benches while their children ran around happily exploring and playing games.

The beauty of natural playgrounds is that they tap directly into children's passions. In traditional playspaces constructed of metal and plastic, decisions about what to play are made by the designers. First you swing. Then you go down the slide. Too often, the result is competition, with kids arguing over who gets to do what, followed by frustration and tears. Conversely, in natural play areas, the child is boss. Imaginations are fired up as kids invent games with the available loose parts. Studies show that interactions tend to be more cooperative as well. Bullying is greatly decreased, and both vandalism and aggressive behavior also go down if there is a tree canopy. And with greater engagement comes longer play intervals, about three times longer compared with old-style play equipment.

Returning to our goal of deepening nature connection, playspaces designed by Bienenstock's group and others are designed to engage not only the five standard senses, but also to help engender a sense of wonder and a sense of place. There are quiet places for contemplation. When on the move, kids improve their balance, agility, and gross and fine motor skills, and they tend to be more engaged mentally. Think about the differing attention levels demanded of evenly spaced monkey bars versus branches within a tree.

Natural playgrounds, which cost about the same as their traditional counterparts, also foster healthy risk-taking, the kind experts say kids need but parents often prevent for fear of injury. Picture a young child climbing on a standard set of monkey bars, the nervous mother standing below with her arms outstretched. Now replace that image with a set of boulders varying in size. Youngers kids can manage to climb onto only the small boulders. But with their enhanced size and strength, bigger kids summit the larger boulders, and safely navigate the leap back to earth. This approach, which Bienenstock calls "graduated challenge," allows children to take only those risks appropriate to their abilities. Proof of this claim comes in the form of statistics showing that the incidence of "catastrophic injuries" such as broken bones is a fraction of that on traditional playgrounds. In short, these natural play areas provide a safe place for all kids to master physical challenges.

The movement to build natural playspaces is gaining steam. Bienenstock Playgrounds and like-minded efforts are getting calls from a wide range of interested parties. Recently, the National Wildlife Federation and the Natural Learning Initiative at North Carolina State University collaborated on the Natural Play & Learning Area Guidelines Project, which sets guidelines for designing, building, and managing natural play environments.

Now, imagine if natural playspaces adorned every school, park, zoo, botanic garden, and museum, not to mention backyards. The result would be safe places for children to play in nature within easy walking distance of virtually every home. We'll return to this dream in the final chapter.

Mentoring Goals

When Jade was between about four and seven years of age, I sometimes walked with her the mile or so to our mailbox along Pacific Coast Highway 1. Typically I picked a time close to dusk and followed a route that avoided the highway, detouring instead across Muir Beach. We inevitably dawdled, picking up bits of driftwood as the glowing western sky deepened from burnt orange to deep rust. She would climb and jump off rocks, choosing bigger ones over time. By the time we headed home with a handful of letters and maybe a small package or two, faint stars pierced the heavens.

For me, the mail was merely a ruse, a Trickster's way for Jade and me to connect in a wondrous outdoor setting. Usually we didn't say much, preferring instead to feel the twilight seep into our bodies. Other than feeling her little hand in mine, my favorite part of these mini adventures was sighting animals whose days were just beginning—swooping bats gorging on an insect smorgasbord; a barn owl heading out for a night of rodent hunting; a gray fox trotting by on the way to who-knows-where. For Jade and me, it felt like we were participating in a grand change of shift: the day creatures like us were heading to bed while the night creatures clocked in and set off to work. A changing of the guard. Tag, you're it.

Heading out at dusk, I found, had other, unanticipated benefits. Small children are often afraid to venture out into the evening blackness. But if they first experience the daylight-to-dusk transition, the fear lessens. In addition, as Rachel and Roger discovered, nighttime has an intangible power, a primal feeling ingrained in us by millennia of intimate contact with the denizens of darkness. With me by her side, these mail trips helped Jade learn to feel comfortable being outdoors at night. Perhaps most important of all, by walking instead of driving, I was modeling my value of, and gratitude for, nature. Without my saying a word, Jade got the message that the natural world matters—that it is a part of us, and we a part of it.

Young children are like wolf pups. They long to venture outside, but not too far from Mom and Dad. They're all about exploring and pushing edges close to home, yet run back regularly for a dose of security. As a nature mentor, the key is to give young kids plenty of time in natural places—backyards, beaches, forests, deserts, creeks, parks—where they can play with all those loose parts until exhaustion sets in. Show interest when they bring you some random object for inspection, but otherwise feel free to let kids hang out and explore with all their senses. The end result for the child will be an amazing experience in which she deepens her bond with you and with nature.

At this stage, one of the major goals is empathy. Talk about the trees and the animals as the amazing life forms they are—each one built to fulfill a role in that place; each with its own unique way of experiencing the world. Fulfill kids' longings for both language and nature by reading animal stories. Encourage youngsters to imagine what it feels like to be a bird or a tree, and to act it out. If you feel so inclined, get in there and stand tall like a tree or fly like a hawk. Remember that this sort of mimicking is a powerful way to foster nature connection and build that sense of empathy.

Rachel Carson underlined the role of adult mentors as co-conspirators, expressing the value of nature as much through actions as words, and unabashedly reveling in the experience of being outdoors with children. She best expressed the spirit of mentoring young children in another of her famous quotes:

> If a child is to keep alive his inborn sense of wonder . . . he needs the companionship of at least one adult who can share it, rediscovering with him the joy, excitement and mystery of the world we live in.

Become one of those adults. Make a huge difference in a young child's life simply by sharing his nature experiences, and enjoying yourself along the way. The path to becoming a wild child starts with being a wonder kid. Wonder deepens connection.

With deeper connection comes empathy, and then caring. And, with time, caring leads to love.

Secret #6 for Raising a Wild Child

Perhaps the greatest secret of being a nature mentor during the early childhood years is at once the easiest and most difficult thing to do. It is, simply, to get kids outside, get out of the way, and let 'em play!

Nature Mentoring Tips

FREE PLAY RULES!

One of the essential rules of nature mentoring is to enable children to fulfill their innate longings. Young kids long to play; it's what they're designed to do. So carve out some regular time for the children in your life to engage in unstructured play, with a portion of it outdoors. *Unstructured* here means free play without adult guidance or supervision. Encourage kids to create their own imaginative games and activities, preferably using readily available natural elements—loose parts like water, sticks, dirt, and rocks. Feel free to gather up some of these loose parts or, better yet, have the kids do it. Bigger elements, such as large sticks, can be used for creating makeshift structures, like forts or bridges. Smaller items can be used in an almost infinite array of activities. Aim for an hour a day of free play outdoors and watch the effect it has on the kids. A rapidly growing mountain of evidence indicates that this kind of nature play is critical for their physical, mental, emotional, and social development, as well as their everyday health. Besides, they'll love you for it!

NATURE CONNECTION IS A CONTACT SPORT

Too often these days, children's encounters with nature are dominated by a look-but-don't-touch directive. Fearing that we must protect nature and our kids at all costs, we often do far more harm than good. Nature connection depends on firsthand, multisensory encounters. It's a messy, dirty business—picking leaves and flowers, turning over rocks, holding wriggling worms, splashing in ponds. Lacking such experiences, children's growth is impoverished and they're unlikely to care for, let alone protect, natural places. So loosen up and find some hands-on nature experiences for the kids in your life. Rather than telling kids "no" all the time when they want to climb a tree, throw a rock, or step into a muddy pond, take a deep breath and offer words of encouragement. Don't worry so much about the dirt and scrapes. Clothes and bodies can be washed, cuts heal.

Most of the time, kids don't need to be shown how to connect with nature. It's engrained in their DNA. Rather than seeing nature connection as something you need to teach young children, the real key is simply to take them outside and let them do what comes naturally! At least on occasion, seek out some wilder places where kids can go off-trail and bushwhack a little. As much as possible, and more so as children grow up, give them space to explore on their own. Nature connection is a contact sport, and nature can take it!

FREE THE BUGS

With the help of children, make a habit of using a cup and a card to catch insects and spiders that find their way into your home or classroom. A clear plastic cup is best so that you can observe the little critters before releasing them outside. Jade and I have done this in our home for years, prompting her to observe the various "bugs" more closely. The unspoken (or spoken, if you prefer) message of this activity is that each of these many-legged animals is an individual with its own life to live, a life worthy of our assistance. If kids show a strong interest, you might work with them to figure out what kind of insect you have, but identifications aren't essential. Alternatively, you might decide to sacrifice a few individuals, pinning them to a card and storing them in a nature collection for future observation. Yes, I understand the intense contradictions of saving versus killing, but the latter can be done in such a way as to demonstrate to children the value and importance of all life. If killing even insects is outside your comfort zone, another option is to collect and pin dead bugs to add to a child's nature table.

NIGHTTIME ADVENTURES

As Rachel Carson discovered with her nephew, there's something powerful about being outdoors at night immersed in a natural setting, no matter what your age. Beaches, deserts, forests, even neighborhoods take on an entirely different feel in the dark. And, of course, different creatures come out after the sun goes down. So, assuming you can find a safe place, seek out opportunities to take children on nighttime adventures, even if it's just a walk around the block or some quiet time in the backyard. Watch them closely and see where their interests (and fears) are directed. Be authentic and open yourself up to rekindling that childlike sense of wonder, chasing their passions as well as your own. If you model this kind of engaged playfulness, the child will feel more secure and do the same. The end result will be a growing sense of wonder in both of you.

If you're a city dweller, escape the urban environment once

in a while to experience truly dark skies. A good litmus test is whether or not you can see the Milky Way, that starry band of light crossing the sky. There are few experiences more powerful than lying beneath a star-filled night sky, particularly during one of the annual meteor showers.

ADD SOME LOOSE PARTS

Whether you're a teacher, parent, grandparent, or some other kind of caregiver, add some loose parts to children's playspaces. Whether it's the schoolyard, backyard, or courtyard, the addition of natural elements such as rocks, logs, water, and sticks will likely transform the play experience outdoors. I've seen amazing places where kids were provided with long, pole-like sticks that could be used to make teepee-like structures. Of course, if you go to the local park, chances are good that plenty of loose parts will be waiting for you. The goal here is to allow children's imaginations, as well as their bodies, to run free and be creative. Feel free to sit back and let the kids run the show. If you do engage, be sure to follow rather than lead. Remember that for free play to be truly free, children must be the bosses.

7

The Age of Competence

Mentoring During the Middle Childhood Years

> For special places to work their magic on kids, they need
> to be able to do some clamber and damage. They need to
> be free to climb trees, muck about, catch things, and get
> wet—above all, to leave the trail.
>
> — ROBERT MICHAEL PYLE

SIR DAVID ATTENBOROUGH, the great naturalist and BBC wildlife presenter, has often been asked, "How did you become interested in animals?" His response is always the same: "How on Earth did you lose your interest in them?"

Sir David's point is that virtually all children possess a strong fascination for animals and nature. Evidence can be found in the plethora of animal-related games, clothing, toys, "stuffies," books, and movies, from *The Lion King* to *Happy Feet*. Annual attendance at zoos, nature museums, aquariums, and the like are another strong indicator. Dominated by family audiences with young children, these institutions enjoy higher cumulative attendance numbers each year in North America than all professional sporting events combined.

For young children, the notion of animals as thinking, feeling individuals—as subjects rather than objects—comes naturally. And the presence of such nonhuman "others" can be very compelling, influencing how kids view themselves and their place in the world. Recall my daughter Jade and her relationship with Reddy, our local red-tailed hawk.

Unfortunately, Attenborough's adult passion for animals is all too rare. Most children enter middle childhood brimming with questions and wonder about animals and nature. Yet odds are great that by the time they hit adolescence, those same youngsters will have "grown out of" this animal phase, and their passion for nature will also have vanished. We consider this transition a sign of maturity, with the unspoken assumption that a child's emotional attachments to wild creatures, and to nature as a whole, are juvenile and somehow delusional. It's likely no coincidence that by fourth grade, a third of boys and girls have already lost interest in science. And by eighth grade that number rises almost to 50 percent.

What happens during those pivotal middle childhood years? Is the declining interest in the natural world an inevitable result of maturity, perhaps linked to brain development and heightened interest in the social realm? Or is the move away from nature driven by cultural trends? Is it possible that the passion children often feel toward animals and nature is the healthy condition, and it is we adults who are the delusional ones, victims of many years of counterconditioning?

We tend to associate early childhood and adolescence with explosive transformations in both mind and body. During the former interval, toddlers learn to walk and talk. In the latter, bodily maturity becomes paired with teen obsessions over peers and sex. By contrast, the middle childhood stage sandwiched between, spanning about six to eleven years of age, is often thought of as a happy, quiescent time—a joy for parents and teachers alike.

Yet recent findings in neuroscience and other fields show that middle childhood is far from static. Behind those smiling, cherubic faces, brains are undergoing dramatic changes, resulting in startling new capacities. While some new synaptic connections are forged, tens of billions of others are intensively pruned. Stronger pathways are reinforced and amplified; weaker ones marginalized or severed. As a result, the brain experiences a major reorganization, enabling more efficient communication between its different domains.

Overall, middle childhood brains retain some of their elasticity from earlier years, yet become sufficiently organized to wrestle with big, abstract ideas. Real logic and reasoning are now possible, so learning makes a huge leap. More and more, children are able to get past their own egocentric inclinations to truly see things from another's point of view. They're also able to reflect on their own successes and failures. With these freshly modified brains, impulse control gets a major boost, along with concentration, short-term memory, and future planning.

Of course, physical changes occur as well. Muscles and bones broaden and lengthen, resulting in leaner, more athletic bodies. Gross motor skills make a huge jump, with kids becoming increasingly more adept at running, jumping, balancing, throwing, and climbing. The same trend applies to fine motor skills, from cutting and pasting to drawing and painting. This is the age when children can finally tie shoelaces, floss teeth, and play a musical instrument.

Middle childhood is often called the age of reason, in reference to kids' newly acquired abilities in abstract thinking. It seems to me, however, that this life stage might be better summarized as the age of competence. For the first time, maturing minds and bodies enable youngsters to perform feats previ-

ously impossible. Coupled with these new mental and physical capacities is a deep longing to demonstrate competence. So
strong is this desire that children who don't see themselves as
competent in academic, social, and other arenas—for example,
athletics or music—tend to become depressed and suffer feelings of isolation. The need to learn skills and have them vali-
dated by others is a prime internal directive during these middle years.

No wonder, then, that these intervening years between toddler and teen are the stage of life when children around the
world are first put to work (though, these days, not typically in
North America or Europe). Babysitting, water hauling, fishing,
planting, harvesting, cooking—all are now well within the kid
wheelhouse.

On the face of it, then, there's no obvious developmental
reason why children lose their interest in animals and nature.
To the contrary, we're born with an innate drive to understand
and master our worlds, and our brains and bodies are finely
tuned throughout all of childhood to help us achieve this biological imperative. Bolstering this claim are the many thousands
of adults (myself included) whose childhood passion for nature
has persisted. Then there are the numerous indigenous societies
for which a deep, persistent, heartfelt nature connection remains
the cultural norm.

No, the answer to this conundrum is to be found outside the
human body. There's something about Western culture in particular that tends to stifle the human-nature bond. The domesticat-
ing tendencies of schooling, outlined in Chapter 4, are certainly
part of the problem. Equally critical is the fact that more and
more, children are no longer given opportunities to soak up the
magic of nature through independent wanderings.

Leveraging Passions

For Jade's eighth birthday, Toni and I brought in San Francisco Bay Area nature artist Zach Pine to join us on Muir Beach, and invited about thirty kids and adults to join in on the fun. Zach is a remarkable fellow who chose to walk away from a career in medicine to pursue a different passion—using art to connect people of all ages with nature. Along with his nature art workshops, he has installed hands-on "Create-With-Nature" zones in schools, parks, museums, and public spaces. In Zach's view, he does as much healing with his nature work as he would have as a doctor. And, while Zach and other nature artists clearly have highly developed skills, beginners need no prior experience. Anyone can be a nature artist!

It was a beautiful late-summer morning with a low tide and two-foot waves breaking lazily on the shore. Zach began by encouraging the kids to spread out and collect raw materials—loose parts, in other words. They enthusiastically ran off to rummage through the flotsam and jetsam, returning minutes later with armfuls of crab shells, rocks, sticks, feathers, and long kelp strands. He then set small groups of kids to work, teaching them such skills as stacking stones (the secret is at least three points of contact between successive layers) and making near-perfect spheres with sand (the key here is to use semi-wet sand and toss the spheres up in the air again and again).

Most of the kids were Jade's friends from school and the local community, immersed in the thick of middle childhood. I noticed that the younger brothers and sisters tended to stay close to one of their parents, continually seeking reassurance. Jade and her friends, meanwhile, were all over the place, working singly and in pairs, Mom and Dad forgotten. I watched as some kids, of their own accord, artfully wove seven-foot-long pieces of seaweed among wavy alignments of rocks and sand globes. Others created shrines of wood, sand, or rocks, topped by carefully arrayed feathers and crab shells. Nature art, I quickly learned, taps into the middle childhood passion for acquiring new competencies. It also offers opportunities for peer connection and collaboration, allowing open-ended creativity.

Zach's passion proved to be contagious. Most of the adults, initially standoffish, soon jumped in, working steadfastly to master rock stacking or sand globes. Ultimately, everyone collaborated to add finishing touches. The centerpiece of this art installation was a ten-foot-wide, heart-shaped "Happy Birthday, Jade" sculpture beautifully rimmed with globes, shells, rocks, seaweed, and feathers. After about ninety minutes, I climbed a nearby hill to get a good look from above, and literally gasped as I turned to survey the scene. The group had transformed a significant chunk of this wild northern California beach into a spectacular nature art gallery! Afterward we all sat down for a delicious picnic lunch and admired our work. Slowly but surely, the encroaching tide began to reclaim its terrain, wiping the canvas clean for the next wave of artists.

Among the greatest longings of middle childhood is the desire for a degree of freedom and independence. Kids at this stage are compelled to put their newfound abilities to use sampling new horizons: geographic, social, emotional, and intellectual. Whereas a backyard with a few bushes and some dirt may be plenty wild for a toddler, wildness for youngsters in middle childhood might mean navigating an urban creek with forested margins. The previous yearning to remain within the intimate Mom-and-Dad bubble is replaced by a hunger to burst out and explore new terrain, often without the accompaniment of grown-ups.

Nevertheless, although spectacular wilderness settings may exert their greatest effects on adolescents, as we'll see in the following chapter, nearby nature remains key during middle childhood. Kids at this stage seek to connect with the local and familiar, be it an empty lot or a creek bed. Ideally, this is a place to be explored without adult guidance, or even presence, a place where children can put down roots and foster a deep sense of connection. For me, this place was "the woods," that protected area of second-growth forest near my home in Vancouver, British Columbia, described in the Introduction.

The power of the familiar and the ordinary is not to be underestimated. In the words of Robert Michael Pyle,

> It is through close and intimate contact with a particular patch
> of ground that we learn to respond to the earth . . . We need
> to recognize the humble places where this alchemy occurs . . .
> Everybody has a ditch, or ought to. For only the ditches—and
> the fields, the woods, the ravines—can teach us to care enough.

Thus, an important element of nature-mentoring children of this age is to loosen the reins enough that they have the freedom and access to find their own place and visit it often.

Children's play during the middle childhood years tends to be more physical and competitive, focused increasingly on testing physical limits. Games such as kick the can become addictive, alongside team sports like soccer and basketball. Middle childhood is also the time when kids begin drumming up the courage for unfamiliar, often risky activities such as skateboarding, surfing, rock climbing, and snorkeling.

The classic activity for kids of this age (all too rarely the case today) was building a fort, preferably somewhere secret, beyond the prying eyes of grown-ups. Why does fort building hold such allure? Because it embodies the central longings of middle child-hood: autonomy, competence, and separation from adults.

Fortunately, this desire to demonstrate competence extends to home life as well. At some point during middle childhood, most kids move from being oblivious of household chores—whether folding laundry or cutting the lawn—to expressing a desire to participate. Coyote mentors can tap into this craving by assign-ing tasks outdoors and giving children responsibility to com-plete them on their own. Harking back to our hunter-gatherer origins, look for opportunities for kids to collect—berries, cher-ries, plums, and apples are all good candidates. Visit a local pick-your-own farm if one is handy. (While not the deepest form of nature connection, most kids will be glad to help you "for-age" at the supermarket, finding items on the grocery list. Jade has always loved this activity.)

What other natural elements would kids want to collect or catch in your local area? Options might include acorns or rocks, lizards or frogs. Many children have learned how to catch liz-ards through dint of sheer speed, or via cleverer approaches like making a "noose" from a long blade of grass. Challenge chil-dren to do some collecting and catching and come back to tell the tales. These expeditions could include catching photographs rather than creatures. The key is to send children out collecting so that they can bring something back. Such challenges make terrific fodder for story of the day, as well as providing you, the nature mentor, with plenty of avenues to dance along the edges of understanding and experience.

Ironically, despite the desire to gain some separation from mothers and fathers, kids in middle childhood also look to par-ents as models and guides.

I recently had a conversation with two outdoorsmen, one an avid fly-fisherman, the other a big-game hunter and accom-

plished animal sculptor. Both claimed that their kids, now adolescents or older, had developed a strong bond with nature.
When I asked how, the fisherman spoke of taking his boys out
camping and fishing, encouraging them to become more aware
of their surroundings. He did this in part by asking questions.
Which flying insects are the fish feeding on? How does the song
of the chickadee change during different seasons? Where do the
fish tend to congregate in the stream, and at what time of day?

The sculptor, meanwhile, happily shared stories of his daughter accompanying him on treks to watch animals in the wild. He
too posed questions. How do the deer's legs move as it walks?
What are the changes when it shifts to a run? How are the pro-
portions and muscles of an adult elk different from those of
a juvenile? She apparently listened closely and learned how to
pay attention. Today she does her own wilderness excursions to
study wolves and other animals up close as a means of inform-
ing her art.

The key here is that both men took their kids with them
while they pursued their own outdoor passions. The children,
feeling that longing for competence, picked up on these passions
and unknowingly used them to deepen their own nature connection. The lesson is that while it's important to observe children closely and support their individual interests, as a nature
mentor you need to be authentic in your own interests as well.
Sharing these sorts of experiences with children will ultimately
strengthen their bond with nature. Are they going to want to do
the same things you're passionate about? Maybe, maybe not. I
suggest not pushing too hard; they'll figure it out on their own.
But kids will be fueled by your energy and create a stronger
bond with nature, perhaps developing expertise in one or more
outdoor pursuits along the way.

So, whether you're a parent, grandparent, teacher, or nanny, what's your nature passion? Birding? Mountain biking? Painting? Whatever it is, think about how you might use it in Trickster fashion to play on the desires of children and deepen their nature connection. If you don't yet have a nature passion or activity, think about finding one. Most such activities—among them, fishing, hunting, gardening, mushrooming, mountain climbing, and birding—entail learning a set of skills that can be improved throughout life. In other words, they involve competencies, exactly the kind of thing that's likely to engage kids in middle childhood.

This is also the age when kids first get the wherewithal to start a daily sit spot routine (Chapter 3). Think about starting with your child, taking a few minutes daily, or at least a few times a week, to return to the same natural place just to listen, look, and share stories about your experiences. Alternatively, if you simply love to walk in the park or go hiking in nearby natural areas, you can leverage this activity by encouraging kids to open their senses, and maybe do some collecting or catching along the way.

With kids in the range of six to twelve years old, your questions can become more abstract, probing and pushing edges well beyond those that existed just a couple of years earlier. The grand opportunity here is to use your nature passion *and* that of children to get kids outdoors, heighten their awareness, and deepen their connection.

Ecstatic Moments

Think back to your childhood and recall a place that was extremely meaningful to you. If so inclined, close your eyes and contemplate a memorable moment in that place. Imagine details: sights, smells, sounds, whether you're alone or with others. I invite you to pause briefly to do this . . .

Now, was your place indoors or out? If you're part of the baby-boomer generation, born between 1946 and 1965, you likely chose an outdoor, nature-rich setting. Chances are also good that you imagined yourself at some age in middle childhood, immersed in a place you found somehow magical.

Boomers like me are part of the last generation raised with abundant nature contact. Yet in conducting this same exercise during many talks that I've given, I've found that the great majority of people born in the late '60s and '70s still choose an outdoor setting. Nature has great power to stir our emotions in memorable ways.

As for middle childhood, there's something about experiences during this life interval that leave lasting impressions. In reviewing the autobiographies of 300 "geniuses"—among them scientists, artists, inventors, and writers—anthropologist Edith Cobb discovered a strong trend. Most individuals highlighted powerful nature experiences that occurred during this in-between phase of their youth.

> There is a special period, the . . . middle age of childhood, approximately from five or six to eleven or twelve—between the strivings of animal infancy and the storms of adolescence—when the natural world is experienced in some highly evocative way, producing in the child a sense of some profound continuity with natural processes . . .
>
> It is principally to this middle-age range in their early life that these writers say they return in memory in order to renew the power and impulse to create at its very source . . . In these memories the child appears to experience a sense of dis-

continuity, an awareness of his own unique separateness and identity, and also a continuity, a renewal of relationship with nature as process.

Louise Chawla of the University of Colorado–Boulder has critiqued some of Cobb's methods and amended a few of her conclusions. Chawla, tapping into her own research, underlines the fact that anyone—not just geniuses—can have this kind of transcendent encounter in the natural world, and that such experiences can inspire creativity. She also makes room for different degrees, or depths, of experience, and highlights the role of "ecstatic places."

Ecstatic, as Chawla uses it, goes back to the word's original Greek meaning of "outstanding," or "standing outside ourselves." She emphasizes that such ecstatic moments and places are delicate and highly dependent on initial conditions. Key ingredients include freedom, discovery, and the use of multiple senses (all of which resonate as I look back on my bootful of pollywogs experience described in the Introduction). Wild nature, however, is not a requirement; many such potent moments feature urban nature. And, as with my frog pond adventure, not all of these experiences are limited to middle childhood, though most seem to fall there.

Kenneth Clark, in his book *Civilization: A Personal View,* nicely captures both the power and the spirit of deep nature experience:

> Total immersion: this is the ultimate reason why the love of nature has been for so long accepted as a religion. It is a means by which we can lose our identity in the whole and gain thereby a more intense consciousness of being.

Chawla concludes from her research that ecstatic moments are rare and lasting gifts that offer us meaningful memories, a core sense of calm, and an understanding of our embeddedness within nature. For at least some people, she adds, they also help foster a creative disposition. Who wouldn't want their children to have such experiences?

Life Under House Arrest

Today, however, nature experience, while not quite teetering on the brink of extinction, is definitely under siege. Overscheduled kids have no time for it. Overprotected kids are kept indoors under constant supervision. And over-screened kids opt for virtual worlds created by others. Many children fall into all three categories—overscheduled, overprotected, and over-screened—living under effective "house arrest."

Saddled with derogatory labels like "helicopter parent" and "tiger mom," dads and (especially) moms are often saddled with the blame for this recent transformation. Yet parents are equally deserving of our empathy and understanding. The past generation has witnessed a cultural transformation in the way we conceive of childhood and parenting, resulting in new and powerful trends that prove difficult to buck.

The truth of the matter is that virtually all parents want the very best for their children. And they go to great lengths to get it. Overworked mothers and fathers seek out the best schools for their kids. Those with financial means shell out heaps of cash for private schools, academic tutors, extracurricular music lessons, sporting teams, and summer camps. In between, of course, there's plenty of driving—to and from school, to the seemingly ubiquitous weekend soccer games, to playdates and sleepovers.

No wonder kids' lives are overscheduled, leaving little time to be, well . . . just kids.

A similar trend applies to overprotecting children. Play-dates—those multihour kid get-togethers orchestrated by grown-ups (and, unfortunately, often involving very little real play)—are a recent invention of risk-averse parents. Prior to the past couple of decades, there was simply no need for them. When most of us were kids and needed someone to play with, we simply walked or biked to a friend's house and knocked on the door. Or we just headed out into the neighborhood, where other kids were already playing. Today, parents who let their children walk to school, or wander the neighborhood during evenings and weekends, run the risk of being labeled as irresponsible or worse. An unattended child roaming the neighborhood is likely to result in a call to the police.

Fear of leaving our children unattended is not only a North American phenomenon. Several studies conducted in Europe and Australia have found that the acceptable radius of independent mobility for children has shrunk drastically, more than 90 percent in the past four generations according to one United Kingdom report. The latter highlights one family's story, contrasting the freedom experienced by the great grandfather (able to go up to six miles from home unattended at age eight) with that of the present-day eight-year-old son (limited to a radius of about 300 yards).

Though the statistics do not support the notion that kids are at higher risk of abduction by strangers, parental fear is all too real. Richard Louv writes, "Does our fear often border on the irrational? Sure. But nobody said that parenting itself is completely rational. If it were, scientists would be raising our kids. In labs. With control groups."

In a recent *Atlantic* article titled "The Overprotected Kid,"

Hanna Rosin describes one of the great paradoxes of our time. As parents, many of us are busier than ever before, with two-income families and longer working hours being commonplace. Yet mothers and fathers spend much more time with their children than ever before. How can this be?

The answer is that when our kids are not in school, they're under near-constant supervision. Rosin writes: "When my daughter was about ten, my husband suddenly realized that in her whole life, she had probably not spent more than ten minutes unsupervised by an adult. Not ten minutes in ten years." Rosin's daughter is hardly unique. Continual oversight of children is the (albeit often uncomfortable) norm these days. Hardly the recipe for ecstatic nature moments.

I know from firsthand experience what it's like to combat these trends. Jade is now a young adolescent. As an elementary school student, she had far more homework than either my wife or I did at her age. We expressed our concerns to Jade's teachers but received little sympathy. "Parents expect us to assign this much homework," we were told. As for extracurricular activities, Toni and I decided that Jade could choose one sport and one musical instrument. She began playing drums in second grade, and started kicking her way through karate classes in third. This music–martial arts combo has persisted, greatly limiting Jade's afterschool free time. When she has managed to hang out with friends, it's largely been through playdates and sleepovers, where grown-ups are rarely more than a wall away.

Yet it's also true that Jade has spent plenty of time outdoors. We're fortunate to have been able to get her out hiking, camping, playing on the beach, and attending various nature-focused summer camps. As a result, she considers herself a "nature girl" and seeks opportunities to spend time outside. Yet that outdoor time has been hard to come by, often requiring considerable planning. And I regret the fact that Jade hasn't had more un-structured playtime, let alone solitude, outdoors.

I think it's important for parents to devote some thought to balancing risks. In protecting our children from certain kinds of risky behaviors, are we risking even greater harms? Of course, if we keep kids indoors, their chances of being abducted by a stranger or being hit by a car will likely go down. And yes, if our kids never climb trees, their odds of experiencing a broken arm or wrist may decrease.

But what are the costs of these choices? What are children losing by not having long stretches of timeless nature experi-ence? A strong argument can be made for the many physical, mental, and emotional benefits of free play. Another potential casualty of a life lived indoors is autonomy. Kids need to test their limits, sometimes beyond the watchful gaze of grown-ups. Then there are those ecstatic, meaning-making moments that may never occur if nature is not an integral part of childhood. Of course, no clear-minded parents would choose to impoverish their child. Yet this is exactly what may be happening when we keep overscheduled children indoors.

Now ponder this. If the present indoor trend continues un-abated, how will people answer in a generation when they're asked to name that meaningful childhood place? And if the overwhelming majority chooses indoor settings, what will we have lost?

Hummingbird Parenting

So, given that most parents are unlikely to let their kids roam freely, at least not in the foreseeable future, let's ask a different question. How can we reduce risk and manage our fears while still getting our kids outdoors and giving them some meaningful autonomy?

Here are a few strategies to consider. First, the best way to get children outside is to go with them. Make family outdoor time a priority and schedule it if necessary. You may be surprised at the results. Renee Limon, a mother of two who cofounded Enviro-Mom.com, claims, "When we go outside, my kids become their best selves. Gone are the petty arguments about whose turn it is to go first or what to do next. Suddenly the kids are creative, digging in the dirt, picking up worms, jumping and laughing."

A second strategy is to plan for outdoor time. With the crazy pace of kids' lives today, it's unlikely that they will get a reasonable amount of nature play unless you get it on the calendar. In other words, if you agree that time outdoors deserves to be an integral part of growing up, make it a priority and insert it into the weekly schedule. Let your kids know that you're doing this and explain why you think it's important.

Given today's parental fears, if outdoor play is going to become an integral part of children's lives, most of it is likely going to have to happen in places such as backyards, school-yards, courtyards, and parks. Fortunately, these environments can be plenty wild, especially for young children, as long as a few natural elements are added—for example, boulders, trees, sand, grasses, and perhaps a garden. The simple addition of native wildflowers attracts native insects and birds. This kind of rewilding creates a variety of miniature habitats ideally suited for engaging young minds in imaginative play.

For kids in middle childhood, the present age focus of our discussion, try to find places that allow for more autonomy, in terms of both distance and freedom. Parents, look to local parks or other kinds of open spaces. Teachers, school grounds can make ideal places for nature play, as we'll see in Chapter 10.

Michele Whitaker offers what may be the most helpful strategy of all. Try becoming more of a "hummingbird parent." In her words: "In the range from helicopter to neglect—I probably fall a bit more toward helicopter. In fact, I call myself a hummingbird parent. I tend to stay physically distant to let them explore and problem solve, but zoom in at moments when safety is an issue (which isn't very often)."

I love the hummingbird metaphor. Whitaker suggests that grown-ups become more conscious of the physical distance they keep from kids, and take steps back as children get older to allow for increasing autonomy. Along this path, we can find potential for us to fulfill our need to keep kids safe while allowing them to take risks and push limits. If we're successful, the end result will be another generation of free-range kids.

But here's the rub. To be most effective, nature mentoring cannot be a solo endeavor. One person may play the primary role, but children need multiple mentors.

It Takes a Village

If you're a parent of a child six or older, I'm willing to bet that you've had firsthand experience with the following scenario:

You: "How was your day today?"
Child: "Good."
You: "What did you do?"
Child: "Nothing."
You: "Ah c'mon. There must have been something exciting that happened."
Child: "Nope."

Then, once in a while, after one of these rewarding interactions, someone else arrives—perhaps a sister, uncle, grandparent, friend, or the FedEx delivery guy—and asks the same question. Suddenly your child erupts in a flurry of animated stories. "In gym class, Evan got hit in the head with a baseball bat and had to be taken to the hospital for stitches . . . Ooh, and in English class, Ms. Fletcher taught us this Greek myth about an awesome one-eyed monster called the Cyclops . . ."

Your first reaction is likely, "What the . . . what am I, chopped liver?" But then comes a sense of relief from hearing at least a few details about your child's day.

The problem is that particularly once middle childhood takes hold, moms and dads are not always the right people to talk with. In fact, for reasons that are rarely clear but likely have something to do with that longing for independence, they can be exactly the *wrong* people. Aunts and uncles in the broadest sense—that is, pretty much any adult who cares for, listens to, and has the trust of your child—are often the preferred go-to people.

Putting this into the context of nature mentoring, you may have all the best intentions, asking questions and trying to pull a story of the day from your child after a nature excursion. But if you're a parent, at least some of the time your efforts will need the backing of another adult. So, in true Coyote fashion, think about whom you might enlist to help you in being a nature mentor. If no one comes to mind, put some effort into finding more people who might fill this role.

The same factors often apply to your child taking risks. Let's say your son wants to climb high into a tree, or your daughter is keen to jump across a raging creek. As a parent, even if you consent to the activity (a long shot for many), you may unwittingly cause your child to have an accident because of your nervous energy and concern for their safety. Meanwhile, that caring "uncle" or "aunt" could be just the person to offer the right mixture of caution and enthusiastic support, resulting in a powerful victory that bolsters your kid's sense of confidence.

Because children in middle childhood tend to idolize teens, yearning for the day when they'll get to walk in those bigger shoes, another great strategy is to mix age groups. Look for trustworthy teens in your extended family or surrounding network who might be willing to help with getting younger children outside having adventures. Contrary to popular belief, adolescents, especially those with lots of nature experience, are often happy to hang out on occasion with younger kids.

Not to be forgotten, grandparents and other elders also have an essential role to play in nature connection. First off, they typically fall solidly within the "caring nonparent" category, making them great targets for hearing children's stories. Second, grandparents are rapidly becoming the only demographic whose childhoods included a deep sense of nature connection. Their generation embodies Richard Louv's "last child in the woods." So grandpas and grandmas are often full of nature stories with potential to engage children's imaginations and help them to stretch limits. "Back in the day, when I was your age, we'd head down to the pond and catch frogs by the dozen. Those slippery little hoppers were tricky, but we learned to be trickier, sneaking up so quietly they never heard us coming."

Today, the Audubon Society, the Sierra Club, and other likeminded environmental organizations are concerned because their membership is so heavily dominated by seniors. Where is the next generation of members going to come from? More importantly, who will be Earth's stewards in future generations if our collective memory of nature experiences dwindles to the point of extinction?

Grandparents and other elders, this is your moment. As the primary holders of the nature connection flame, you are ideally positioned to make a real difference in how younger generations see themselves in relation to the natural world. Seek out children with whom you can share your nature stories and, in doing so, provoke the creation of new ones. We need your passion and your wisdom to help us spawn the next generation of nature lovers!

The great news is that no matter who you are, you shouldn't feel like you need to be the sole nature mentor for the children in your life. In fact, kids' nature connection will likely go much deeper with multiple mentors of various ages. The more problematic news, perhaps, is that you need to find others willing and able to help.

Around now you may be thinking, "Okay, this sounds like a terrific approach, but it ain't gonna happen with my extended family, and I really don't have any friends that I can see playing this role." Before you fall into the depths of despair and heave this book into the fireplace, let me offer one possible solution.

Family Nature Clubs

The premise is simple. Get two or more families outdoors together on a regular basis—say, once a month. Let the kids run around and play, while the adults enjoy food, drink, and each other, talking adult stuff. Sound interesting? Thousands of families have already signed up. The Children & Nature Network currently has about 200 registered family nature clubs, with that number doubling in just the past few years. With names such as High Park Rangers, Muddy Boots, and Dangerous Dads, some clubs consist of a few families; others include hundreds.

Chip and Ashley Donahue were looking for ways to get their

three kids outdoors around their home in Roanoke, Virginia. Inspired by *Last Child in the Woods*, they started a free family nature club: KIVA, or Kids in the Valley, Adventuring! With the help of a couple of newspaper articles and some supportive word of mouth, more than 600 families joined. What does the club do on their monthly outings? Hiking, picnics, nature reclamation projects; anything with an outdoor bent. On cold or rainy days, guess what? They still bundle up and head outside. Only one rule applies, aimed at safety and family bonding: Parents or guardians must stay with their children at all times. The Donahues send out a free monthly newsletter recommending outdoor places to visit and let kids play.

Richard Louv has been perhaps the biggest proponent of family nature clubs, eagerly sharing their many advantages. He notes that these clubs can be formed by any family in any neighborhood, from inner city to rural farmlands. They're free to create, with free membership (in most cases), and generally involve free activities. Nature clubs help fight off the specter of fear with the safety of numbers. They offer engaging outdoor activities with minimal effort and planning. They allow parents and other caregivers to share knowledge about nearby nature, increasing the understanding of all. Finally, there's the all-important motivation factor. Because let's face it, we're all more likely to show up for a weekend nature outing if we know that other families are there waiting for us.

I think Louv is really on to something, and I would add a trio of additional benefits to his list. First, children are likely to be excited to go anywhere that involves playing with other children, so family clubs have potential to bust kids out of their electronic doldrums and get excited about nature. Second, it's much easier to develop your talents as a hummingbird parent when there are plenty of other adults around keeping an eye on the little ones. Third, a family nature club has potential to become a community of nature mentors—teens, "aunts," "uncles," and elders—harnessing the power of multiple generations and relieving parents from being the sole nature mentors. With minimal guidance, these other mentors can ask edge-stretching questions, listen to stories and share their own, and help kids navigate risk safely. And don't forget about yourself. You need support as well, including like-minded adults with whom you can share your own stories of growing nature connection.

Louv envisions a time when such clubs become the norm in every community. To help achieve this dream, the Children & Nature Network, which he cofounded, offers a free online toolkit to start your own club. New clubs are popping up almost daily. There may already be one in your neck of the woods. If not, why not get one started?

How do we stem the tide of children falling out of love with nature during middle childhood? One part of the answer may just be communities formed around family nature clubs.

Secret #7 for Raising a Wild Child

For children in middle childhood, tap into their longings by fostering nature experiences with plenty of exploration, autonomy, and demonstrations of competence.

Nature Mentoring Tips

BECOME A HUMMINGBIRD PARENT

Beginning in middle childhood (snd sometimes earlier!) children long for some separation and independence from adults. One of the greatest challenges of being a nature mentor for children of this age is honoring this need, fighting the urge to be ever present. So instead of helicopter parenting, work on developing your flight skills as a hummingbird parent. This means giving kids space and autonomy to take risks, staying on the periphery sipping nectar most of the time and zooming in only when necessary. If the idea of hanging back makes you nervous, start off close, slowly work your way back, and see how it feels. Monitor how the children are feeling about your distance too. As they get older, it will be more and more important to increase that separation so as to give children the freedom to take some risks, make some mistakes, and deal with consequences. The goal should not be to eliminate risk; children must learn eventually how to cope with risky circumstances, or face much larger consequences as inexperienced adolescents and adults. If you follow this pathway of expanding freedom, children will become ever more confident and capable.

BRING OUT THE ARTISTS

Follow Zach Pine's lead and turn your kids into nature artists. You can find the necessary raw materials in most outdoor settings. Dirt, sticks, rocks, feathers, pinecones, flowers—all are terrific artistic elements. One favorite subject of smaller children is fairy houses, or even mini-villages, made from small sticks and plant matter. This kind of art fuels imaginations and stories. Alternatively, nature art can be big and showy, like the beach examples described in this chapter. Of course, feel free to engage your inner artist as well. If you do, chances are you won't need to teach the youngsters anything. They'll watch you closely and mimic what you do. After all the artistic creations are completed, think about photographing them to keep a record. Kids love to go back and see how their artistic abilities transformed as they grew up. For teachers, get creative and consider ways that art and science might be interwoven.

STREAMING ADVENTURES

Our notion of wildness matures with age. A backyard with trees, bushes, and rocks is plenty wild for a preschooler. But for kids in middle childhood, between about six and eleven years of age, nature connection is best fostered by adventures a little farther afield. Forests are exceptional settings, as are beaches. And among the most effective and commonly available options are streams, preferably lined with greenery rather than buildings. Even semi-wild watercourses in urban areas are typically home to fishes, frogs, butterflies, and birds, among many other creatures. For maximal effect, encourage the children to take their time and look closely. If appropriate, let them get into the water and navigate their way upstream, making observations along the way. A small net is always good for catching passerby critters. Make a game out of it once in a while, splitting the kids into pairs or small groups to see which one can count the greatest number of plant and animal types. And—again, if appropriate—let the youngsters take off without immediate adult supervision or guidance. Middle childhood is the time to begin exploring one's home terrain, and autonomy is a powerful ingredient in fostering a passion for place.

DISCOVER YOUR OWN NATURE PASSION

I have long been fascinated by birds, though so far I have yet to become a serious birder. Nevertheless, because I am always looking at birds and listening to their songs, my daughter Jade has become something of a birdwatcher too. My personal favorite is to combine hiking and birding. If you haven't found a nature activity that you're passionate about, consider putting some effort into it. Yes, most of us are extremely busy and find it difficult to carve out time for anything new. But the reality is that with rare exceptions, most young kids these days aren't going to get out into nature unless we take them there. And let's face it: You're unlikely to do that unless there's some compelling reason to get you there. So try to find an activity—whether it's close to home, like gardening, or far away, like fly-fishing or snowshoeing—that you can engage in with the children in your life. Along with actually getting you and the kids out into nature, potential pluses include deepening your own nature connection, allowing you to model the value of nature (and your own connection), providing a ready source of narratives for telling stories, and establishing a skill that children can also work on developing over time.

GO CLUBBING

Perhaps the biggest reason that children today don't get out into nature is that we grown-ups don't make it a priority. Most of us will need to schedule nature into our busy lives if it's going to become a part of what we do and how we live. This is where family nature clubs can make all the difference, offering a group of other families to connect with outdoors on a regular, scheduled basis. Family nature clubs make the process of getting into nature easy, with the organization of outings shared by the group. They offer a ready source of children for your kids to play with, and a cadre of like-minded adults to interact with. Check to see if a family nature club already exists in your area. And if not, consider starting one. It's free and there's a simple kit to get you started at the website of the Children & Nature Network. Among the greatest benefits of partnering up with other "natural families" is the instant community you'll access that can assist you in your mentoring efforts. So go ahead. Unleash the power of community and watch your nature connection and mentoring efforts take off!

8

The Social Animal

Mentoring Adolescents

There is nothing in a caterpillar that tells you it is going to be a butterfly.

— R. BUCKMINSTER FULLER

TWO HUNDRED ADULTS stood side by side, forming a giant circle in the middle of a forest clearing. It was day four of the Art of Mentoring, the weeklong intensive in the Santa Cruz Mountains introduced in Chapter 3. The group, now an intentional community, had rallied in similar fashion each of the previous mornings to share announcements and talk about the day's activities. But this circle was to be different.

Following the usual preamble, a group of ten teens accompanied by a pair of twenty-something counselors—one male, one female—entered the clearing. They were a ragtag bunch, a few tall and gangly, still finding their bodies; others, more childlike, awaiting that adolescent growth spurt. The ring of adults briefly parted, and the teen group entered, forming their own much tighter ring at the center. In unison, the adults then slowly moved in, packing up around the teens while leaving perhaps a meter's separation.

One of the staff members announced that we were gathered

to celebrate the teens' departure as they headed off on a multi-day wilderness trek. This was much more than a backpacking trip, he added. These youths were about to venture off on an expedition to discover themselves, their peers, and the mountains, and raise their awareness along the way.

He asked that each of the teens declare their intentions for the trip. "My intention is to get to know my fellow teens better," said one girl. "My intention is to push my edges and have fun," declared one of the gangly boys.

After all the teens had spoken, the grown-ups were given the opportunity to share words of support, which rang out from around the circle. "Live the trip to the fullest." "Take care of each other." And so on.

Finally, all the younger kids, who until then had been on the sidelines, were invited into the narrow gap between the adults and teens. They entered full of smiles and nervousness, some peeking between the legs of the teens in search of an older brother or sister. They too were given the chance to share their words of wisdom. "Don't kill yourselves," offered one girl. "Don't kill each other," her friend added.

The teens were then informed that the entire community would sing a song to usher them off on their trip, that we would keep singing until they were well out of sight. And so we did. Now, imagine 200 people singing a brief yet meaningful song of farewell to drum accompaniment, again and again. The intensity of the feeling is hard to describe. It was like being on a remote beach as enormous waves repeatedly pound the shore. In a word, powerful.

After a minute or so, the teens exited the circle, hoisted their backpacks, and began walking up the hill. Several looked back and waved. A few minutes later, they rounded the corner out of sight. We sang a while longer, raising the volume even higher in case they could still hear us. And then we stopped. The energy that had united us only moments prior began to dissipate. Suddenly dropped from timelessness back into the present, I noticed tears flowing down some of the faces around me. Jade stood on the opposite side, a look of wonder on her face, still staring at the place where the teens had disappeared into the forest.

Teen Brains, Teen Longings

Adults sometimes speak of teenagers as if they're part of an alien species, or at least humans whose minds have been temporarily hijacked. This is by no means a recent sentiment, as adolescents have long been regarded as enigmatic works in progress. Aristotle and Socrates bemoaned them. So too did Shakespeare:

> I would there were no age between sixteen and three-and-twenty, or that youth would sleep out the rest; for there is nothing in the between but getting wenches with child, wronging the ancientry, stealing, fighting . . .

Only in the past couple of decades have neuroscientists made great strides in understanding the inner workings of the adolescent brain. Not long ago, it was thought that all major brain development was completed in the early years of life, no later than early in middle childhood. New imaging technologies, however, have allowed us to take photographs and video of the living brain. These new tools reveal an organ that, though nearing adult size by age six, continues to develop and change throughout the teens and twenties.

In general, three things happen to brain cells. They proliferate, growing rapidly and forming new connections. They're pruned, with unused cells cut away like unwanted branches on a rosebush. And they're insulated, coated with a substance called myelin that increases speed and efficiency of transmissions. Proliferation of brain cells, we now know, peaks during early adolescence, with pruning and insulation thereafter becoming dominant. Experience is the X factor in this use-it-or-lose-it process. Brain cells activated by experience are retained; the leftovers are pruned away.

To complicate matters, the twenty-first-century teen brain seems to be falling victim to an imbalance of forces involving risk and reward. On the one hand, puberty triggers physiological and chemical changes within the brain that cause adolescents to overvalue rewards, especially social rewards involving peers. An inordinate amount of energy is spent worrying about projecting the "right" image, whatever that may be. These brain changes explain why teens are so highly motivated—let's say compelled—to take risks. Hark back to the intense feelings surrounding teen love interests and athletic pursuits.

Thankfully, there's an area of the brain, known as the prefrontal cortex, that controls impulses, guides decision-making, and enables long-term planning. This lump of brain matter just behind the forehead is also involved with self-awareness and preventing inappropriate behaviors. However, experience emerges again as the critical factor. As we face challenging decisions, the prefrontal cortex is modified, allowing us to hone our expertise and impulse control through trial and error.

According to one hypothesis now garnering support, these two systems—one driving motivation, the other enabling inhibition—were more in sync during our hunter-gatherer and farming days. Back then, the emotional drive of puberty was countered by early and abundant experience received through apprenticeships and adult mentoring. In these societies, kids were put to work hunting, gathering, cooking, babysitting, and the like during middle childhood. By engaging the prefrontal cortex of the brain early, youngsters were honing important, often risky skills—say, wielding a machete or tending a fire—well before the chemical cocktail of puberty kicked in.

Today, most North American kids do little else beyond school, not just through middle childhood but adolescence as well. Gone, it seems, are the teen babysitting jobs and paper routes. Parents would rather endure a dinner of stale granola and sour milk than have their eight-year-old cook. For twenty-first-century youths, then (at least in the developed world), that all-important control and inhibition system, so highly dependent on experience, is underdeveloped when adolescence strikes. Consequently, so the hypothesis goes, teens are ill prepared to deal with risk and often make poor decisions.

One Berkeley psychologist puts it this way: adolescents develop an accelerator well before they can steer and brake. Hardly the ideal setup.

Okay, let's look at some upsides. With all those proliferating brain cells, adolescents are ideally suited for learning and creativity. Compared to their middle childhood predecessors, they possess a greatly enhanced capacity for abstract and conceptual thinking, as well as moral and ethical reasoning. This is the time of life when the brain first learns how to comprehend the greatest temporal and spatial scales (at least as much as human minds can). Although the big ideas of evolution and ecology—including the story of the universe and the flow of matter and energy through ecosystems (see Chapters 4 and 5)—can and should be introduced in early and middle childhood, it's during the teen years that we finally begin to grapple with their meaning, and to understand our place in this vastness.

Perhaps most important for the purposes of our discussion,

we know that adolescents long to take risks with high potential for social rewards, especially those involving peers. Ideally, these risks will consist of challenges with which the teen has minimal prior experience, clearly demonstrating movement away from childhood. Self-esteem, self-awareness, self-identity—these are the targets of adolescent arrows, even if the archers are often blindfolded.

So what role can nature play?

Adolescents and Nature

If you were to head outside right now and ask a large, random sample of people to rate a series of images taken in various places—urban, rural, and wild—the great majority would show a strong preference toward natural settings. Odds are also excellent that you'd get the same result if you repeated the survey in different cultures around the world, even if the natural settings ran the gamut from spectacular to mundane.

This finding has been repeated multiple times over the past four decades in several countries. Many believe that this bias is genetic, built into our DNA, reflecting a deep ancestry lived in intimate contact with the natural world. Remarkably, people often show greatest preference toward savannah-type settings with grassland, patches of trees, and water, leading some to argue that this penchant too is hard-wired within us, evolutionary baggage carried from our African origins. I'm skeptical of this last claim, given that humans have lived in a variety of settings worldwide during the past 70,000 years, and that we now know that genes can evolve very quickly.

What interests me more is another finding of these studies. Adolescents differ from younger and older age cohorts in showing a weaker preference for natural settings of all kinds. They don't rate images of lush forests or mountainous settings as high, instead showing a stronger preference for active urban settings—say, city streets with cars and buses. After reviewing the evidence, Rachel and Stephen Kaplan concluded that this teen propensity does not so much reflect a dislike of nature; the participants' selections still indicated appreciation and enjoyment of natural settings. Rather, nature no longer has the same pull for adolescents because of their heightened enthusiasm for peer interactions in urban areas.

Does this mean we should forget about nature connection during the adolescent years, and let them take a "time out"? By no means. Wild nature offers amazing settings to undertake daring yet controlled challenges with peers. And teens tend to be passionate about doing outdoor activities if other teens are present.

The problem is, they aren't spending much time in nature.

In 2012, an online blogging community called StageofLife .com surveyed more than 4,000 American teens and college students, asking about their attitudes toward nature. The results go a long way toward helping us understand the challenges faced by anyone who wants to foster nature connection among teenagers.

About 89 percent of respondents agreed that their generation is disconnected from nature. When asked if they care about the effects of "man" on nature, the same high percentage reported either, "yes, I care passionately," or "yes, I care but I don't take an active role." These same adolescents averaged about four to five hours per week outdoors (including work, sports, and hobbies)—far less, they reported, than during their elementary school years.

The survey was accompanied by an essay contest, which revealed several prominent themes. The adolescents were in strong agreement that they and their peers use technology too much and should spend more time, even an hour a day, connecting with nature. They used words such as *peaceful* and *simple* to describe the natural world, contrasting it with the frenzy of the digital world. Many wrote of previous impactful, even life-changing nature experiences—some recent, others years in the past. And there was strong consensus that we need to treat nature with respect and take care of it.

In short, nature's great, it's good for us, and we need to care for it, but we just don't manage to get outside much. Why not? The survey didn't ask specifically, but other sources point to homework, technology, lack of experience, and "bugs" as frequent deterrents. And presumably there's minimal incentive to head outdoors if one's peers are digitally "wired" indoors.

So how might we apply Coyote mentoring methods to transform our new understanding of teenage proclivities into nature connection?

In fact, the nature formula for this age group is pretty straightforward. Put adolescents together in outdoor situations where they can take calculated risks with each other while demonstrating new skills and strengths. Make sure they have a degree of autonomy from adults and strong peer support. Exactly this approach is already used by Outward Bound and many other successful programs that work with teens around the United States and elsewhere.

Finding Yourself

On April 29, 1992, a terrified kid named Juan Martinez hid in a bathtub in south-central Los Angeles while shots rang out and riots savaged his neighborhood. Several years later, as an angry ninth grader considering a career in the local gang, Martinez was given a choice. Serve weeks of detention or join the "eco-club." Despite fears of being stuck with the "geeks and dorks," he chose the latter. At the end of that school year, the fifteen-year-old had his first wilderness experience—a transformative two-week eco-club trip to Wyoming's Grand Tetons. Martinez returned home passionate about getting more urban youths outdoors. He helped form an environmental justice youth league academy in L.A., the first of its kind in the country. Today he is an ambassador for North Face, a National Geographic Emerging Explorer, and the youngest member in the history of the Sierra Club Foundation Board. He also heads up the Natural Leaders Network for the Children & Nature Network. As a result of Martinez's efforts, many thousands of youths, many of them also inner-city kids, are connecting with nature.

Juan Martinez's amazing story embodies several lessons. First, he is walking proof that nature connection can begin in the teen years. While it's always best to start as young as possible, Martinez and many others show that it's never too late. The second lesson is that given the right mentoring, youths often make excellent leaders. Martinez has quickly become a powerful role model for young leaders seeking to connect other youths with nature. And the third lesson is that service can be a powerful form of nature connection. By working on behalf of people and nature in a given place, we almost cannot help but deepen our own sense of nature connection.

"Find your place on the planet. Dig in, and take responsibility from there." This quote from poet Gary Snyder nicely sums up the nature connection pathway to service. Indeed, in very general terms, we might even equate Snyder's three steps with the three growth stages. You find your place in early childhood, dig in during middle childhood, and take responsibility for that place in adolescence. And yet, as we shall see, this equation is too simplistic, in part because service can begin as soon as early childhood.

Nevertheless, teens and younger kids can easily be empowered to identify local problems and devote their energies toward solutions. School gardens, reclaimed streams, recycling programs, and fish ladders are examples of service-based projects with the potential to build on one's understanding of local nature and deepen connections with it.

If you're a parent wondering how to find an engaging service project for your child, the best way to start is simply to ask her: "If you were going to get involved in doing something for our community, what do you think it might be?" Feel free to throw out ideas, particularly if there are some with which the child is already familiar.

If you don't hit on anything that strikes a chord, another great strategy is to seek a confluence of passions, or at least interests. First, try to determine where kids' nature interests lie. Do they seem most attracted to, say, birds, streams, or plants? If you've been nature-mentoring awhile, you'll likely have a good idea of the answer already. Second, what kind of local problem are they most concerned about? Threatened species? Social injustice? Water quality? With answers to these two questions, you can search together for an activity that interweaves both.

Yet another way to identify a great service opportunity is to make a list of local opportunities and simply go and try out some that sound interesting. When our family still lived in California, a large-scale project was undertaken near our home to improve the health of Redwood Creek, which flows through famous Muir Woods National Monument to empty into the ocean at Muir Beach. One of the primary goals was to improve the stream habitat for coho salmon because Redwood Creek is part of the southernmost North American watershed still hosting stable runs of coho.

Jade and I got involved by working with the Golden Gate National Parks Conservancy to plant elderberry and blackberry along the creek margins. We were each given a vest, a hardhat, gloves, and a digging tool. After a short orientation, we were handed seedlings and told where to plant them. For each seedling, we dug a hole just deep enough to cover the roots. We then removed the plant from its protective plastic casing, carefully placed it in the hole, and filled the remainder with dirt. After completing this process with seven or so seedlings in a small area, we covered the plants with a loose matrix of sticks to prevent deer from grazing away all our hard work. Ever since, Jade and I have both felt a sense of pride whenever we stroll past that beautiful flowing creek.

If you're a teacher, perhaps start off by thinking about service activities that your students might lead right on the school grounds: say, planting a vegetable garden, putting in bird boxes to attract nesting birds, or starting a recycling program. And consider ways to integrate the curriculum so that these service projects become service-learning projects. Off site, seek out local organizations that offer service opportunities for school groups.

If beauty is symbolized by the heart, and truth by the brain, goodness might be considered the domain of the gut—a moral compass guiding our decision-making. It is during the teen years that we begin to fine-tune our moral compass. Although service can begin at almost any age, I know of no better moral fine-tuning activity than teen service learning. As Gandhi once observed, "The best way to find yourself is to lose yourself in the service of others." The message here is that those "others" extend beyond human communities to encompass natural communities as well.

Going Wild

Wilderness offers entirely different, exceptionally powerful opportunities for nature experiences, a grand sensory banquet that taps our emotions deeply. No virtual simulation can compare to a face-to-face encounter with a moose, coyote, or glacier-capped mountain. Nature viewed on a screen is detached, almost imaginary. In contrast, a growing body of research suggests that immersion in wilderness not only awakens the senses and provokes deep thoughts and feelings. It also leads often to transcendent experiences that deepen the bond with nature. Does falling in love with nature require regular wilderness experiences? No. Does a deep and lasting connection require at least some wilderness time? Almost certainly.

A number of studies have examined the effects of wilderness on adolescents. Perhaps the most comprehensive, conducted by Stephen Kellert and Victoria Derr of Yale University, involved more than 700 participants and three leading wilderness adventure providers: Outward Bound, National Outdoor Leadership School, and the Student Conservation Association.

In case you're not familiar with these sorts of organizations, most follow a similar pattern. Take participants into an unfamiliar setting for a week or two and design challenging experiences that push mental, physical, and emotional edges. Whatever the activity—perhaps canoeing, canyoneering, or mountaineering—participants learn to work as a team and to support each other through the inevitable highs and lows, always placing risk management and safety first. The education that occurs on these trips is less about naming plants and animals, and more about developing character. Even from this brief description, you can get a sense of why adolescents might respond favorably: interacting with peers in challenging activities that push limits, increase skill levels, and build character.

Kellert and Derr investigated the impact of wilderness programs using a double-pronged approach. First, through a combination of surveys, interviews, and observations, they looked at responses immediately before, just after, and six months after adolescents experienced one of these programs. Second, they examined the longer view, engaging adults who had participated in one of these three wilderness experiences during the previous twenty-five years.

A large majority of the participants stated that the experience of being in a wilderness program was one of the most important of their lives. Years later, they reported cascading effects on their personality and character development. Surprisingly, rather than diminishing through time, the effects seemed to deepen, with respondents claiming that the experience boosted self-confidence, as well as their capacity to cope with life challenges. Between 66 and 75 percent reported lasting increases in self-esteem, autonomy, initiative, independence, interpersonal skills, and problem-solving abilities. A large majority claimed that their wilderness adventure resulted in a heightened respect and appreciation for nature. And despite the fact that these experiences occurred many miles from the nearest Starbucks or Walmart, most said that their wilderness adventure bolstered their ability to function in urban settings. Talk about a full spectrum of social benefits!

The participant responses tell the story best. Here's just one example:

> It gave me an unbelievable confidence in myself. I found a beauty, strength, and an inner peace that I never knew was present . . . I learned the most I ever learned about life, myself, and the skills that I still use every day . . . It made me more confident, focused, and self-reliant. I have become more compassionate toward not only nature but toward other people . . . I learned about respect, setting goals, working to my maximum and past it. These are skills I consider to be important in everything I do, and I feel they will help me continue to be successful through life.

Granted, not all the responses were so glowing. Caution must be exercised in particular with youth who have had no previous outdoor experiences. In such instances, a more gradual approach is often best, with individuals first gaining some experience and confidence through, say, hiking and overnight camping.

Nevertheless, the consistently positive responses from the great majority of program participants speak to the power of wilderness. Whereas the local and familiar exert their greatest impacts during early and middle childhood, the wild and unfamiliar tend to resonate deeply with adolescents. These sorts of intense wilderness trips are experiential education on steroids, with lessons encompassing not only the external world of nature, but also social interactions and the internal world of self—just what the teen brain thrives on.

One caveat. A study by Louise Chawla and Victoria Derr found that although wilderness programs with adolescents do tend to promote personal growth, many are less effective at cultivating environmental understanding, awareness, and responsibility. So if nature connection is a goal, as emphasized throughout this book, activities that deepen this connection must be integrated explicitly into Outward Bound–style programs.

Mother Nature Is Colorblind

Dondre Smallwood was stunned. The skinny eight-year-old stood gaping, straining as the huge fish fought madly at the end of his line. "It's a northern pike," someone yelled. Whatever that was. For Dondre, the most remarkable thing was that he'd hauled this monster from a lake within walking distance of his house. He had no idea such creatures existed in Denver!

Dondre lived in Montbello, a low-income, often dangerous, mostly African American and Hispanic neighborhood, and the place he still calls home today. Prior to encountering that tasty hook, the pike was living in a lake within nearby Rocky Mountain Arsenal National Wildlife Refuge.

Now a handsome twenty-year-old with short-cropped hair, diamond stud earrings, and a goatee tuft on his chin, Dondre laughs as he tells the story. He had been on his very first ELK trip that day. He didn't really know what the group was all about, but his older sister decided that it'd be good for him and his brother Dwayne to join. So there they were, fishing for the first time and talking about going hiking and camping up in the mountains. Crazy stuff. As far as he knew, black people didn't do such things.

A dozen years later, he and Dwayne are both attending college, the first in their extended family to do so. Dondre plans to major in environmental science, Dwayne in biology. Dondre, who still works closely with ELK, is now a big-time mentor to kids from the same neighborhood, and he credits the group with giving him the desire and confidence to really make something of his life. His goal is to continue this work as a career, connecting people of color with nature.

ELK stands for Environmental Learning for Kids, a group cofounded in 1996 by husband-and-wife team Stacie and Scott Gilmore, both Montbello residents. Stacie still heads up ELK today, thrilled at the organization's great success. The group conducts science programs in local schools, as well as a multi-week afterschool program. These activities provide plenty of opportunities to recruit promising kids for the year-round student program, offered free of charge to about 180 youths ranging from five to twenty-five years in age. About thirty new full-time students are added each year as existing members leave, and there's plenty of competition for these slots. More than 1,000 fortunate kids like Dondre have gone through the program in the past eighteen years.

Stacie and Scott were both trained as biologists. Stacie smiles recalling the days when they first established ELK, determined that the students would learn a large series of facts, like the state tree, bird, and insect, and the names of local plants and animals. It wasn't long, however, before she realized that this academic approach was fatally flawed. Rather than factual knowledge, the real goal was changing behaviors and empowering lives. And the pathway to get there was hands-on experience with like-minded others ranging in age from middle childhood to adult. Instead of a bunch of "little scientists," Gilmore wanted ELK to foster role models for the entire neighborhood.

What do the ELK kids do? Camping, hiking, fishing, river rafting, ropes courses—even, on occasion, big-game hunting (under the watchful guidance of Colorado Parks and Wildlife). They regularly head to nearby state and national parks, and occasionally visit more distant locales such as Arizona's Grand

Canyon and Utah's Lake Powell. They also participate in various service activities, from garbage pick-up and invasive plant removal locally to trail building and tree planting in national parks.

Throughout all of these activities, emphasis is placed on community. ELK provides a second family, or in some cases the only meaningful family, for their kids, many of whom deal with difficult home situations. Just as youngsters are nearing adolescence and perhaps considering less desirable life paths, like joining one of the local gangs, ELK offers an enticing alternative. The program places major emphasis on respect: for self, for family, for community, and for nature. Scott and Stacie host regular events at their house, often hanging out in the backyard. The kids know that if they're ever in trouble, or even if they hit rock bottom because of some bad decisions, they can reach out and find help.

When I asked what role nature plays in the ELK community, Stacie and Dondre both responded with the same word: *awe.* They spoke of spending a night under a pitch-black sky in Rocky Mountain National Park, listening to the oohs and aahs of kids watching their first meteor shower. Dondre said it was that feeling of awe that hooked him in the beginning, and still fuels him today. At first he was scared to go out into nature. Today it's "my escape from everyday life," a "humbling experience that allows me to be present in the moment." He looks forward to teaching others how to experience this kind of presence in nature.

One of the greatest challenges facing the growing movement to connect people with nature is its largely white, affluent constituency. One survey found that only about one in five visitors to national parks in the United States is nonwhite. Another study revealed that only about 30 percent of outdoor activity participants belong to racial minorities, with African Americans being the least represented group.

When it comes to people, Mother Nature is colorblind. She doesn't recognize skin color. Yet we humans still contend with the deep roots of racism. The "new nature movement," as it's now called, simply cannot succeed unless it becomes everyone's movement, regardless of ethnic background and annual family income. In North America, this statement is underlined by the fact that the population is becoming increasingly diverse over time. One of the greatest challenges before us, then, is ensuring equal access to resources, including healthy foods, safe neighborhoods, unpolluted environments, quality education, and access to parks and other green spaces.

Stacie Gilmore is doing her part, and receiving major accolades along the way. In 2014, the White House formally recognized Gilmore as a "champion of change" for "engaging the next generation of conservationists." ELK is now fundraising for an education center to be placed on a five-acre property in the heart of Montbello. The plan is to transform this barren piece of land into a nature-rich open space for the entire community.

Several other organizations around the United States are now working hard to connect people of color with the natural world. For example, Juan Martinez is actively engaging ethnically diverse youth in the Natural Leaders program. The Trust for Public Land, a national nonprofit, is busy creating and revitalizing parks, the bulk of these in underserved communities. In Oakland, a fireball of a woman named Rue Mapp heads up Outdoor Afro, whose slogan is, "Where black people and nature meet." Also in the Bay Area, Jose González recently established Latino Outdoors, with the aim of connecting underserved Latino audiences nationwide with nature.

González told me that his approach has been to ask: What's

unique and different about the way Latinos engage with nature? And how can we use existing cultural traditions, from food and clothing to holidays and celebrations, to leverage nature connection? To give one, perhaps trite, example, many Hispanic cultures have a tradition of hosting weekend picnics in parks, where the adults sit and talk while the kids run around and play. Here, then, is a family nature club of sorts. González has offered programs at some of these picnic outings, using games and other interactive activities to engage kids (and often adults). He sees great potential for efforts like these to raise awareness about the workings of local nature and redefine the story of how Latinos engage with the natural world.

We need many more groups out there connecting people of color with the natural world. It's time to scale up the successes of programs like ELK to reach all children in all neighborhoods, in countries worldwide. And although this chapter focuses on adolescents, the nature connection process should be initiated as early in life as possible.

Rites of Passage

One might sum up adolescence as a quest for meaning. Who am I? How do I fit into the world? What is my own unique voice and how do I find it? These are the kinds of vexing questions that teens must grapple with as they navigate the transition from childhood to adulthood.

In many cultures, ceremonial rites of passage mark this transition (and others). The adolescent enters as a child and emerges as an adult, prepared to take on new responsibilities. Think of bar and bat mitzvah in the Jewish tradition, and quinceañera in many Latin American countries.

Most rites of passage involve three steps. First, the individual is separated from his previous daily life. Sometimes this separation is literal, with the person leaving the community. Other times it is symbolic—involving, for example, tattooing or cutting of hair. Second is the in-between, or *liminal*, phase, in which the person goes through some kind of new experience. Finally comes reincorporation, with the individual formally recognized by the community as having a new role and status. Among the strong feelings typically catalyzed by this trio of experiences is a sense of belonging.

Such ceremonies were likely the norm throughout much of human history. Recently, however, despite their recognized potential for generating meaning, rites of passage have become increasingly rare, at least in the industrial world. Lacking structured, community-sanctioned paths for venturing into adulthood, the adolescent thirst for risk is often expressed in less formal, more dangerous activities. Joining a gang is the modern urban equivalent of warrior initiation rites. Even driving at excessive speeds or taking nonprescription drugs can symbolically take the place of more formal ceremonies.

Recognizing the gap created by the loss of rites of passage, a number of groups have sprung up to provide age-of-transition ceremonial experiences. In the United States, Wilderness Awareness School, founded by Jon Young, teaches nature mentoring and offers adolescents rites of passage. Others, like Weaving Earth and Rites of Passage, both based in California, provide similar kinds of transition experiences. Meanwhile, Feet on the Earth, out of Boulder, Colorado, creates transition ceremonies aimed specifically at adolescent girls. And across the border in Canada, Rediscovery conducts nature connection and ceremonial transitions for native and nonnative participants, informed by First Nations cultural traditions. Less formally, many adolescent participants of wilderness adventures like those offered by Outward Bound report that the experience was like a transformational rite of passage that helped launch them into adulthood.

Should all teens head off for a couple of weeks into the wilderness to experience a challenging rite of passage with peers? It is clearly a great fit for many, but I wouldn't make the pitch for all. As a nature mentor—or better yet, a small community of nature mentors—you can choreograph rites of passage for adolescents that need not involve wilderness, let alone formal programs. Surfing that big wave, catching a marlin, or skiing that double black-diamond run for the first time can all be influential nature experiences that help propel a teen toward adulthood.

It's all in the lead-up and follow-through. Many folks think that a multiday solo into the wild constitutes a vision quest. Yet without the proper training and lead-up experiences, four days in the woods is just, well, a four-day camping trip. And if no one knows you went, it can hardly be considered a rite of passage. Don't forget that third phase of reincorporation into the community, along with a new status.

So the nature mentor participates beforehand, typically for several years, by preparing the mentee—opening awareness, building skills, fostering edge-stretching experiences. Training is important for achieving any goal worth its salt, let alone one worthy of adulthood. There must be challenges, setbacks, and mini-victories along the way to fuel further exploration and experiences. As the rite of passage approaches, whether it is to be formal or informal, others in the community should be informed. This is a big deal! If the task is successfully completed, the adolescent will have made a significant step toward adulthood, complete with new responsibilities. Afterward, a true community celebration—or at least a fancy, festive family dinner—is in order.

Before adolescence sets in, contemplate ways that shared outdoor adventure might help forge a relationship with your children, grandchildren, nieces, or whomever. If kids learn that nature is the place to take on challenges, they're more likely to look there when adolescence sets in and the compulsion for risk-taking is magnified. Nature can help provide that much-needed sense of inner strength, of being part of a world that you will never master but can operate in with confidence.

In the end, often one of the most difficult tasks for nature mentors is celebrating the separation and independence of teens. We know it is the right thing to do, that it's part of their journey, but we have a tough time letting go, particularly if risky challenges are involved. Kids need some autonomy during middle childhood, but this need peaks in adolescence, and it is a huge part of the transition to adulthood. So don't hold on too tight.

There you have it. In the course of three chapters, we've examined nature connection during early childhood, middle childhood, and adolescence. David Sobel offers this synopsis of how nature connection changes through the three age groups discussed in this trio of chapters:

> If the task in early childhood is to bond with family and develop empathy for nature; and in middle childhood to bond with the earth; the task in adolescence is to bond with the self, and nature provides setting and opportunity for challenging rites of passage.

To this I would add that the bond with nature can, and should, be deepened during all of these life stages. And if done well, together with emotional connection and understanding, another important outcome likely to emerge in adolescence is wisdom—the capacity to know what is true and right, and to make sound judgments.

Coming Home

Back at the Art of Mentoring, three days after the teens departed on their wilderness trek, around midday, word spread through the camp that they had returned. By arrangement, the teens were met by a couple of adults and kept on the camp margins. Their reincorporation into the community was to be as symbolic and memorable as their departure.

On the road beside the kitchen, the same one the teens had taken when they departed, the rest of the community gathered. Men and young boys on one side, women and girls on the other. Jon Young, guitar in hand, began playing the Elderberry Song, and the men's voices joined in close to 100 strong.

We had learned the song the previous day. As Jon tells the story, it was gifted to the world in two halves. The first half came to a man in Santa Barbara, California, sitting beneath an elderberry tree. A second elderberry tree, this one in Toronto, Canada, passed the second half of the song to a woman. Jon was fortunate enough to meet both people and help bring the two halves together, uniting masculine with feminine. The Elderberry Song has no words. Rather, it is driven by deep, vowel-rich sounds, different for each gender. For me, the resulting effect is strongly reminiscent of some southern African drum and mbira music.

The men sang their part several times, taking a step toward the women with each repetition, as if in serenade. Then the women joined in, rounding out the music and sending pulses soaring. They too took a forward step at the start of each rep-etition, until there was perhaps a two-meter gap, or passage, between the masculine and feminine sides of the road.

The teens then appeared at the top of the hill and began walking toward the singing community. A slight hesitation marked their step as the adolescents first surveyed the scene cre-ated for them. By the time they got close, the music had reached a fever pitch and some of the singers were jumping like Maa-sai warriors. (Okay, I may have engaged in a little jumping.) As the teens entered the pulsing corridor, we could see green-ery and sticks woven through hair and hanging from packs. As they passed by, their expressions were a mélange of pride, awe, and gratitude. And this time around, the flowing tears streamed down not only adult faces, but those of adolescents as well.

As Jade and I drove out of camp the next day, heading back to Colorado, she turned to me and said, "Dad, I'd like to come back here again to go on that teen trip."

"Yeah," I replied. "Me too."

Secret #8 for Raising a Wild Child

Create opportunities for regular time in wild nature where ado-lescents can engage in challenging, adventurous activities with one another.

Nature Mentoring Tips

MAKE TIME FOR NATURE

Meaningful nature connection cannot happen without actual time spent in nature. One of the biggest challenges for adolescents is finding time to get outdoors. You can help by limiting screen time and encouraging teens to get outside. Up the ante by seeking out cool activities and getting peers involved. That way, they can challenge each other and you have an opportunity to guide the risk-taking. Importantly, the kinds of nature activities that adolescents engage in tend to be healthier than many urban activities. As noted earlier, family nature clubs offer an excellent tool to promote nature connection during the teen years. Before deciding that your teen would never agree to participate, give it a shot. Such groups can be a great source of peers. You might even find your teen begging to head out on the next nature club adventure!

MAKE NATURE *THE* PLACE FOR ADVENTURE

Preferably by middle childhood, and certainly by adolescence, think about making nature the place for adventure. To heighten the odds that you'll actually get out there regularly, pick an activity that you're passionate about, whether it's snowboarding, biking, or hiking. Better yet, try to identify one for each season. Ideally, these activities will be challenging enough to allow for increasing skill levels over time, fostering that all-important sense of accomplishment. Even if you simply like to camp or hike, you might think about adding in navigation skills with a GPS device, or identification of edible plants. Whatever your chosen activities, try to get some time in wilderness because of its power to stir teen emotions. During the latter teen years, look for opportunities for adolescents to get out on their own, or with twenty-something leaders who can watch over them. When youths discover that natural settings can be ideal for challenging activities with their peers, their enthusiasm is likely to be very high indeed!

CORE ROUTINES FOR ADOLESCENTS

Don't forget about the core nature connection routines. Whether the adolescent you're mentoring is a novice or a seasoned adventurer, it's still essential to maintain these routines, including regular nature experiences (wandering, sit spot, etc.), story of the day, and questioning. And remember that as with kids of middle childhood age, sometimes parents are the wrong people to do the questioning! So try to get others involved who are passionate about the teen and about nature. If you yourself simply are not into pursuing nature connection in depth, but you still want it for the teens in your life, consider finding a mentor who can help guide them toward deeper nature connection. Organizations like Wilderness Awareness School can likely help you find a mentor in your area.

THE POWER OF SERVICE

Service can be a great way to promote nature connection at almost any age, but it's particularly powerful among adolescents. Work with teens to find a local service project they're passionate about, even if it requires their time only once a month. As a parent, let them try out a few alternatives if necessary, but after settling on one, encourage them to commit their efforts for at least one year. Help them understand the connections between their efforts and the health of your place. On those occasions when reluctance kicks in, remind them of their commitment, as well as the fact that prospective employers tend to think very highly of job candidates with a history of service experience.

If you're a middle or high school teacher, consider working with your students to select a service project that the entire class can work on, and be sure to tie it into the curriculum. Their efforts could be focused in the schoolyard, out in the community, or in a nearby state park. The most important thing is for teens to be able to see the transformational power of working together to achieve a service-based goal.

PREPARE FOR A RITE OF PASSAGE

For parents, I suggest identifying some nature-related activity that your adolescent is passionate about, and then defining a specific, difficult-to-attain goal. Perhaps it's a multiday solo in the wilderness, or a canoe trip with a big portage, hiking to the top of a particular mountain, or planting and tending a backyard garden. Work with her to build up skill levels with that goal always in mind, and engage peers if possible so they can progress together. If wild nature isn't your thing, but you want your teen to have those experiences, consider finding an organization like the National Outdoor Leadership School (NOLS) to help out.

For teachers, particularly of high school seniors, consider adding an end-of-year wilderness trip. Yes, this may be a major challenge logistically, particularly in a public school, but it will be well worth the effort if you pull it off. Perhaps call it "Vision Quest" or something similar to entice teens with the challenge. Through the year, have them learn about the place and the activities they will encounter on the trip. Whatever rite of passage you create, be sure to assemble a "community" of some sort (for example, extended family or classmates) to witness and celebrate the teens' success.

Part IV

OBSTACLES
AND SOLUTIONS

9

Dangerous Liaisons

Balancing Technology and Nature

The more high-tech our lives become, the more nature we need.

— RICHARD LOUV

"CALIFORNIA TOWHEE!" an earnest voice exclaimed in hushed tones. The metallic chirps pierced the air from a coast live oak just off the trail. "Sounds like a smoke alarm running down," someone quickly added, offering a memorable image for the birding novices like me. Several of our group checked a box on their smartphone screens. I wrote a note in my journal, feeling old-school.

"Pacific-slope flycatcher." "Wilson's warbler." "Dark-eyed junco." "Cedar waxwing." "Hutton's vireo." The colorful names spilled out fast now as our binocular-toting band rose to the challenge of identifying as many bird species as possible. Some IDs were made visually, others by ear. Several of our group were clearly serious birders.

A bewildering chorus of songs emanated from the surrounding greenery. I smiled wide as a distinctive, upward-spiraling trill rang out from the valley to our right, recalling childhood memories of camping in British Columbia. "Swainson's thrush," two women said in unison.

It was 7:20 a.m. and the bioblitz had just begun. Bioblitzes—brief (typically 24-hour) surveys of living species within a particular area—are a relatively recent invention. The focal area can be as vast as a national park or as pint-sized as a schoolyard. Bigger events attract biologists with such specialties as fungi, microbes, birds, wildflowers, insects, spiders, mammals, lichens, reptiles, trees, and amphibians. Smaller events like this one in Tilden Regional Park, California, are populated more by enthusiasts than experts, with abundant help from "citizen scientists"—that is, people like you. Beyond documenting species diversity, bioblitz goals often include environmental conservation and connecting people with nature.

This particular event in the Berkeley Hills was organized by "Nerds for Nature," an informal San Francisco Bay group with the upbeat mission of "bringing together technologists and environmental professionals to collaboratively build awesome tools to understand, protect, and revive the natural world." This loose collaboration of nature lovers hosts monthly meet-ups and occasional outdoor affairs like this one. Dan Rademacher, one of the group's founders and organizers, told me that Nerds for Nature was formed with the explicit goal of attracting a younger audience to the outdoors. They seem to be succeeding.

A large proportion of the attendees on this sparkling April day were young, thirty and under, with plenty of kids in the bunch. A few were nerdy in appearance, sporting thick-rimmed glasses and multipocketed vests overflowing with gadgets. But most of us looked like a random sample of humanity drawn from nearby San Francisco. While some folks were clearly knowledgeable about local nature, or at least a portion of it, the majority appeared to be along for the ride, enjoying the chance to be in a beautiful natural setting on a weekend morning and learn a few things along the way.

By ten o'clock, our birding group had spotted or heard forty-three different kinds of avians, which to me seemed highly respectable. Shortly afterward, I headed out with the pond and stream group. Led by Tilden Park naturalist James Wilson, we loaded up with long-handled nets, microscopes, posters, and boxes filled with ice cube trays, small nets, tweezers, TV dinner–style trays, and guidebooks. Most of us also carried some sort of electronic tablet or smartphone. Stopping first at a large pond, James demonstrated how to collect water samples and use spoons to carefully isolate the tiny critters found there. Among the denizens were water striders, red worms, and even a squirming California newt. Each newly identified animal was carefully documented with photographs and notes.

The kids squatted in rapt attention as naturalist James shared the amazing story of another discovery—horsehair worms. While still in the guise of larvae, these minute creatures are often ingested by drinking grasshoppers. Once inside, they exit the grasshopper's gut and begin moving through the body, feeding on blood and various tissues. After these parasitic wrigglers reach adult size, some surpassing a foot in length, they infect the brain of the hapless insect, eventually causing it to leap unnaturally into the nearest body of water. At this point the horsehair worms exit their dying host to meet other worms and mate.

"Cooooool," one of the boys declared.

Next we headed off to Jewel Lake, where maybe a dozen western pond turtles basked motionless on sunlit logs. Our group was enchanted by the pipevine swallowtails, butterflies with mostly black wings rimmed in iridescent blue. One family scouting the lake margin netted a three-spined stickleback, which James artfully maneuvered into a clear plastic, water-filled, fish-size container. After the fish was photographed and enjoyed by all, a four-year-old girl in a pink shirt, tights, and a tutu skirt was tasked with returning it to the lake. Although convinced that the little swimmer would much prefer to come home with her, with some gentle coaxing she eventually gave in and released it.

Over the course of the day, other naturalist-led groups headed out in search of insects, fungi, and evidence of mammals. During the evening, there was an opportunity to search for nocturnal creatures, among them bats and owls. The total species count for the day, 219, was modest. But the main purpose of the Tilden Park event was engagement rather than science. By comparison, just the month before, 320 volunteer scientists and over 6,000 participants had conducted a large-scale bioblitz in the Golden Gate National Recreation Area, bagging in excess of 2,300 species, 80 of them new additions to the park's list. All identifications from both of these Bay Area events were uploaded to a global database using an app called iNaturalist. In this way, the nonexpert participants became "citizen scientists," collecting real data for real research.

At these bioblitz events — now becoming increasingly common across the United States, Canada, and Europe — one common factor stands out: digital technologies are all but ubiquitous.

Fearing for the Natives

As a society, we've rapidly become a throng of techno-addicts, shifting obsessively between smartphones and tablets, laptops and televisions. During my lifetime, our information consumption has more than tripled. Recall that the bulk of young people, the so-called digital natives, now spend seven to ten hours each day staring at screens. By the time most children enter kindergarten, they have consumed over 5,000 hours of television — enough time to earn a college degree.

Of course, those of us over 35 — the "digital immigrants" — are compulsive users as well. One study of computer users at work found that people change windows or check e-mail about 37 times an hour! Awash in a sea of digital information, we rarely stop to consider the impact of this rampant technophilia on ourselves, our children, or our communities.

What influence is all this frantic screen time having on our brains? Chances are you're a digital consumer with plenty of firsthand experience. If so, some of the findings generated by recent studies will likely come as no surprise. Heavy consumption of information technologies reduces attention spans and makes us more easily distracted. Regular interruptions (for example, e-mail and text messages) tend to increase stress and decrease short-term memory, making it more difficult to learn or perform even simple tasks. Brain researchers are becoming increasingly convinced that excessive screen time makes us more impatient, impulsive, forgetful, and even narcissistic.

More surprising perhaps is the multitasking myth. That is, with the exception of a few "supertaskers" (only 3 percent of us), simultaneous use of multiple technologies actually lowers efficiency. One study of Microsoft employees found that stopping even briefly to check e-mail set back the main task at hand by about fifteen minutes. Overall, committed multitaskers tend to be slower than nonmultitaskers when attempting to solve several problems simultaneously. The problem, it seems, is that multitaskers train their brains to be highly sensitive to new information and are thus easily distracted, always seeking that next digital tidbit.

What about the effects of digital technologies on children in particular?

Electronic media use has been linked to decreased well-being of kids. For example, one study concluded that girls' risk for emotional problems increases twofold with each additional hour of digital media consumed. Boys, in contrast, showed heightened risk of peer problems with increased TV and electronic game use. Another study reported that kids whose electronic game-playing is unmonitored by parents tend to have a significantly higher body mass index (BMI) by age seven than children with more grown-up supervision.

In his book *The Dumbest Generation: How the Digital Age Stupefies Young Americans and Jeopardizes Our Future*, Mark Bauerlein argues that despite having fingertip access to a vast library of knowledge, young people today tend to be less informed, less literate, and more self-absorbed than in any preceding generation. Rather than living up to its promise as the "great source" accessed by an information superhighway, for most digital natives the Internet functions more as the "great communicator," enabling youngsters to stay connected to one another 24/7 through e-mail, chat, instant messaging, blogs, and social media sites.

Bauerlein is by no means a lone voice. A quick search will reveal a bevy of books with similarly alarming titles—for example, *Distracted: The Erosion of Attention and the Coming Dark Age*, and *The Big Disconnect: Protecting Childhood and Family Relationships in the Digital Age*. Growing numbers of psychologists fear the impacts to children's self-identity wrought by our gadget fixation. One Stanford researcher, Elias Aboujaoude, refers to the "fracturing of the self" caused by excessive reliance on technology. Some neuroscientists specializing in the brain's frontal lobe speculate that abusing digital technologies could stunt youngsters' normal growth, "freezing them in teen brain mode." Others researchers suggest that heavy technology use by the current generation of youth is redefining the human relationship, reducing our empathy. Ironically, the more interconnected we become in the digital age, the more isolated we may feel. As human-technology specialist Sherry Turkle points out, if we don't teach our children to be alone, they're only going to be lonely. We need to value solitude, she says, and model it for our children.

Less than two decades ago, researchers thought that the brain ceased developing at the onset of adulthood. A slew of recent studies demonstrates that the brain continually adapts and changes throughout life, including in our senior years—a phenomenon dubbed *neuroplasticity*. To cite one fascinating example, a study of Tibetan monks showed much higher gamma wave activity in the prefrontal cortex of the brain during meditation than in a control group, resulting in stronger feelings of happiness and compassion in the former. The remarkable truth of the matter, then, is that we "train our brains" throughout life, actually rewiring parts of our neurocircuitry based on the activities we choose to engage in. So it's best to give serious consideration to the things we allow to dominate our minds, and those of our children.

Some psychologists compare our dependence on screen technologies to an eating disorder. Like food, technology is now an essential part of our daily diet. And just as food addicts struggle to limit their consumption of calories, so too we must develop habits to moderate our consumption of technologies, for both ourselves and our children. Success will require setting thoughtful constraints. The American Academy of Pediatrics recommends restricting kids' screen time to no more than two hours per day (less than a quarter of their present daily consumption). For children under two years, the AAP recommends no screen time at all.

I remain skeptical about some of the dire predictions coming out around technology consumption. After all, my generation consumed more than our fair share of *Happy Days* and *Gilligan's Island*, and yet the world is still turning. Nonetheless, the bottom line is that despite their numerous advantages, phones, tablets, computers, and televisions are potentially dangerous tools. Although we're only beginning to understand the impacts of electronic technologies on growing children, researchers are becoming increasingly worried. The central concern seems to be that overuse of digital technologies is somehow rewiring our brains in ways that diminish our health, and even our humanity. If we are to set sail and navigate a healthy course into the future, for both our children and our communities, it will be important to restrict the amount of time we allow youngsters (and ourselves!) to be immersed in the digital ocean.

To be clear, I'm no technophobe, no Luddite. On a personal level, I'm a major technology user myself, and I battle the daily siren call to "stay connected." And on a societal level, I cannot envision a path forward, sustainable or otherwise, that does not embrace technology. So, as I see it, the key question is this: Given our penchant toward digital obsession, how can we embrace both nature and technology?

The Hybrid Mind

Author Richard Louv argues convincingly that "The more high-tech our lives become, the more nature we need." In my view, he's right-on. But in the age of iPhones, Game Boys, and Google, how are we to forge this balance of seeming opposites? Clearly there's no turning back to simpler, low-tech times. No, the twenty-first-century wild child will need to learn how to balance and integrate both technology *and* nature.

Louv offers us a provocative goal—what he calls the *hybrid mind*. Individuals with a hybrid mind are capable of switching easily back and forth between the digital and physical worlds. This cognitive flexibility marries our ancient capacity for multisensory wonder with a more recently acquired, narrowly focused digital prowess. The hybrid mind is a powerful notion, one that appears to be grounded in two fundamentally different ways of thinking.

Recall the two kinds of consciousness described by psychologist Alison Gopnik, whom we first met back in Chapter 6. The first, called *spotlight consciousness*, involves the kind of narrow, directed attention that blocks out external stimuli. This is the mental state you'd expect to have when, say, reading a book, just as you're doing now. The second mode involves a broader, more diffuse kind of attention that Gopnik refers to as *lantern consciousness*. Picture a meandering stroll through a redwood forest with your senses wide open to the spectrum of sights, sounds, and fragrances.

Spotlights are purpose driven, focusing their beam tightly on a particular subject. Lanterns illuminate broadly, shedding light on a broad range of subjects.

Near the end of early childhood, and even more so during middle childhood, youngsters become increasingly skilled at spotlight consciousness and devote far more time to this more focused brand of attention. The transformation is in part genetic, associated with changes in brain development, and in part cultural, accelerated by the proddings of grown-ups.

Today we value the spotlight far more than the lantern, a fact reflected in the recent trend to push academic-style learning back into kindergarten and even the preschool years. Modern schooling—from reading and writing to science and social studies—demands focused attention. Similarly, digital screens, fast becoming ubiquitous in elementary classrooms, require the kind of highly directed, selective attention linked with spotlight consciousness. Unsurprisingly, then, despite the fact that we begin life as highly adept lantern thinkers, with our senses open to the entire world, we tend to lose this proficiency by middle childhood simply through disuse.

Human attention biases haven't always been so imbalanced. As noted previously, for most of the last 200 millennia, *Homo sapiens* consisted entirely of hunter-gatherers. We made the switch (at least most of us) to agriculture-based subsistence only in the past 10,000 years—a mere 5 percent of our total duration. If studies of living hunting and gathering cultures are any guide, lantern consciousness was highly valued in these earlier, nomadic cultures. After all, individuals with a developed ability to broaden their awareness likely had a big advantage detecting predators, prey, plant foods, medicine, and other items essential to survival. Indeed, societies that lacked this ability would not have lasted long.

Is diffuse, lantern-style consciousness no longer necessary, the cognitive equivalent of horse and buggy? Hardly. Directed attention and spotlight consciousness tend to be fatiguing and stress-inducing, robbing us of energy. Think about how you feel after staring at a computer screen for hours on end. In contrast, being outdoors in, say, a park or a forest encourages a less focused, more diffuse mode of attention, the sort that opens up our senses, relieves stress, restores energy, and fosters clear thinking. This explains at least in part why even a brief walk outdoors can be so rejuvenating. I know that it works for me.

In addition, whereas directed attention severs us from our surroundings, diffuse attention engages our senses and embeds us within the larger world. That's why lantern consciousness tends to be the genesis of wonder and fascination, sparking those rare but invaluable moments when we feel intimately connected with nature.

Without doubt, lantern consciousness is also a factor in the success of outdoor, place-based education. Learning improves when we engage more of our senses. Why? In part because not all of us are visual learners. Some learn best through bodily movement, or hands-on activities, or with music. Engaging more senses means experiencing more sounds, more smells, more tastes—in short, collecting more sensory input for building knowledge and lasting memories.

Richard Louv highlights the rights of children to experience both facets of hybrid consciousness:

> Today, students (and the rest of us) who work and learn in a dominating digital environment expend enormous energy to *block out* many of these senses, in order to focus narrowly on the screen in front of the eyes. That's the very definition of being less alive. Who among us wants to be less alive? What parent wants their child to be less alive? . . . Few today would question the notion that every person, especially every young person, has a right to access the Internet, whether through a school district, a library, or a city's public Wi-Fi program. We accept the idea that the divide between the digital haves and have-nots must be closed. But all children also have a right to develop a wider spectrum of their senses and mental abilities, to know the real world, and to be fully alive.

In short, we're given multiple senses, but our ability to use them is based on experience. We can develop these senses, or they can deteriorate and leave us impoverished.

What does all this mean for nature mentors? For kids in early childhood, it means that in addition to learning directed attention, youngsters should also be encouraged to continue honing diffuse, lantern consciousness. Digital technologies (for children over two years of age) will help with the former, nature with the latter. Balance will come from engaging regularly in both.

For youth in middle childhood and adolescence, the task of nature mentoring becomes increasingly difficult because the gravitational pull of technologies is bolstered by both schooling and peers. All the more important, then, to make time for outdoor experiences in which you model the kind of diffuse, senses-open attention style that will enable kids and teens to form a deeper connection with the nonhuman world.

Ultimately, children who develop this hybrid mind will be able to interact deftly with both technology and the natural world. Technological tools will be used to augment, rather than block, human senses. Just as a birder uses binoculars to look closely at a robin and then lets the optics hang while she absorbs its lovely song, so too, with practice and mentorship, will kids learn to migrate between digital experience and the real, multi-sensory world. In this sense, the litmus test for nature-friendly technologies might be how long it takes to transition from a digital focus back to the multisensory world.

Using High-Tech in the Great Outdoors

Lovers of the outdoors sometimes bemoan the excessive use of technology in nature. But human interactions with the natural world have always included technologies. After all, stone tools are technology. Millions of years prior to the first true humans, our prehuman ancestors used skillfully crafted stone blades to kill and carve up their prey, as well as to process plant foods. Humans later took technologies to new heights, inventing bone hooks for catching fish, bow and arrow for taking prey from a distance, and eventually plows for tearing into the land. Viewed in this light, carbon fiber fishing rods, binoculars with precision optics, and GPS units communicating with Earth-orbiting satellites are merely exemplars of the latest gear used to interact with nature. The same holds for hiking boots, backpacks, and thermal clothing.

Of course, as noted earlier, most of us concerned with technology abuse are referring to screen-based technologies. Certainly all of us, children and adults, need to unplug at least some of the time when outdoors. Quiet reflection and engaging the full suite of senses is difficult when a glowing screen beckons, perhaps even more so for kids than grown-ups. Nevertheless, we'll also need to leverage those electronic screens to get children (and adults) out into nature.

So how might we begin establishing a tech/nature balance? What kinds of digital devices are best for switching back and forth between directed and diffuse attention?

Digital photography offers perhaps the easiest and most obvious electronic pathway to connect kids with nature. Cameras encourage children as young as two years old to use technology as a fun, creative tool. Nature is so full of sensory stimuli that it can be overwhelming, particularly for the uninitiated. Taking pictures enables youngsters to focus briefly on a single subject—an insect, flower, or bird—and see it in a meaningful way before experiencing it again with multiple senses (for example, smelling the flower or hearing the bird). (The critical caveat here, and one that may require some mentoring, is that it's easy to think only about taking photos and never fully engage with one's surroundings. So make sure the camera is put away most of the time.) Photographs allow kids to take away vivid mementos of nature interactions, fostering lasting memories.

Photos can be used to create various kinds of art, or they can be linked together into slide shows. And these days, with the heavy emphasis on social media, children can easily share their nature experiences with others through imagery.

Many of the same benefits apply to video. Videography enables an even higher degree of creativity, combining visuals and sound. Miranda Andersen, a native of Vancouver, British Columbia, began making films about nature when she was nine years old. Her first effort celebrated a woman who cofounded a salmon hatchery. Later, at the ripe old age of thirteen, Miranda made a beautiful film, *The Child in Nature*, aimed at highlighting the potential power of nature in children's lives. So video too can be a great digital tool for enhancing nature connection.

Beyond capturing still or moving images, there's now a plethora of downloadable nature apps, with new products added weekly. Many are aimed at birders, enabling identifications in your backyard or any other setting. Similar offerings are available for mammals, reptiles and amphibians, fishes, and insects and spiders. Other apps target enthusiasts of trees, wildflowers, or other plants. Want to ID those tracks and scat you encounter while out hiking? There are apps for that too. Are pests your concern? Fear not. A downloadable tool will give you abundant information on everything from cockroaches to rodents. Still other online offerings allow you to track your nature sightings in real time and tag each one with its geographic location. And a growing number of these applications are aimed specifically at kids.

Not to be left out, rock hounds can find apps dedicated to rocks, gems, and minerals. And other, almost magical offerings enable you to locate and identify planets, stars, constellations, and other denizens of the night sky. While I was attending a recent conference in La Jolla, California, one of the participants, phone in hand, announced that the International Space Station would be flying overhead momentarily. So a bunch of us (geeks) quickly gathered outside to watch the bright, starlike object perform its slow-motion tumble across the sky. Those with a penchant for geocaching can easily locate literally millions of geocache sites around the world, many of them in natural areas. Or you can augment your backcountry escape with online products that will enable you to count your steps, track your journey, determine your elevation with pinpoint accuracy, access maps to help you find your way, or identify that random peak on the skyline. Of course, armed with the ever-popular Google Earth, you can zoom, godlike, into any place on the planet, perhaps to preview a hike or get a bird's-eye view of your favorite park or camping spot. Finally, a social media app called Yonder now allows you to share digital images and video of nature experiences with a network of other nature enthusiasts and discover what they're up to. Bewildering, right?

Dinosaurs, Trains, and Indoor Nature

Several years ago, I received a phone call from an executive at the Hollywood-based Jim Henson Company. She told me that they were creating a new educational television series aimed at preschoolers, with dinosaurs as the main hook, and she asked if I'd like to get involved. The ensuing conversation went something like this:

"What's it going to be called?" I asked.

"*Dinosaur Train*," she replied.

"What?" I stammered. "You can't call it that."

"Why not?" she asked calmly.

"Because dinosaur paleontologists like me have to remind

people regularly that humans and dinosaurs did not live at the same time. Sticking them together on a train just perpetuates the myth."

"No problem," she said. "We're only going to put dinosaurs on the train."

I paused, took a deep breath, and blurted out, "Well, that's just brilliant!"

And so it has been. Since its 2009 debut, *Dinosaur Train*, brainchild of creator Craig Bartlett, has been a roaring hit for PBS KIDS. Viewed in millions of households per month in the United States, the show's reach has expanded to more than 100 countries worldwide. Since its inception, I have had the dual honor of serving as the series science advisor and on-air host. Each episode consists mostly of colorful, eye-popping animation of dinosaurs and other creatures. The main character is Buddy, a kid *T. rex*, who, together with his adoptive family of flying reptiles (*Pteranodons*), heads out on a magical train to explore places and times during the Age of Dinosaurs. Appearing as "Dr. Scott," I show up at the end of each episode to talk about the science behind the story and connect the content back to present-day nature. In more than 100 episodes, we've used dinosaurs as a powerful vehicle to address a wide variety of nature-related topics—from plants, animals, and poop to hurricanes, volcanoes, and shooting stars. For preschoolers, the marriage of dinosaurs and trains is like mixing chocolate and peanut butter—almost irresistible.

While immersed in preparations for season one of *Dinosaur Train*, I began to get concerned that the series would become yet another compelling product tethering kids to indoor screens. So I negotiated a tagline that would encourage kids to get outdoors. My wife Toni came up with the final version that I still exclaim enthusiastically at the end of every show: "Get outside, get into nature, and make your own discoveries!"

I must confess that I had no idea if a television show could successfully convince large numbers of children to turn off the TV and head outside. But after hearing anecdotally from many hundreds of kids and adults, I'm happy to report that the premise seems to work. Numerous moms and dads have told me that their little Johnny now continually asks to play outside, where he digs holes in search of fossils. (Sorry about that, parents.) Meanwhile, Jenny is heading out regularly to check out those living dinosaurs known as birds as they fly, sing, and make nests full of babies. Some parents are even using the series as leverage to get their kids outdoors. ("Remember what Dr. Scott says. Time to get outside and make your own discoveries!") PBS KIDS and the Jim Henson Company fully embraced the "get outside" message, creating a Nature Trackers Club on the show and on the accompanying *Dinosaur Train* website. Here, then, is an example of technology being used as a potent tool to encourage kids to explore and connect with local nature.

A few other kid TV shows currently out there have a science and nature focus. Of course, you can always dip your cup into that flowing river of information known as the Internet, where you and your kids can seek answers to just about any kind of nature-related question. By focusing on kids' most pressing queries, particularly after returning from the great outdoors, the digital and natural worlds can mesh almost seamlessly in the making of a wild child. A growing number of websites also help you find local outdoor activities and connect you with other like-minded folks. On a national level, The Nature Conservancy hosts Nature Rocks, a website that offers an excellent guide to outdoor possibilities near you.

Closely related are the growing numbers of educational, nature-related digital games for kids, among them Name That Shark, Bird Brains, and Be Bear-Aware. While some will cringe at the prospect, it seems to me that online gaming offers a vast, virtually untapped landscape for connecting kids with nature. What if there were games that gave you points and access to higher levels for identifying and learning about local nature? Or how about games with a broader focus, encouraging you to delve deeper and deeper into the flow of energy and matter in your local ecosystem? We've barely scratched the surface in nature gaming.

Distance learning is another terrific platform for engaging kids with nature. In the fall of 2013, I stood on a blustery hilltop deep within the rugged, gray-and-white-streaked badlands of southern Utah, talking via satellite to students in classrooms around the country. I showed them a few tools of the paleontological trade—among them a jackhammer, shovel, paintbrush, and dental pick—and briefly described how we use them. Next I held up the serrated tooth of a predatory tyrannosaur and the massive, blunt hoof of a duck-billed dinosaur plant-eater, both fossils found just the day before. The camera operator zoomed in for a closer look. The students asked me in real time about the ancient creatures being unearthed in this remote chunk of the American West, and what life was like in this part of the world 75 million years ago. It would be impossible, let alone impractical, to transport thousands of youngsters to a remote dig site. Through the magic of distance learning, we now bring the dig site into the classroom. Here, then, is an effective, high-tech pathway for exposing elementary, middle, and high school students not just to paleontology, but to the entire spectrum of scientific professions.

In short, although outdoor experiences in direct contact with nearby nature are essential, indoor experiences augmented by digital technologies also have an important role to play in the raising of a wild child.

Just Ask Nature

What do kingfishers, Namibian beetles, and humpback whales have in common? Are they primary targets of a new conservation effort? Namesakes of professional sporting teams? Nope. Instead, all three have inspired amazing new human technologies. And together, such innovations have sparked an entirely new field at the intersection of nature and technology, a field with potential to help lead us back toward a thriving human-nature relationship.

Kingfisher bills inspired a Japanese engineer to redesign the nose of the Shinkansen bullet train, reducing noise and energy consumption while increasing top speeds. A dime-size beetle living in the harsh Namibian desert prompted biologists and engineers to join forces to create a superefficient water harvesting material that combines a Teflonlike, water-repellent surface with water-attracting bumps. And the bumpy flippers of humpback whales have inspired aerodynamic blades that now spin in a variety of machines, from wind turbines to computers.

I could cite hundreds of other high-tech inventions founded on nature's genius. Together they're part of a nascent yet rapidly growing field called *biomimicry* (from *bios*, meaning life, and *mimesis*, meaning to imitate). Biomimicry seeks answers to human problems by turning to answers already invented by Mother Nature. The most famous example is Velcro, inspired by burrs that stuck tenaciously to the canine companion of a Swiss engineer.

Contrary to popular belief, evolution isn't a random process. Detractors often compare evolution to thousands of monkeys hammering away on typewriters until one, by chance, generates a lengthy book with all the letters and words in correct order. This metaphor could not be more erroneous. Evolution is highly creative, constantly developing new solutions through a relentless trial-and-error process. The core idea of biomimicry is that nature has already solved most of the problems now facing human engineers and designers. By tapping into these solutions, or "adaptations," we're learning to grab solar energy like a leaf, create color like a butterfly, grow food like a grassland, and recycle our wastes like a swamp.

Today, when speaking of cutting-edge technological innovations, we often refer to *high technology*. In contrast, nature's technological solutions might be called *deep technology*, the result of evolutionary R&D conducted over billions of years of deep time. My strong hunch is that the future sweet spot of technology will reside at the interface of high-tech and deep-tech. Here we'll eventually learn to model not just our materials and gadgets but entire societies after nature's wisdom. In such a place, buildings would behave like trees, harnessing the sun's energy and regulating temperatures without expensive heating and cooling. Such innovations are already well under way in the world of architecture. Ultimately, through linked infrastructure networks, cities might function much like ecosystems, funneling local resources where they're needed and using the waste from one sector as the raw materials of another. A dream? Yes, but a glorious and attainable one—the true melding of nature and technology.

Meanwhile, biomimicry is now making inroads into K–12 and higher education. Pioneering teachers are quickly finding

ways to place nature-based thinking into the heart of the curriculum. Today, you can even attain a master's degree in this
field. No question: biomimicry is a powerful lens through which
to view science education, encouraging children and adults to
reach creative new heights inspired by the nonhuman world
around them.

Yet the thing that excites me most about this new field is its
revolutionary shift in perspective. No longer merely something
to learn *about,* nature is transformed into something to learn
from. Rather than a bunch of raw materials, nature becomes
mentor and model. Deep technology and biomimicry are potent tools that unite the Epic of Evolution—the story of all of
us—with a thriving future, one in which humans are fully embedded within the natural world. "We live on a wildly diverse
planet surrounded by genius," says Janine Benyus, founder and
leader of the biomimicry movement. Got a pressing problem to
solve? Just ask nature!

The Digital Naturalist

As outlined back in Chapter 1, the early twentieth century was
a heyday for naturalists. Spending time outdoors immersed in
nature was commonplace, and most people had at least a rudimentary knowledge of local plants and animals. Remarkably, a
large proportion of Americans and Europeans, perhaps even a
majority, considered themselves naturalists. Back then, a typical
naturalist would head outdoors armed with a pen and a notebook. If fortunate, his backpack might also contain a pair of
binoculars, a magnifying glass, and a field guide or two. Those
who were socially inclined gathered periodically to share dis-

coveries and insights, but for the most part their nature-related passions were played out in solitude or, at most, in the company of one or two others.

Today, naturalists are an all-too-rare breed. For most of us, the word, if it means anything, connotes a uniformed national or state park employee, someone who takes visitors on nature walks by day and offers slide presentations by night. But I think a new heyday for naturalists may be dawning.

This time around, things will be very different, thanks in large part to digital technologies. The quintessential twenty-first-century digital naturalist may once again carry binoculars in her backpack. But the pen and notebook will be long gone, as will the guidebooks. In their place will be a single handheld digital device with built-in phone, camera, video, magnifying glass, and various field guides, ranging from plants and animals to rocks and stars, making identifications a cinch. That same device will record the exact location of each observation using a built-in GPS and augment this fine-tuned geographic placement with weather conditions, elevation, and other relevant bits of information. Another app on the device will enable her to upload observations to a national database, contributing to multiple citizen-science projects. Despite being alone or with a small group, maybe miles from civilization, chances are that she'll be in contact with other, like-minded individuals who can assist in identifying plants and animals. Our digital naturalist will feel that she's part of a cohesive, action-based community that cares for its local place and acts on its behalf. On days when she becomes absorbed and stays out after dark, a built-in flashlight app will help her get home safely.

But before we can realize this new Age of Naturalists, a key initial step will be rewilding our cities. After all, that's where most of us now live. So, as our journey nears its end, let's turn to the revolutionary notion of urban rewilding.

Secret #9 for Raising a Wild Child

Mentor the children in your life to embrace both technology and nature, to establish a balance where high-tech and nature-loving become the thriving norm.

Nature Mentoring Tips

SNAP SOME NATURE PHOTOS

Screens are a major part of the lives of most children today. So think about ways to use digital technologies to leverage nature connection. Here's one idea.

Encourage kids to take a camera outside and take photos of five natural things that interest them—flowers, bugs, rocks, whatever. Then invite them to open their senses and spend at least five minutes closely observing their surroundings, including tiny things like ants and giant things like clouds. After that, their challenge is to take five additional photos and compare them with the first five. What did they find different about the two shoot sessions? Did opening their senses and taking time to observe closely change anything? If so, how? At this point, the kids might use the photos to create a slide show or an art project, or they could pick their favorite image and write a poem about it. Be creative or, better yet, co-creative. The key is to use the camera as a tool to heighten observation and awareness skills, and then to reflect on the results. Afterward, feel free to encourage electronic sharing of the results. This activity is a great one for parents, teachers, and other caregivers, offering an easy avenue to blend the digital and natural worlds.

TAP INTO THE GREAT SOURCE

Take kids to a wild or semi-wild place and once again ask them to find (and, if desired, photograph or sketch) a few things that they find interesting. If desired, use probing questions to build awareness, exploring the subject together. When you get back home, head to the computer with the kids and use the Internet to find out something you didn't know about one or more of the chosen objects. Consider having kids keep a natural journal to record their discoveries and findings. An alternative that encourages kids to move beyond eyesight is to record some bird songs using a smartphone and then go to one of many websites when you're back home to identify the song makers. If time is your concern, remember that the whole activity, outdoor and in, can be done in as little as thirty minutes. In addition to spending quality time with your kids, these activities are a terrific way of reinforcing that you, the mentor, need not be a nature expert. The only requisites are a show of interest in whatever the child comes up with, and an enthusiasm for doing some co-investigating afterward.

GO ON A GEOCACHING ADVENTURE!

Geocaching is a fun, high-tech form of treasure hunting that has exploded in recent years. Armed with a GPS-enabled device, participants navigate their way to specific coordinates to find the geocache hidden there. Geocachers typically sign a logbook and, in some cases, remove an object or place another inside.

They then share photos and stories with others online. As of this writing, there are about 2.5 million geocaches and more than 6 million geocachers worldwide! You can find geocache sites in every major city, as well as in suburban and wild areas. So chances are excellent that you'll find plenty of geocaches close to home or wherever you go. To find out how to get involved, check out www.geocaching.com.

GET NATURE APPED

Try downloading one or more nature apps to your smartphone and giving them a spin. Stars, rocks, trees, birds, mammals—whatever your nature interest, chances are there's an app out there. Ask your kids what intrigues them the most and download apps on those topics too. Alternatively, iNaturalist is a great starting point because it allows you to upload observations of just about any kind of living organism, learn about it, and connect with like-minded nature enthusiasts (no, they didn't pay me for the plug). Nature apps are popping up and evolving so quickly that you can be sure to find something that strikes your fancy, and that of the children in your life. Be sure to model hybrid mind behavior—that is, a balance between digital and real world, demonstrating how they can complement each other. And make youngsters aware of the different modes of consciousness involved: typically narrow for screens and broad for nature.

MAKE A NATURE FILM

Whether you're a teacher, parent, or other caregiver, a great way to foster hybrid mind thinking is to encourage kids (sometimes best in teams of two or three) to make a nature video. This process can be as simple or sophisticated as you like, but is often best when it includes several of the elements cited earlier, including (1) observation time outdoors to identify elements of greatest interest, (2) Internet time indoors to discover background information, (3) time for reflection and discussion, and (4) filming and editing time. These days, a number of easily available, inexpensive software packages make it simple to overlay music and special effects. (And if you have no idea how to do this, your kids probably do.) For older children and teens, video can be a terrific vehicle to increase awareness of sights, sounds, and shadows, among other things. Videos can also be a powerful format for storytelling; consider having kids identify an important cause in local nature—say, a stream overrun with nonnative plants or an effort to plant milkweed to sustain migrating monarch butterflies. Of course, you can always share any resulting products in the digital realm, or merely with family, friends, or other students.

10

The Rewilding Revolution

Growing Nature Lovers in the Big City

Hope is a verb with its sleeves rolled up.

— DAVID ORR

WORLD WAR Z. Mad Max. The Hunger Games. Planet of the Apes. Night of the Living Dead. Armageddon. Escape from New York. Terminator. The War of the Worlds. If these Hollywood hits are any guide, we have a bit of an obsession with apocalypse. According to the omniscient source, Wikipedia, the number of apocalyptic films has steadily increased over the past several decades. Prior to 1950 there were only five. The progression from there goes as follows: 1950s, 11; 1960s, 20; 1970s, 33; 1980s, 33; 1990s, 34; 2000s, 58. And during the first four years of this decade, 42 end-of-the-world-style movies have already premiered.

This phenomenon was undoubtedly driven in the post–World War II era by the bomb and our entirely rational fear of nuclear holocaust. But a nuclear explanation can't account for the persistent upward trajectory of the holocaust film genre. Public fear of nuclear war has decreased, yet the number of apocalyptic films nearly doubled in the first decade of the twenty-first century, and we're on track to double that number again in the current decade. Maybe there are a few new fears in town.

A few years ago, when Jade was eight, I asked her, "When you're the age of your grandmother, do you think the world will be the same as it is today, or worse, or better?" For emphasis, I used a flat hand, a downward-pointing hand, and an upward-pointing hand to illustrate each of the three conditions.

With barely a moment's hesitation, she calmly replied, "It's gonna be worse."

"Whaaaat?" I stammered, dumbfounded. "Who told you that?"

With a look almost equal in incredulity, she came back with, "Daddy, everyone knows the world is getting hotter, and that it's going to be worse for people."

Eight years old.

Jade is not alone in her views. Indeed, it seems the majority of people, both children and adults, see things getting much worse in the decades to come. And no wonder. Fear of nuclear war (which now has its own name: *nucleomituphobia*) has been surpassed by fears of environmental decline involving such causes as global warming, species extinctions, and destruction of rainforests and coral reefs. As Jade's reaction demonstrates, kids as well as adults are getting this message loud and clear.

Of course, renegade aliens, zombies, and robots carry more box-office cachet than the yellow brick road to utopian bliss. Yet, whether or not the frequency of *Terminator*-style films shares a cause-and-effect relationship with our environmental fears, it's worth asking: If all we hear about is things getting worse, don't we risk a self-fulfilling apocalyptic prophecy? Martin Luther King Jr. taught us that no movement can be successful unless it presents a vision that people feel compelled to move toward. Where is the powerful vision for humans and nature—the one without zombies and aliens?

The buzzword these days for a healthy path into the future is *sustainability*. But folks don't seem to put much stock in it, and we really aren't getting a strong, consistent vision of what sustainability might look like. At its heart, sustainability is all about establishing a healthy human-nature relationship. Yet, like many others, I struggle with this concept. The word *sustain* connotes a lack of change, hardly the stuff of a compelling vision. As green architect William McDonough once observed, "Who would want, simply, a 'sustainable' marriage?" All of us would prefer a partner with whom we're likely to flourish, even thrive. That's why I speak more these days about *thrivability*. Now, there's something worth fighting for.

In many respects, thrivability is a local challenge. Yes, some pressing issues demand global cooperation, climate change topping the list. Others, like the banning of certain pesticides and laws to protect endangered species, demand federal legislation. Yet numerous ecological problems, including habitat destruction and species losses, also require local solutions. How local? You might define it as the city or town you live in plus the surrounding bioregion. Bioregions are ecological communities of plants, animals, and environmental conditions bounded by natural borders. Each is unique in terms of its diversity of life, soils, watersheds, landforms, and seasonal weather patterns, not to mention cultures. So at its root, thrivability, our capacity to thrive, is first and foremost a local bioregion phenomenon. To underline this claim, people are unlikely to alter their behavior on global issues, including climate change, if they're not engaged locally.

Engaging people locally, however, is challenged by an invisible bias. If you go outside and look around at nearby nature, whatever it is, chances are you'll consider it normal. I currently live near City Park on the east side of Denver, Colorado. The park has plenty of nature: big trees, foxes and squirrels, cormorants and Canada geese, a surfeit of rabbits. Yet a century ago, black-footed ferrets hunted prairie dogs in this place. And prior to the great slaughter in the 1800s, bison herds numbering in the thousands roamed what is now eastern Denver, hunted by grizzlies and Native Americans. So "normal" changes with each passing generation. Or, to put it another way, there is no normal.

The confounding factor is that human lifespans are typically less than a century. And whatever we see around us as we grow up tends to be interpreted as the norm. Psychologist Peter Kahn interviewed African American children living in inner-city Houston about their environmental opinions and values. The kids showed a surprisingly high level of moral concern for nearby nature, and most understood concepts like pollution. Yet they also tended to think that Houston, one of the most polluted cities in the United States, did not have a pollution problem.

Kahn concluded that these children lacked an experiential baseline to compare the ideas of polluted versus not polluted. And he proposed that almost all of us make the same error across generations because we see the natural world experienced in our childhood as environmentally normal. The real problem arises when we realize that for most places, the quality and diversity of our local environments have been steadily declining for at least a century, and much longer in most places. Yet this degradation is effectively invisible to us, a phenomenon Kahn refers to as *environmental generational amnesia*.

One way we might work around the shifting baseline behind this unique brand of amnesia is to change the environment for the better over a brief time span, establishing a new and improved norm. How might we accomplish such a feat? Easy, just go native!

Going Native

Richard Louv makes a strong case that whereas the twentieth century was the time of nature conservation, the twenty-first century must be the era of nature restoration. Doug Tallamy, professor in the Department of Entomology and Wildlife Ecology at the University of Delaware, could not agree more. And Tallamy has a simple, yet powerful idea that could help realize the restoration dream. As described in his terrific book, *Bringing Nature Home*, native plants could help us re-nature the places we live and save countless species from extinction.

Thanks to natural selection operating over many millennia, all plants and animals have evolved to play specific roles in particular ecosystems. In other words, evolution has endowed organisms with features that improve their odds of surviving and reproducing in that place. So when a plant from one continent is transplanted to another, it now exists within a web of relationships entirely different from those of its ancestors. Sometimes these green "aliens" (there they are again) struggle and die off. Other times they thrive, often because of a lack of predators or parasites. Meanwhile, shaking things up by adding invasive species often causes their native counterparts to diminish or disappear locally—even to go extinct.

Tallamy has shown that plant-eating insects feed mostly, often only, on native species. That is, they eat plants from their ancestral habitats, foodstuffs the insects have coexisted with for millennia. Environments dominated by nonnative plants, then, make things rough for the local insect herbivores. Insects support a bevy of bug-eating predators, especially birds, which in turn are fodder for larger predators like hawks. So the increase of alien plants in a given area creates cascading effects, often diminishing the diversity of life forms at multiple ecological levels.

Now consider our present-day cities. Today, the vast majority of urban plants (80 percent by some measures) are not native to the built environments they grow in. According to Tallamy, about 3,400 alien plant species have been introduced in North America alone. That is, we've imported them, either intentionally or unintentionally, from other parts of the world. Think about the Australian eucalyptus trees found over much of northern California, or the plethora of Asian roses adorning European and North American gardens.

To make matters worse, we've disposed of most of the ancestral plant diversity, opting instead for monotonous expanses of one or a few kinds of greenery. The prime example is our thirsty lawns, dominated by a single species — Kentucky bluegrass (which, despite its name, originated in Eurasia). With native plants decimated and replaced by fewer varieties of aliens, our cities support only a tiny fraction of the native insects, birds, and other animals from the local bioregion.

Tallamy's solution is to seed our cities, our suburbs, indeed all human-dominated landscapes, once again with native plants. This *wildscaping* reverses the recently imposed negative cycle, attracting more native insects, which are quickly followed by birds and other animals. The local web of life becomes more robust and diverse, more capable of fighting off unwanted intruders. Nearby nature wins by boosting its diversity and staving off extinctions. We win by living in nature-rich settings that improve our health and well-being.

And if saving species isn't motivation enough, there's another great reason to seed native plants in any patch of soil you can stick a trowel into: they provide an amazing tool for nature connection.

Most of the time we're oblivious to the comings and goings of blossoms and birds. We might pause to breathe in the fragrant springtime or listen to the morning bird chorus. But how many of us celebrate the return of warblers, tanagers, vireos, and thrushes from their wintering grounds in Central and South America? These birds interweave our local web of life with others in distant lands. By consciously encouraging the return of these birds with native plants and insects, we weave ourselves into this mysterious, long-distance ebb and flow of life.

As a nature mentor, you might work with kids to seed some native plants in the backyard, perhaps along the fence or just next to the barbeque. If you live in an apartment, why not do the same in a windowsill planter? If you work in a library, museum, or community center, wildscaping the building's periphery could become an important experiential learning tool. And for all you nature mentor teachers, school grounds offer an excellent platform for native greening, as well as for engaging students in the resulting biodiversity boost. What if migrating birds became part of the biology curriculum, or social studies, or art?

The Greening of Cities

To my mind, cities are by far the best focal level for addressing thrivability. A large nation such as the United States is far too big and unwieldy for this task, as are most states. On their own, neighborhoods are much too small for the large-scale, systemic change we're after. Cities, on the contrary, although huge in some cases, seem to fall into the Goldilocks zone—neither too big nor too small. Cities are the places where most of us now live—more than 80 percent of North Americans, with that number expected to reach 90 percent by 2050. Mayors are the politicians with arguably the greatest capacity to really get things done. And most do. If we can find city-level solutions, likely implemented one community at a time, there's a strong likelihood that these can be exported to urban areas in other regions.

Yet cities also present a fundamental problem. Traditionally, they're the human-dominated places where the wild things aren't. Until recently, the most celebrated urban areas were those where nature was banished to the outskirts and beyond. Manicured gardens, stately tree-lined streets, pigeons, crows, rats, maybe some bunnies—these weren't nature. The natural world was that untamed, unruly stuff with gnashing teeth beyond the urban boundaries. The pioneering Swiss-French architect and urban planner Le Corbusier considered the city to be "a human operation directed against nature" and the house "a machine for living in." In a very real sense, cities have been symbols of human domination over the natural world.

Over the past century, continuous expansion of urban areas has disturbed or destroyed habitats, forcing many animals to adapt to unfamiliar conditions. Many others have disappeared entirely. We've blurred the lines between urban, rural, and nature, resulting in many more, often contentious human encounters with coyotes, raccoons, deer, beaver, even bears and mountain lions.

Maybe it's time to rethink both nature and cities. What if nature were reenvisioned as the greater matrix from which we arose, and within which we're still inextricably embedded? And what if cities, rather than banishing nature, welcomed native

plants and animals within their boundaries and actively con-
tributed to the health of local ecosystems? Imagine if buildings
behaved like trees, harnessing the energy of sunlight and recycling their wastes back into the local environment. Extending
this metaphor, cities would become forests. This is the vision of a
growing number of architects and urban planners, recently embodied in a new building certification program called the Living
Building Challenge.

Timothy Beatley, a professor in the University of Virginia's
School of Architecture, has traveled the world seeking out *biophilic cities*—his term for cities that put nature first in design,
planning, and management. You may recall that *biophilia* trans-
lates as "love of life." A parallel movement toward "green" cities
focuses on such elements as mass transit, energy-efficient buildings, and renewable energy production. But with biophilic cities,
the emphasis is on conserving, restoring, and celebrating nature.
Rather than being optional, nature is considered "absolutely essential to living a happy, healthy and meaningful life." These
urban areas often feature green roofs, green walls, and plenty
of green spaces interconnected by trails. Beatley cites Helsinki,
Finland, subdivided by green wedges, broadest at the city's forested margins and narrowing toward the urban core. Anchor-
age, Alaska, is another example, with an astounding 250 miles
of trails wandering through its nature-rich boundaries.

For Beatley, biophilic cities are equally about creating nature-
rich environments and engaging people with them. Along with
ramping up access to green spaces, he argues that we should
measure the success of cities by the amount of time people spend
outdoors in natural settings, the percentage of the population
that's active in outdoor clubs and organizations, and the percentage of the population that can recognize common species of

plants and animals. Equally important are biophilic institutions and governance—for example, the adoption of a biodiversity action plan and the priority given to environmental education. Beatley recently founded the Biophilic Cities Network to create a platform for partner cities to identify obstacles and work toward shared solutions.

On a similar front, in 1996 a group of passionate people representing multiple organizations in the Chicago area established Chicago Wilderness, with the aim of restoring and sustaining local biological diversity. Today more than 250 partner organizations manage a vast nature reserve of 370,000 acres strewn across southwestern Michigan, northwestern Indiana, northern Illinois, and southern Wisconsin. In recent years, similar kinds of green-space alliances have popped up in cities around the United States. Examples include the Bay Area Open Space Council in San Francisco, the Intertwine Alliance in Portland, and Amigos de los Rios in Los Angeles. In Denver, we're working on a parallel effort, also with a coalition of diverse organizations at the table.

Inspired by Richard Louv and Doug Tallamy, in 2013 Toronto embarked on the Homegrown National Park Project, which aims to create a vibrant green corridor along the former path of Garrison Creek, in the city's west end. Rather than building an actual park, the project has appointed community leaders, known as "park rangers," to head up the transformation of backyards and public spaces, using such strategies as guerilla gardening and moss graffiti (yes, that's graffiti made with moss). In short, the aim is to crowdsource a major urban park into existence.

We live in exciting times. Projects like these are reenvisioning the very idea of a city, and the relationship between humans and nature.

Rewilding

One of the most pressing questions of our time, worthy of consideration by all of us, is: How can humans and nature thrive in my local place—my bioregion? Another, more anthropomorphic way of asking the same question is, What does this place want to be?

In recent years, a concept has emerged that may offer a profound answer. It's called *rewilding*. This word generally refers to large-scale conservation efforts to protect, restore, and connect wilderness areas. Reestablishing big carnivores such as bears, wolves, and mountain lions often appears as a central element. In most instances, the overarching aims of rewilding efforts are preserving functional ecosystems and curbing species losses. To give a single example, the Yellowstone to Yukon Initiative (Y2Y) seeks to preserve and connect mountain ecosystems between Yellowstone National Park in the United States and the Yukon in the Canadian north, forming an expansive wildlife corridor for grizzly bears, migratory birds, and other animals.

Yet the notion of rewilding can be applied to cities and surrounding natural areas as well. Here the focus is less on big carnivores and more on native plants and birds. In this sense, Doug Tallamy's goal of spreading native greenery throughout cities, as well as Toronto's Homegrown National Park, can be thought of as urban rewilding projects. Rewilding also applies to people's minds, bodies, and spirits, an antidote to the domestication caused by denatured lives. We might even think of this sort of internal rewilding as the primary aim of nature mentoring.

How might we begin the rewilding process? Certainly we can seed some native plants, but we're still lacking that all-important compelling vision, a castle in the sky to strive for. Try as we might, we won't find the answers solely by looking at present-day nature. Remember that the natural world has been severely degraded, and that this degradation has been largely hidden from us by Kahn's environmental generational amnesia. Before determining how people and nature can thrive within our local bioregions, we need to know what our places were like in the recent past, when nature last thrived there. But how far back in time do we look? One hundred years? One thousand years?

For the New World, a good place to start is with the arrival of humans, sometime prior to 13,000 years ago; people likely followed vast herds of mammals across the Bering land bridge from Asia into North America. What those first pioneers found after navigating their way southward through the northern ice sheets is hard for us to fathom today. You could describe it as the Serengeti on steroids—vast plains brimming with mega-beasts. Mastodons, giant ground sloths, broad-horned bison, camels, horses, and tanklike glyptodonts were among the plant eaters. Flesh eaters included saber-toothed cats, hyenas, dire wolves, cheetah, lions bigger than any today, and the short-faced bear, dwarfing the largest living grizzlies. Giant California condors soared above the grassy plains, cleaning up the carnage. By all estimates, the plants too were highly diverse.

Humans and nature did not thrive together for long, however. Within 300 years of the first people arriving, the North American megafauna was gone, or nearly so. Although much debate still ensues over the cause of this extinction, with climate and humans as the primary culprits, the evidence is strong that people played a key role. Not long afterward, a second wave of big mammals arrived, mostly from north of the ice sheets, to fill the ecological gap. The colonizers included moose, elk, gray wolf, grizzly, and vast herds of short-horned bison. Humans eventually decimated the numbers of these animals as well.

We always eat the big ones first. As humans spread around

the globe from their natal continent of Africa, they tended to wipe out, or at least greatly diminish, most of the big animals before becoming more proficient at coexisting with those that remained. Many cultures (though not all) became expert at modifying the landscape so as to maintain a high diversity of plants and animals. For them, an intimate connection with nature was essential to survival. Today, we associate vast numbers of large animals with African savannahs, the birthplace of humans. But if we look back in the distant past, over millions of years, the presence of large animals was the thriving norm globally.

Thirteen thousand years may sound like an awfully long time, but it's in the range of 400 human lifespans. From Mother Nature's evolutionary perspective, it's a mere eyeblink, given that species of backboned animals tend to persist on the order of one million years. Many native plants and animals living among us today still carry adaptations intended for those Pleistocene landscapes. J. B. MacKinnon, in his book *The Once and Future World*, cites several examples of such "ecological ghosts." The classic is America's sole surviving antelope-like mammal, the pronghorn. If you've ever driven through the western plains, you've likely seen these fleet-footed, white-rumped creatures. Pronghorns can run at speeds approaching 60 miles per hour, taking about five seconds and a dozen steps to sprint the length of an American football field! This blinding pace far exceeds that of even the swiftest carnivores in its environment today. Why so fast? The solution to this high-velocity mystery is that the running abilities of pronghorns are left over from the ice age glory days, when cheetah and long-legged hyenas still crouched in the grass.

There's no question that ecosystems in the American West and elsewhere were far more diverse in the past than they are today. Grasslands and big animals often form a symbiotic cycle.

Grasses feed a wide range of herbivores, which in turn stimulate growth of diverse varieties of grasses and other plants through trampling and nitrogen-rich dung. That's one reason why many rewilding proponents argue for bringing back megafaunal species such as bison, bears, and even elephants. Some propose we put African elephants on the American plains as a proxy for the extinct mammoths and mastodons. Others suggest that we figure out how to "de-extinct" mammoths and mastodons by merging cloning technologies with ancient DNA, returning these Pleistocene giants to their natal homelands. Still others make the case for reintroducing vast herds of American bison.

For other places, we may not need to reach so far back into time. And we must avoid the fallacy that the presence of people inevitably leads to the destruction of nature. A large literature now demonstrates that some indigenous cultures learned to live within, and even to cultivate, diverse natural settings. A prime example are the pre-Columbian peoples of Amazonia, who built networks of roads and canals, cultivated crops such as maize and manioc, and managed plantations of bananas and palms, all within the wild rainforest. Indeed, knowledge of how indigenous peoples lived on the land offers an essential source for understanding how we might work with that same land in the future. Some of this understanding has been lost to us, but much is now available thanks to the work of anthropologists, archaeologists, and, most importantly, the living descendants of these cultures. We have much to learn from such traditional ecological knowledge.

Our goal here should *not* be to go backward in an attempt to revive some lost ecosystem. It should be about cocreating a thriving future based on an understanding of the biological diversity previously supported in our home bioregion. We simply cannot answer the question about the future thriving of humans and nature in a particular place unless we first know something of the plants and animals that existed there in the past. Natural history museums, as the primary keepers of the objects and stories of past worlds, have a crucial role to play in this effort. And in keeping with Doug Tallamy's vision, perhaps we should look to kick off our rewilding efforts not with those charismatic megafauna, but rather with native plants and insects.

As we acquire and disseminate an understanding of the past, our attention also needs to be directed to an exploration of the present. What kinds of creatures and plants inhabit our cities and bioregions today? A range of tools and techniques is available to assist in conducting such biological inventories, including those 24-hour surveys called bioblitzes described in Chapter 9. Equally critical is an understanding of how our local place works, the relationships between organisms and the flow of energy and matter highlighted in Chapter 4. Only then, through comparisons with the past, can we begin to gain an accurate sense of an ecosystem's strengths and weaknesses, including what has been lost in recent generations.

With some knowledge of the past and the present, we're finally ready to turn our attention to the future and begin to answer the question of what it means for humans and nature to thrive in a particular place. Here we immediately stumble into a fascinating temporal imbalance. Looking backward, we see a single, sinuous path that has brought us through 14 billion years of time to the present moment. But turning to face the future, an infinite number of paths lie before us. Which one do we take? Are we destined to stumble along blindfolded, or do we have the wisdom to plot a clear, thrivable course forward?

What if all cities were reimagined as nature-rich places, with abundant space set aside for native plants and animals, or at least some of them? Nature already provides services essential to our existence, among them clean air and water, productive local farms and fisheries, temperature control, resilience to climate change, and quality of life through green spaces and educational opportunities. How could we revitalize our urban areas to nurture these services?

We might start by crowdsourcing the future. Guided by scientific institutions like museums of natural history, communities in every city in every bioregion could initiate discussions about the kind of future they want, informed by what is known of the past and present of those places. Once a community has chosen a desired destination—that is, which of the infinite number of futures they want to pursue—then it's a matter of "backcasting," plotting a path from where they are now to where they want to go.

Of course, rewilding will not be simple. The process will entail plenty of trial and error, along with inevitable debates. Our knowledge of the past will always be limited. And visions for the future will undoubtedly change with each passing generation, as knowledge increases and social values shift, resulting in a zigzagging pathway. But that's okay. The essence of this rewilding process is communities co-creating the future, modifying the path forward as the situation demands.

Revolution

Today, almost every major city in the developed world features multiple organizations that aim to connect people, and especially children, with nature. The list includes independent schools, natural history museums, environmental education organizations, botanical gardens, zoos, planetariums, aquariums, science centers, wilderness outfitters, nature centers, and nature kid camps. The great majority of these organizations are doing amazing things, positively impacting the lives of dozens, hundreds, even thousands of children. Yet, despite this plethora of nature-related offerings, the disconnect between children and nature has ballooned to an all-time high, while science literacy levels have dwindled. Youths in America and elsewhere continue to break records in technology consumption while becoming increasingly detached from the natural world. In short, despite the concerted efforts and successes of so many, we haven't yet figured out how to "move the needle" on nature connection at an urban scale.

With relatively few exceptions—among them the growing number of green space alliances—the many institutions involved with nature connection function independently of one another, each attempting to carve out a niche with potential for long-term persistence and growth. One possible solution is to double or triple the number of organizations working on these problems. Yet this experiment has been run again and again in cities around North America and elsewhere, thus far without scalable results.

A new approach is needed. Rather than adding more organizations, a thrivable answer is more likely to emerge through collaborations that scale nature connection efforts by leveraging the assets of multiple partners. Researchers at Stanford University recently dubbed this approach "collective impact" and published a set of guidelines gleaned from comparing successful collaborations with unsuccessful attempts. Key conditions of success include a common agenda, shared and consistent measurement of results, mutually reinforcing activities, ongoing communication, and the support of a backbone organization to coordinate efforts.

How might a major metro area apply the collective impact

model to rewilding their urban, suburban, and rural regions? A first step would be bringing together representatives from local governments, corporations, nonprofits, higher education, K–12 schools, and foundations. Ideally, this group would act like a Swiss Army knife, each organization functioning as a distinct tool with unique capacities.

One subset of partners might work on past ecological baselines, establishing an understanding of how nearby nature has thrived during relatively recent centuries and millennia — say, since humans arrived. Another subset would work on the present, conducting a biological inventory of the bioregion and beginning work to restore native plants and animals. And a third group would focus on the future, developing an inspiring vision based on widespread community input. All of these efforts could be aided by citizen scientists and citizen naturalists, children and adults who may not have formal expertise, yet nevertheless serve a critical role in collecting information and acting on it.

Success in the rewilding revolution will likely require both top-down and bottom-up elements. The top-down portion consists of a compelling vision and strategy, combined with a publicity campaign and needed changes in legislation to permit widespread greening. The bottom-up component includes the full spectrum of grassroots efforts, from you mentoring your child and planting some native plants to collaborative, community-based projects aimed at achieving wins and demonstrating progress. In all communities, even ones we might think of as hopeless, there are people who possess great passion to care for one another and their surroundings; if we find those people and work with them, we can spark great change. True success and transformation would arrive when bottom-up and top-down efforts become fully interwoven. Toronto's Homegrown National

Park is one example of a powerful top-down vision paired with grassroots efforts.

In Denver, our nascent green-space alliance is contemplating an even more ambitious goal: a great urban park. As envisioned, this park, a patchwork of engaging green spaces, would be within a ten-minute walk of *all* metro Denver residents, regardless of ethnic background or family income. The plan would be to build on the existing network of parks, refuges, and trail systems, revitalizing some green spaces while creating new ones, all with the help of local communities. In addition to boosting access to nature, a host of educational providers would generate opportunities to engage people with these rewilded spaces.

Schoolyards may hold the greatest potential to accomplish some early, bottom-up victories. In the United States alone, more than 132,000 schools teach students in over 13,000 school districts. Every community has a school. What if all those schoolyards were greened into diverse ecosystems, outfitted with natural playgrounds, vegetable gardens, outdoor classrooms, and native plants? What if all teachers were trained in place-based education and confident to teach just about any subject outdoors on the school grounds? And what if those many thousands of schoolyards were open after school hours, providing ready access to captivating natural settings? In a sense, schools are microcosms of cities, complete with communities, buildings, and outdoor areas. They are also the places where our children spend a substantial proportion of their youthful waking hours. We could begin the transformation of both childhood and cities simply by making schools more nature rich.

Libraries offer additional, abundantly available opportunities to collaborate in promoting nature connection, including through after-school programs. To give one exciting new example, the Sun Ray Library in St. Paul, Minnesota, has partnered with the Children & Nature Network and the local parks and recreation department to create a nature-rich place that goes well beyond a book-filled building. As planned, this library will have an outdoor reading garden, a rain garden, wildlife-friendly plantings, and a play area festooned with dozens of trees. Youths and adults will have opportunities to be trained as "Natural Leaders," hosting educational events focused on local place, and backpacks full of nature-related gear will be available for checking out. The Children & Nature Network hopes to build on this success, fostering many more "green libraries."

Add to all this the rewilding of backyards, courtyards, and parks with native species, and you can see that it wouldn't take long to transform urban and suburban landscapes into a thriving new norm. Best of all, this rewilding revolution, particularly in its initial stages, doesn't require oversight or permission or even much in the way of expertise. Anyone can participate simply by planting some native plants.

The elements for a rewilding revolution, both people and place, are all there: Jon Young's core routines for nature connection, emphasizing a mentored blend of nature experiences and stories. John Dewey's experiential learning, featuring hands-on, multisensory engagement with the real world in real time. Thomas Berry's Universe Story, the epic of everything with potential to help root us in local place. Adam Bienenstock's natural playgrounds, offering children easy access to imaginative free play in a safe, challenging setting. Sharon Danks's green schoolyards, weaving kids and communities into the fabric of nearby nature. Stacie Gilmore's strategies for inner-city youths, connecting underserved human and natural communities, one child at a time. Richard Louv's hybrid mind, balancing attention-narrowing technologies with awareness-expanding nature. Doug

Tallamy's native plants, a vibrant green pathway to restore wild nature in urban areas worldwide. And Timothy Beatley's biophilic cities, urban settings that resonate with the natural world.

And we now understand how a collaborative, collective impact approach can help weave these diverse pieces together, leveraging the work of all partners. Warp and weft. Top-down meets bottom-up. Mother Nature has kicked in as well, providing our inner drive to bond with nature, together with resilient native plants and animals that will return in abundance if only we invite them. Now we just need the will to do it.

A compelling case can be made that a healthy population is impossible without a healthy place to live. After all, our bodies and minds are deeply interconnected with local place through air, water, and food, as well as the psychological effects of nature on our brains. The reverse is also true: truly healthy urban and suburban settings likely cannot exist without a healthy population. Why would people act on behalf of a place unless they care about it and engage with it through a variety of activities? The key, then, may be tackling both problems simultaneously, bootstrapping healthy people and places into existence through rewilding.

Revolutionaries

Who will drive urban and suburban rewilding? For the most part, it will be nature mentors—people like you and me. Scaling efforts to foster deep nature connection depends on two things: access and engagement. The access half of the equation involves rewilding cities and their suburbs, from domestic gardens with their bevy of wild critters to wilder settings with foxes and hawks. The engagement half is all about rewilding minds.

Who else other than caring nature mentors are likely to take on the heavy lifting? But here's the fun part: odds are excellent that this work will be some of the most enjoyable and satisfying any of us will ever do.

We've seen how nature connection is founded on three elements: experience, mentoring, and understanding—EMU. Hands-on, multisensory experience is essential, as is understanding of some key ideas. Yet given that children will get neither the experience nor the understanding in the absence of caring adults, the foundation for nature connection—or, perhaps more accurately, the fuel—is mentoring.

We need nature mentors to engage youngsters in routines such as sit spot, story of the day, and artful questioning aimed at stretching edges. Rather than focusing on nature's nitty-gritty—the names of plants and animals or random facts about their biology—ask questions that nudge kids toward big ideas. At the top of the list are the horizontal connections that embed us within the local, moment-to-moment flow of energy and matter, as well as the vertical connections cascading from our shared heritage with stars, planets, and other life forms. These overarching concepts—embodied by ecology and evolution, respectively, in the grandest sense of both—can form a scaffold upon which to add accumulated knowledge. Equally crucial is rooting learning in local place. An experiential, place-based approach offers perhaps the most potent pathway for engaging young learners. Oh, and remember to tell nature stories, lots of them, throwing yourself wholeheartedly into the task.

As we've seen, the process of nature connection changes dramatically as children grow. For early childhood, the key ingredient is plenty of unstructured nature play, with kids taking the lead. Your role as mentor is to let them learn and engage like the playful scientists they were born to be. Make a habit of heading outdoors daily, even if it's just for a walk around the block. Watch carefully to see where interests and passions lie, and encourage these with additional activities. Begin the nature connection process early, preferably during infancy, taking advantage of captivating settings like beaches, forests, and nighttime stars whenever possible. Let these experiences deepen the bond between you and the child. Get used to dirt. Nature connection is a contact sport, so encourage kids to engage bodily with all of their senses. That's what bathtubs and laundry machines are for. Throughout these early childhood years, the primary goal is wonder, and more wonder.

In middle childhood, tap into kids' growing longing for autonomy, risk, and competence. Abundant nature experience continues to be essential. Work on becoming a hummingbird parent, taking steps backward with each passing year, and zooming in only when necessary. Let children find their own special place(s) outdoors. These spots are the most likely sources of ecstatic moments, where kids will sense a deep connection with the natural world. Send them off on collecting expeditions, whether for berries, lizards, or photographs. Tap into the power of nature art to awaken awareness and creativity. Think about layering in more formal nature connection tools like wandering and sit spot, and follow up with journaling and a few probing questions. Consider establishing similar nature habits yourself, even if you manage to get out only once a week. Better yet, find a nature activity that you're truly passionate about and bring children along for the ride. Your level of engagement is critical for keeping them engaged. Don't forget to develop at least a small cohort of others to help you in your quest; from this age onward, nature mentoring must extend beyond parents. Establish and maintain strict limits for screen time, replacing many of these hours with nature time. Continue to foster wonder at every opportunity.

Finally, adolescence is also a time when youngsters long to take another step outward, not only away from parents but away from home and often into wilder landscapes. Nature mentors need to give teens this needed space, and with it increasing autonomy and responsibility. In particular, teens are strongly compelled to engage in challenging adventures with other teens. So think about establishing nature as the place for those adventures, and ensure that adolescents are mentored in the skills necessary to be confident—whether backpacking, fishing, skiing, or surfing. Service learning, although powerful at any age, offers an exceptional avenue for teens to take on additional responsibility, engage in challenging activities with peers, and fine-tune their moral compass. If this service occurs outdoors, it's also a powerful way to deepen nature connection. We all need rites of passage, though few of us now experience them. Find a rite of passage that works for your teen(s) and mentor them beforehand (preferably over a period of years) to ensure the necessary skills and confidence are in place. At the right time (you'll know when it is), orchestrate a transformational event, and celebrate afterward with community. In this way, nature can play a pivotal role in the transition from childhood to adulthood, ultimately fostering wisdom.

By now I hope you've fathomed both the art and the science of being a nature mentor. Thanks to growing numbers of empirical, science-based studies, we've begun to glean what sorts of approaches are likely to be most effective at specific stages of life. But the application of those approaches is a true art that, like any other, requires practice and diligence.

In the end, raising a wild child is much more about seeding love than knowledge. So nature mentors must work their Coyote magic more in the realm of emotions than intellect. Antoine de Saint-Exupéry expressed this point beautifully:

> If you want to build a ship, don't drum up people to collect wood and don't assign them tasks and work, but rather teach them to long for the endless immensity of the sea.

Nature connection is the ship we're trying to build. Our goal as mentors is not to share facts or assign tasks. It is to be matchmakers, to help children fall in love with nature so that they long to be immersed within it. That emotional pull, if deeply entrenched, will nourish a lifelong sense of wonder and a desire to seek answers. If you help to cultivate that longing, children will figure out the rest.

Secret #10 for Raising a Wild Child

Rather than sharing knowledge and expertise, your chief goal as a nature mentor is to help instill a deep longing for nature.

Nature Mentoring Tips

OFFER A POSITIVE VISION

One of the greatest gifts we can give to children is an optimistic outlook on the future. Particularly for kids in early childhood, avoid negative stories about the natural world and the declining environment. These can lead to emotional detachment rather than caring. Recognize, however, that kids in middle childhood will likely be getting a doom-and-gloom message about the state of the world, even if it doesn't come from you. It's important to listen to kids' fears for the future, to respond honestly, and even to share your own fears. Equally important, however, is balancing any fears with positive, hopeful stories of change, stories that demonstrate how people are working to solve the problems, and how youths can be part of this critical work. Ultimately, think about how you might instill a vision of a thriving future for both people and nature, particularly in your local place. Engage kids in actively imagining and realizing this future.

For teachers, consider a class project in which the students work together to envision a thriving future in their local place. How would that place look different than it does today? What kinds of plants and animals might live there? How would the relationship between humans and nature change? And what might they do to realize this vision, perhaps starting at home, school, or in the local community?

GO NATIVE

Whether you're a parent, grandparent, teacher, informal educator, or someone else who cares for kids, one of the simplest and most profound ways to be a nature mentor is to cultivate plants native to your region. Work with kids to research which plants are best for your area, and what kinds of animals they are likely to attract. To give one example, Project Milkweed aims to empower people to plant milkweed to create nutritious flyways for the endangered monarch butterflies. Other kinds of plants attract bees or hummingbirds (though it's important to select pesticide-free plants). Engage youngsters in caring for the plants, and then watch for the arrival of your target animals, like migrating birds. If you happen to have a sit spot close by that you visit regularly, it should be easy to monitor comings and goings during the year. Let children know that their actions can help transform the community, providing habitat for a variety of plants and animals.

GREEN SOME SCHOOLS

Greening schoolyards is one of the most powerful ways to foster nature connection, especially if the kids themselves are directly involved in the design and construction. Begin in your own neighborhood, perhaps at your child's school. Start talking with neighbors, teachers, the principal, or district administrators. Invite them to imagine the school building and grounds revitalized through ties with nearby nature. If you're a teacher, think about combining efforts with other teachers to plant a garden, add a native plant trail, or make a simple outdoor classroom. Start small and build up, so that you can achieve some quick successes. Watch how these new green spaces change the learning and activity patterns of children, and make sure that others see these changes too. Through you, communities have the power to reenvision how we educate our children. Sharon Danks's excellent book *Asphalt to Ecosystems* offers a great resource to aid in this effort, as does Rusty Keeler's *Natural Playscapes*. Dream big, build consensus, and make your vision a reality!

ENGAGE LOCALLY

Take advantage of the nature connection organizations already present in your community. Chances are that there are more than you think, possibly including a zoo, natural history museum, botanical garden, family nature clubs, and nature center(s). If you're so inclined, look for ways that these varied efforts might be interconnected so as to scale them up. Many cities now celebrate National Get Outdoors Day. Events like these are a great place to find out about what your area has to offer and to talk with others about possible collaborations. Tell others about your own nature mentoring efforts and why you think they're important. Have conversations about how local people might work together (with kids!) to rewild your hometown. Once again, start small and build from there.

FALL IN LOVE AGAIN

At its root, nature mentoring is matchmaking, helping children fall in love with nature. All youngsters share this built-in bias to bond with nature. But a love for nature must be nurtured, or it will desiccate, disappear, and be forgotten. Children tend to value and care about the things we value and care about. So one of the surest paths to raising a wild child is to rewild your own mind and fall in love again with nature. Schedule time in wild or semi-wild places, even if it's just hanging out for a picnic in the local park. Make nature a priority, for you and for the children in your life. Slow down and leave time for relaxation and reflection. Make a conscious effort to expand your awareness and comment on the beautiful things you see—clouds, flowers, trees, birds. If you lead by example, the kids will follow.

Widening Circles

IMAGINE FOR A moment that within the next generation we are successful in kicking off the rewilding revolution across North America and elsewhere. In what ways might the world be different? How would we change the way we raise children? And how would cities be altered in response? Finally, in what ways might the relationship between people and nature evolve? In the following fictional piece, which takes place a generation from now, I offer a glimpse into one possible future as viewed through the eyes of a conservationist.

Ladies and gentlemen, the 2040 winner of the Rachel Carson Conservation Award, Audubon's youngest honoree to date, Gabriela Ferguson.

Good evening. I'm deeply honored to receive this award, standing on the shoulders of amazing women conservationists, including the towering Rachel Carson. Throughout my life I've walked the path created by these women, reveling in the blue sky, the soil beneath my feet, and the wild air between. And tonight I find myself bursting with gratitude for all these trailblazers.

Several personal mentors have also graced my life, and I could not be here without them. Three in particular stand out. First is my father, Donald Ferguson, who demonstrated the value of nature through his daily actions. It was Papi who taught me how to open my senses and fully experience the world. Second is my Aunt Mariana, whose passion for plants proved contagious, and whose stories ignited my imagination. She helped me see not only the beauty of plants, whether garden vegetable or alpine wildflower, but also their myriad interconnections with surrounding landscapes and creatures.

Finally, the most influential of my mentors has been Mother Nature herself.

I've always been drawn to nature, my first and most enduring love affair. I'm told that even as a baby learning to crawl, I escaped outdoors at every opportunity. The backyard was my first wilderness, and the catalyst for some of my earliest memories. While exploring those dirt-filled nooks and crannies, I discovered iridescent beetles, winding trains of ants, and huge wolf spiders. Back then, the yard seemed immense, with a great spruce tree in one corner and hiding places galore among the rocks and bushes and grasses. There was even a small pond where I could sneak up on frogs. My parents—through their desire to bring nature close to our family—revitalized that tiny slice of southeast Denver to be a paradise for nature play.

Birds especially fascinated me, even in those early years. I developed this penchant from my father, who regularly roused himself early on weekends to sit in the backyard with a cup of steaming coffee, reveling in the morning avian chorus. Papi recognized my growing passion and worked with me to build a birdhouse, followed by a birdbath and a feeder. I soon found myself tiptoeing outside first thing in the morning to my "secret place" between the fence and a wall of chokecherries. From there or some other hidden spot, I watched robins hunt for worms and bugs, and sometimes feed these critters to squawking babies. I marveled at goldfinches, magpies, and hummingbirds.

By far my favorites were the western tanagers. Crimson heads, coal black wings, and brilliant yellow chests. A male in flight is a flash of flame. Some of my earliest artistic efforts depicted tanagers, usually with greatly oversize heads. I even went through a phase of wearing dazzling yellow dresses with red hats! Papi and I discovered online that tanagers are warm-weather devotees, wintering in Central and South America and migrating north to bask in our midlatitude summer heat. Sometimes on snowy winter days in Denver, I imagined those tanagers frolicking in the tropical sun and dreamed of joining them.

Occasionally, during the long hot Colorado summer, I did join the tanagers, camping out in the backyard with my brother Carlos, and in later years, with my girlfriends. It was all a great adventure, even with the screaming sirens and growling motorcycles. Mama and Papi also took us camping up in the mountains. We had several favorite spots, usually along rushing rivers, spending our days hiking, fishing, and exploring.

My love of nature, and of learning, deepened during my school years. I attended two amazing place-based learning schools, the first of which was Hampden Heights Expeditionary School. Back then expeditionary learning—with its focus on hands-on, multisensory experiences, many of them outdoors—was still an alternative form of education. Hampden Heights had a wonderful, amphitheater-like outdoor classroom on the banks of Cherry Creek, where many of our lessons were held. The school grounds also had a pond and wetland that served as a learning laboratory. We caught frogs, water striders, and fish, and learned all about wetland life.

It was through those schoolyard experiences that I first

learned about invasive and endangered species, and developed an interest in conservation.

The abundant native plants all over the campus were accompanied by a student-run vegetable garden, which produced abundant food for the school cafeteria. I vividly remember picking a newly ripened tomato and biting into it on a dare, the red juice spilling down my face and shirt. Until that day, I'd hated tomatoes. From that moment, I loved them. After all, I had grown that tomato!

My friend Margaret and I rode our bikes to and from school along the Cherry Creek trail, sometimes on our own, other times with Carlos and various friends. We loved stopping on the way home to explore the creek, often emerging muddy and scratched, but also grinning and elated.

About halfway between school and home was an abandoned field where we sometimes hung out and talked. One fall day we lay on our backs in the tall grass and imagined all kinds of creatures in the billowing clouds swirling overhead. After a while, we fell silent. Time slowed and then vanished. I remember feeling suspended, suddenly part of the clouds and the sky and the sun. It was glorious! When Margaret and I finally roused ourselves, we were late for dinner and our mothers were not happy. But it was worth it!

Another of those ecstatic moments occurred a few years later in the Rocky Mountain Arsenal National Wildlife Refuge. During World War II, the U.S. Army appropriated 15,000 acres of prairie just north and east of Denver to build weapons. In all, well over 150,000 tons of chemical and heavy metal contaminants were released there. The Arsenal was declared a Superfund site in 1987 and then, somewhat ironically, a wildlife refuge in 1992. An intense cleanup effort was completed in 2010. Today, in 2040, the site is one of the largest urban wildlife refuges in the country, home to mule deer, white pelicans, burrowing owls, black-footed ferrets, coyotes, and bald eagles.

A bison herd was established there too, expanding in size over time. We used to visit the Arsenal when I was a kid, mostly to see these great beasts and imagine long-ago times when their vast, thundering throngs dominated the prairie. During one of those visits, our family and several others stood admiring a group of perhaps forty bison from what we thought was a safe distance. But some teenage boys snuck behind the herd and spooked them, triggering a stampede directly at us. Everyone turned and ran for the fence.

Everyone, that is, except me.

For some reason, I stood perfectly still and just stared wide-eyed as the shaggy giants pounded toward me. I felt neither fear nor bravery—just an overwhelming, full-bodied sense of awe. I was thrilled to be in the presence of such majestic animals, and felt as though I was one of them. Fortunately, Papi turned around and sprinted back to get me. As he tells the story, fear was definitely his dominant emotion! Recognizing that he didn't have time to make it to the fence, he picked me up like a football and ran perpendicular to the bison's path, leaping behind a tree at the last moment.

My mountain phase began at age ten, shortly after my mother passed away. The Rockies became an escape for Papi and me, a place to grieve, and then to begin to heal. Papi and Mariana took me up my first 14,000-foot peak, Mount Quandary. I'll never forget the sense of pride, or the fight for breath, as I stood on top of the world. On our way back down, we were lucky enough to see mountain goats perform death-defying feats while navigating a rocky precipice.

Mariana joined me on many subsequent hikes as well, becoming a key figure during my adolescent years. With her as my guide, I came to understand the various life zones we passed through, from grassy plains to alpine tundra, raising my awareness to new heights. Later in my teen years I took Margaret and other friends on those mountain treks, sometimes backpacking for multiple days. I can't imagine a better proving ground for young women, a place to build strength and confidence, and to bond with one another along the way. I've now summited more than twenty "fourteeners," and those alpine meadows are an integral part of my being.

Ironically, then, the bulk of my conservation work has been in cities. The Rocky Mountain Arsenal National Wildlife Refuge has continued to be important in my life. As a teen conservationist, I volunteered with a nonprofit working to connect local, underserved communities with the refuge. Our organization then collaborated with a much larger green-space initiative working to provide all residents of metro Denver with easy access to beautiful green spaces. These efforts included revitalizing parks and schoolyards, creating new open spaces, and connecting these places with crisscrossing greenways overflowing with native plants.

It was through this work that I discovered my calling as a facilitator, working with diverse constituents to cocreate vital green spaces in low-income neighborhoods. As my name suggests, I was spawned from hybrid stock, Scottish and Latino to be exact. I've taken advantage of that mixed heritage to build bridges across cultural chasms, bringing people together to seek shared values and work collaboratively to build stronger, greener, more vital communities.

I'm proud to say that today, because of our intensely collaborative work, Denver and the entire Rocky Mountain Front Range have become a national model for connecting urban and suburban populations with nearby nature.

And those vibrant greenways aren't just for people. Many other animals use them as well, from migrating birds in spring and fall to elk herds in winter. A generation ago, it would've seemed unthinkable to welcome elk herds into the city. Now they're an annual spectacle, attracting visitors from around the country. Before, when Front Range residents thought of wild nature, they looked westward, to the mountains. Thanks to rewilding efforts on lands previously devoted solely to farming and ranching, the short-grass prairie to the east has made a roaring comeback, highlighted by growing herds of free-roaming bison. Many ranches and farms are still there, but a substantial portion of those grassy plains are once again home to a bounty of native plants and animals, creating another major attraction for locals and for ecotourism.

Even grizzlies have returned to Colorado, now sighted in the mountains not far from Fort Collins and Denver. I wonder what will happen when they enter urban areas.

It's hard to believe that a generation ago, children stayed indoors, captivated by glowing digital screens. For most kids today, in this country and elsewhere, those screens are balanced with time in local nature, including plenty of free play.

During those intervening years, the human population of the Front Range has come close to doubling, annual temperatures have slowly risen, and water supplies have dwindled. Yet we've responded with nature-rich, energy-efficient cities, with efforts to retain and recycle water, and with thoughtful planning aimed specifically at meeting the needs of future generations, human and nonhuman alike. Our communities are far healthier as a result, as are the surrounding ecosystems. More and more we embody our state slogan: "Colorado: Where People and Nature Thrive."

Not so long ago, it would have seemed odd for a conservationist to focus her efforts in cities. But somewhere along the way we learned a critical lesson. Preserving truly wild places begins in backyards and schoolyards. It begins in city parks and empty lots, in ditches and streams, experienced bodily. If fueled by freedom and mentorship, the sparks of childhood wonder will erupt into a burning, persistent passion for the natural world.

Today, the overwhelming majority of us live in cities. If we don't grow up interacting with nature nearby to our homes, chances are slim that we'll ever seek out, let alone preserve, national parks or other wilderness. When I think of my own journey, I reflect on the fact that my family was different from others in my neighborhood. Spiraling out from our backyard, they took me to museums, botanic gardens, and nature centers. They took me to the Denver Mountain Parks and to national parks. They appreciated and respected nature, and made sure that I absorbed these values. When I realized later in life that many of my peers lacked experiences like these, I became passionate about creating entry points. Our job is to set children off on a voyage of discovery that never ends. This voyage is essential not only for healthy bodies and minds. It also happens to be exactly what children need to stoke their spirits and to truly embrace life. I am thrilled to see that this perspective is fast becoming the norm here in America and elsewhere.

In the words of poet Rainer Maria Rilke,

> *I live my life in widening circles*
> *that reach out across the world.*

I may not complete this last one
but I give myself to it.

I circle around God, around the primordial tower.
I've been circling for thousands of years
and I still don't know: am I a falcon,
a storm, or a great song?

Last month, I completed one of those widening circles. For the first time, I traveled to Chiapas, Mexico. While there, I uncovered cultural roots from my mother's side, meeting distant relatives and gaining a much stronger, more intimate sense of my Latino heritage.

I also spent a glorious week in the rainforest exploring another set of roots. Yes, I finally had the chance to frolic with my childhood companions, the western tanagers, in their wintering grounds. It was like finding a long-lost friend and experiencing a side of them you'd never known. I wore a red cap and yellow shirt to celebrate the occasion. Best of all, my tanagers spent their days in boisterous, mixed flocks, foraging with flycatchers, antbirds, woodcreepers, and their breathtaking cousins, the scarlet tanagers.

I returned home rejuvenated, ready to embark on the next circle, wherever it might take me. Warm thanks to all of you for being part of my journey.

Notes

1. Wilding the Mind

23 *Sebastián Vizcaíno:* Barth 1990, p. 96.
   William Waddell: Wikipedia, Big Basin Redwoods State Park: http://en
   .wikipedia.org/wiki/Big_Basin_Redwoods_State_Park, accessed November 7, 2014.
   David Quammen: Quammen 2003, p. 3.
25 *G. E. Hutchinson:* Hutchinson 1962, p. 74.
28 *Henry David Thoreau:* Wikiquote entry for Henry David Thoreau, http://
   en.wikiquote.org/wiki/Henry_David_Thoreau, accessed May 19, 2014.
32 *nature's health benefits are now undeniable:* See references in the following compilations: Frumkin 2012; Selhub and Logan 2012; Children &
   Nature Network 2012. The Children & Nature Network (www.children
   andnature.org) is the most in-depth source for research relating to connecting children with the nature world. The "Research and Resources"
   portion of the website includes descriptions of literally hundreds of publications detailing the value of nature and nature connection strategies.
   One early study: Ulrich 1984.
   Another found similar effects: Moore 1981.
   Yet another investigator found: Berman, Jonides, and Kaplan 2008.
   Shinrin-yoku, or "forest bathing": Tsunetsugu et al. 2010; Frehsée 2014.
   Animals are another form of nonhuman nature: Kahn Jr. 1999; Frumkin
   2012.
33 *Research into so-called human-animal bonds:* Barker and Wolen 2008;
   Walsh 2009; Johnson 2010.
   Americans currently spend an astounding: Sterba 2012.
   One researcher found that post-surgery patients: Park and Mattson 2008.

"Horticultural therapy" has proven its mettle: Haller and Kramer 2006.
Even a few trees can make a real difference: Kuo 2001; Kuo and Sullivan 2001a, 2001b; Taylor, Kuo, and Sullivan 2002.
"park prescriptions": Brody 2010; NPR 2014.
National Park Service has even gotten in on the act: National Park Service's Park Prescription Program, http://www.nps.gov/indu/planyourvisit /parkrx.htm, accessed October 5, 2014.

34   *wilderness has been prescribed as therapy:* Frumkin 2012.
Peter Kahn: Kahn Jr. 2011.

35   *What about children?:* Largo-Wight 2011; Charles and Senauer 2010.
Additional kid bonuses arising from nature interactions: Taylor and Kuo 2011; Bixler, Floyd, and Hammutt 2002; Fjortoft 2001; Malone and Tranter 2003. See also the references and descriptions listed on the following fact sheet compiled by Louise Chawla of the University of Colorado: http://www.colorado.edu/cye/sites/default/files/attached-files/Benefits _nature_fact_2011_0.pdf, accessed October 5, 2014.
Finally, children apparently mimic adults: Kahn Jr. 2011.

37   *recent research indicates that unstructured play in natural settings is essential:* See the following and references therein: Kellert 2002; Lester and Maudsley 2006; Munoz 2009; Hughes 2012.
children who regularly play in nature show heightened motor control: Fjortoft 2001.

38   *96.5 percent of a large sample of adults:* Sebba 1991.
"forest kindergartens": Coyle 2010.

39   *When Louise Chawla of the University of Colorado:* Chawla 1999.
Another study of 2,000 urban adults: Wells and Lekies 2006.

40   *Nature Kids Institute:* www.naturekidsinstitute.org.
Nature Connection Pyramid: http://naturekidsinstitute.blogspot.com/2014 /03/the-nature-connection-pyramid.html, accessed August 3, 2014.

41   *Indigenous peoples on this continent:* See, for example, Nelson 2008; Abram 1996.
Luther Standing Bear quotation: Native American Legends: Great Words from Great Americans, http://www.legendsofamerica.com/na-quotes.html, accessed November 8, 2014.
Marlowe Sam: Sam 2008.

42   *By the close of the 1900s:* Cain 2012.
Anna Botsford Comstock: Comstock 1911.

43   *But nature study took an abrupt and precipitous decline:* Pyle 2001.

45   Sharing Nature with Children: Cornell 1998.
I Love Dirt: Ward 2008.
Fed Up with Frenzy: Lipman 2012.
Bringing Nature Home: Tallamy 2007.

46   *If your school doesn't have an outdoor classroom:* Broda 2011.
Organizations like The Nature Conservancy and the David Suzuki Foundation: The Nature Conservancy 2014a; David Suzuki Foundation 2015.

2. The Power of Place

48 *Terms like* traditional ecological knowledge *(TEK):* Semali and Kincheloe 1999; Peat 2002; Martinez 2004; Settee 2008.
49 *home to about 200 billion neurons:* Micheva et al. 2010.
    Other species of upright primates: Smith et al. 2010.
50 *some researchers have focused:* Broad, Curley, and Keverne 2006.
    Other, more ecologically minded investigators: For example, Kaplan, Hooper, and Gurven 2009.
51 *Current anthropological consensus:* Tattersall 2009.
    Wade Davis: Davis 2009, pp. 23–24.
53 biophilia: Wilson 1984.
    A wide range of evidence: For example, Kellert and Wilson 1993; Kahn Jr. 1999; Beck and Katcher 2003.
54 topophilia: Auden 1947.
    Yi-Fu Tuan: Tuan 1990.
    topophilia hypothesis: Sampson 2012.
    Bonding is a powerful and oft-repeated theme: Mock and Fujioka 1990; Hurtado and Hill 1992; Konner 2010.
55 *human bonding with nature:* Sobel 1996.
    Another implication is that: Nabhan and Trimble 1995.
56 *It's ergonomics:* I thank expert naturalist, tracker, and mentor Jon Young for sharing this ergonomic perspective on nature connection.
59 *"bird language":* Young 2012.
    What the Robin Knows: Young 2012.
68 Keeping a Nature Journal: Leslie and Roth 2000.

3. The Way of Coyote

71 *E. O. Wilson:* Wilson 2006.
73 What the Robin Knows: Young 2012.
74 *8 Shields Institute:* http://8shields.com. A nonprofit organization, the Nature Connection Mentoring Foundation (www.natureconnection.org), has recently emerged out of the 8 Shields Institute and promises to play an important role in this work in the future.
75 *The word* mentor: Wikipedia entry, http://en.wikipedia.org/wiki/Mentor.
78 Coyote's Guide: Young, Haas, and McGown 2010.
83 Keeping a Nature Journal: Leslie and Roth 2000. See also Claire Walker Leslie's terrific book, *The Nature Connection* (2010).
87 Coyote's Guide *recommends the following balance:* Young et al. 2010, pp. 96–98.
89 *"The antidote to Nature Deficit Disorder":* Young et al. 2010, p. 44.
90 *Henry David Thoreau:* ThinkExist's entry for Henry David Thoreau, http://thinkexist.com/quotation/you_cannot_perceive_beauty_but_with_a_serene_mind/340895.html, accessed July 8, 2014.
94 *"firekeeper":* Young et al. 2010, p. 362.

4. Hitched to Everything

96 *John Muir:* A discussion of this John Muir quotation, and its misquoted history, can be found at http://vault.sierraclub.org/john_muir_exhibit/writings /misquotes.aspx, accessed July 27, 2014.

97 *more than 700 distinct* kinds *of bacteria:* Aas et al. 2005.

98 *100 trillion bacterial cells:* Conniff 2013.

101 *The origins of the American education system:* This discussion was derived in large part from Mercogliano 2007.
Paul Shepard: Shepard 1998, p. 87.
Horace Mann: Mercogliano 2007, p. 24.

102 *John Gatto:* Mercogliano 2007, p. 26.
"Nation's Report Card": http://nationsreportcard.gov/reading_math_2013/ #/state-performance, accessed May 29, 2014.

105 *place-based education:* For summaries of this approach and its efficacy, see Sobel 1996, 2004, 2008; Orr 1992; Capra 1996; Stone 2009; the Cloud Institute for Sustainability Education, http://cloudinstitute.org/brief -history, accessed January 14, 2014; the Center for Ecoliteracy, http:// www.ecoliteracy.org, accessed January 14, 2014; Place-Based Education Evaluation Collaborative, http://www.peecworks.org/index, accessed January 14, 2014.

106 *"forest kindergartens":* For a general description of this phenomenon, and a list of some places where it is practiced, see http://en.wikipedia.org /wiki/Forest_school_(learning_style), accessed July 27, 2014.

107 *David Orr:* Orr 1992.
John Dewey: Dewey 1938.
David Sobel: Sobel 1996, 2004, 2008.

108 *One nine-year survey:* Place-Based Education Evaluation Collaborative 2010.

109 *A study conducted by King's College London:* King's College London 2011; see also Suzuki 2014.

110 *John Muir Elementary School:* Stone 2009.
School gardens are an amazing and rapidly growing phenomenon: When talking about connecting children with nature, particularly through gardens, it's important to point out that this sort of nature should not be sprayed with pesticides. Gardens and native plants coated in pesticides can easily become unhealthy places for children. For more information, go to Beyond Pesticides (www.beyondpesticides.org) and the Pesticide Action Network (www.panna.org). See also the references and descriptions listed on this fact sheet compiled by Louise Chawla of the University of Colorado: http://www.colorado.edu/cye/sites/default/files/attached-files /Child_Friendly_Lawns_Gardens_2011.pdf, accessed October 5, 2014.

112 Asphalt to Ecosystems: Danks 2012. See also Moore and Wong 1997, and the references and descriptions listed on another of Louise Chawla's fact sheets: http://www.colorado.edu/cye/sites/default/files/attached-files /Gardening_factsheet_2011.pdf, accessed October 5, 2014.

113 *natural terrain schoolyards tend to reduce stress:* Chawla et al. 2014.

114 *International School Grounds Alliance:* http://greenschoolyards.org/blog
/entry/3741099/the-westerbeke-declaration-on-school-grounds, accessed
October 27, 2014.
Green Schoolyards America: http://www.greenschoolyardsamerica.org/.

118 *from a "collection of objects" to a "communion of subjects":* Berry 1990.
Barry Lopez: Lopez 2012.

120 *a number of terrific teachers' guides online:* The Nature Conservancy
2014; David Suzuki Foundation 2015; see also Louv 2014b.

5. Mothers All the Way Down

124 *Albert Einstein:* Wikiquote entry for Albert Einstein, http://en.wikiquote
.org/wiki/Albert_Einstein, accessed May 10, 2014.

125 *Yet, just as Jade and I did:* I thank cosmologist and friend Brian Swimme
for bringing the experiential sunset activity to my attention in his wonderful little book, *The Hidden Heart of the Cosmos.*

126 *Author Jonathan Gottschall:* Gottschall 2012.

127 *Scientist-author Jared Diamond:* Jared Diamond quoted in Sanders 1997.
The best stories help us not only to live: For example, see Sanders 1997.

128 *In the words of author David Abram:* Abram 2011.
A recent review of seven decades: Williams et al. 2012.

130 *The range of tales is important:* For a more in-depth discussion of storytelling and levels of stories, see Young, Haas, and McGown 2010.

134 *Variously called the Universe Story:* See, for example, Spangler 1986;
Berry 1990; Swimme and Berry 1992; Christian 2004; Chaisson 2006;
Sampson 2006; Swimme and Tucker 2011.

135 *Theologian John Haught:* Haught 2008, p. 2.
Thomas Berry and Brian Swimme have argued persuasively: Berry 1990;
Swimme and Berry 1992.

136 *Muriel Rukeyser:* Wikiquote entry for Muriel Rukeyser, http://en.wiki
quote.org/wiki/Muriel_Rukeyser, accessed July 25, 2014.

137 *Cosmologist Brian Swimme summarizes:* Bridle 2003.

143 *Albert Einstein's injunction:* Wikiquote entry for Albert Einstein, http://en
.wikiquote.org/wiki/Talk:Albert_Einstein, accessed May 14, 2014.
The Other Way to Listen: Baylor 1997.
North American Indian Tales: Larned 1997.

144 *Jennifer Morgan:* Morgan and Anderson 2002, 2003, 2006.

145 *"Council of All Beings":* Seed and Macy 1998.

6. The Playful Scientist

149 *Walt Streightiff:* Goodreads quote entry for Walt Streightiff, http://
www.goodreads.com/quotes/614926-there-are-no-seven-wonders-of
-the-world-in-the, accessed July 31, 2014.

Rachel Carson's world-changing book: Carson 2002 [1962].
Carson's biographer, Linda Lear: Lear 2009.
The Sea Around Us: Carson 1951.
The Edge of the Sea: Carson 1955.
"Help Your Child to Wonder": Carson 1998 [1956].

151 *Judy Swamp:* Jon Young shared this story with me during an interview on July 11, 2014.

153 *"Children aren't just defective adults":* Gopnik 2009, p. 9.
much of youngsters' thinking: Gopnik 2012a.
Fei Xu and Vashti Garcia: Xu and Garcia 2008.

154 *the observational learning abilities of preschoolers:* Buchsbaum et al. 2011.
Another experiment: Sobel, Tenenbaum, and Gopnik 2004.

156 *Albert Einstein:* This quotation has been attributed to Einstein at least since the 1970s. http://en.wikiquote.org/wiki/Talk:Albert_Einstein, accessed July 4, 2014.

157 *"a kind of evolutionary division of labor":* Gopnik 2009, p 11.

158 *play equals learning:* Hirsh-Pasek and Golinkoff 2003.
Another growing body of research: For example, see discussions and references in Hirsh-Pasek and Golinkoff 2003; Mercogliano 2007; Gopnik 2009; Hughes 2012; Wilson 2012.
bodily benefits: Hughes 2012.

159 *American Academy of Pediatrics:* Ginsburg 2007.
One of the most profound and disturbing discoveries: Tough 2012.

160 Wired *magazine:* Liu 2011.

161 *Rates of childhood obesity:* Centers for Disease Control, "Obesity and Overweight," http://www.cdc.gov/obesity/childhood/, accessed July 15, 2014.

162 *vitamin D:* American Academy of Pediatrics 2012.
nearsightedness: American Academy of Ophthalmology 2011, "More Time Outdoors May Reduce Kids' Risk for Nearsightedness," http://www.aao.org/newsroom/release/20111024.cfm, accessed July 15, 2014. This press release summarizes a study by Anthony Khawaja of the University of Cambridge.
environmental conservation: Wells and Lekies 2006.
Playful scientists: Hughes 2012.

164 Why Dirt is Good: Ruebush 2009; Brody 2009, http://www.nytimes.com/2009/01/27/health/27brod.html?_r=0.
first year of life: Lynch et al. 2014.
Ilkka Hanski: Hanski et al. 2012.

166 *Imaginations are fired up:* Moore and Wong 1997; Taylor, Wiley, Kuo, and Sullivan 1998; Fjortoft 2001.
Bullying is greatly decreased: Malone and Tranter 2003.
vandalism and aggressive behavior: Kuo and Sullivan 2001b.
longer play intervals: A. Bienenstock, personal communication, August 7, 2014, unpublished data.
kids improve their balance, agility: Keeler 2008.

167 *incidence of "catastrophic injuries":* Fuselli and Yanchar 2012.
Natural Play & Learning Area Guidelines Project: Natural Play & Learning Places, http://natureplayandlearningplaces.org/wp-content/uploads/2014/09/Nature-Play-Learning-Places_v1.2_Sept22.pdf, accessed November 9, 2014.
169 *Rachel Carson:* Carson 1998 [1956].

7. The Age of Competence

174 *Robert Michael Pyle:* Quoted in Kahn Jr. and Kellert 2002, p. 319.
David Attenborough: Discover Wildlife 2012.
than all professional sporting events combined: CNN Travel 2013; Khalil 2014.
the presence of such nonhuman "others": Myers Jr. 2007.
175 *by fourth grade:* Murphy 2011.
176 *Yet recent findings:* Angier 2011.
age of reason: Rogoff et al. 1975.
177 *children who don't see themselves as competent:* Eccles 1999.
178 *Zach Pine:* http://www.naturesculpture.com.
180 *nearby nature remains key during middle childhood:* Moore 1986; Kellert 2002; Sobel 1996; Nabhan and Trimble 1995.
Robert Michael Pyle: Quotation in Kellert 2002, p. 138.
184 *"There is a special period":* Edith Cobb quotation in Sobel 2011, p. 100.
185 *Louise Chawla:* Chawla 1986, 1990; see also discussion in Louv 2006, pp. 93–95.
Kenneth Clark: Clark 1969, p. 291.
187 *more than 90 percent in the past four generations:* Derbyshire 2007.
Richard Louv writes: Louv 2014a.
In a recent Atlantic *article:* Rosin 2014.
189 *Renee Limon:* Quotation in Burnette 2010.
This kind of rewilding: For ideas and inspiration, see Keeler 2008.
191 *Try becoming more of a "hummingbird parent":* Whitaker 2010.
It Takes a Village: Thanks to the 8 Shields Institute and the Art of Mentoring 2014 participants, especially to Jon Young, for emphasizing the role of community in nature connection.
194 *Family Nature Clubs:* Louv 2011, pp. 148–151.
195 *Kids in the Valley, Adventuring (KIVA):* http://kidsadventuring.org/blog/?page_id=297.
196 *Children & Nature Network:* For more information about the "Natural Families" program, including both existing family nature clubs and how to start your own, see http://www.childrenandnature.org/movement/naturalfamilies/.

8. The Social Animal

203 *Aristotle and Socrates:* See discussion in Kaplan and Kaplan 2002.
Shakespeare: William Shakespeare, *The Winter's Tale.*
photographs and video of the living brain: Here I refer to magnetic resonance imaging (MRI) and functional magnetic resonance imaging (fMRI),
respectively.
204 *To complicate matters:* Gopnik 2012b.
changes within the brain that cause adolescents to overvalue rewards:
Casey and Caudle 2013.
206 *a strong preference toward natural settings:* Kahn Jr. 1999; Clayton 2003.
207 *let them take a "time out"?:* Kaplan and Kaplan 2002.
StageofLife.com: Stage of Life 2012.
208 *Juan Martinez:* Martinez tells his story through a short YouTube video for
North Face: https://www.youtube.com/watch?v=DK-n3wr9d9w, accessed
July 8, 2014.
209 *Natural Leaders Network:* http://www.childrenandnature.org/natural
leaders/.
"Find your place on the planet": Goodreads quote entry for Gary Snyder.
http://www.goodreads.com/quotes/172404-find-your-place-on-the-planet
-dig-in-and-take.
211 *Golden Gate National Parks Conservancy:* http://www.parksconservancy
.org.
teen service learning: If you are a high school teacher interested in initiat-
ing a service learning program, I recommend Witmer and Anderson 1994.
212 Mahatma Gandhi quotation: BrainyQuote, http://www.brainyquote.com
/quotes/quotes/m/mahatmagan150725.html, accessed November 9, 2014.
Stephen Kellert and Victoria Derr: Kellert and Derr 1998.
the Student Conservation Association: https://www.thesca.org.
Outward Bound: http://www.outwardbound.org.
National Outdoor Leadership School: http://www.nols.edu.
214 *Louise Chawla and Victoria Derr:* Chawla and Derr 2012.
215 *within walking distance of his house:* As of this writing, a tall fence still
keeps residents of Montbello out of the Rocky Mountain Arsenal National Wildlife Refuge, which borders the northern side of their neighborhood. Access can be gained several miles away only through the Refuge's
main entrance. However, efforts are under way to remedy this situation,
creating an entrance into the Arsenal adjacent to Montbello.
216 *Environmental Learning for Kids:* http://www.elkkids.org.
217 *One survey found that:* Johnson 2013.
Another study revealed that: Outdoor Foundation 2013.
218 *The Trust for Public Land:* http://www.tpl.org.
Outdoor Afro: http://www.outdoorafro.com.
Latino Outdoors: http://latinooutdoors.org.

220 *Wilderness Awareness School:* http://wildernessawareness.org/.
Weaving Earth: http://www.weavingearth.com. Weaving Earth staff were also intimately involved with the Art of Mentoring week described in this chapter.
Rites of Passage: http://www.ritesofpassagevisionquest.org.
Feet on the Earth: http://feetontheearth.org.
Rediscovery: http://rediscovery.org/.
222 *David Sobel:* Sobel 2011, p. 163.
227 *National Outdoor Leadership School (NOLS):* http://www.nols.edu.

9. Dangerous Liaisons

232 *"Nerds for Nature":* http://nerdsfornature.org.
234 *bioblitz in the Golden Gate National Recreation Area:* San Francisco Unified School District, Science Department 2014. See also http://voices .nationalgeographic.com/blog/bioblitz/.
iNaturalist: http://www.inaturalist.org.
By the time most children enter kindergarten: McDonough 2009; National Wildlife Federation 2010.
235 *One study of computer users:* Smithstein 2010.
the findings generated by recent studies: Richtel 2010; Jackson and McKibben 2008; Steiner-Adair and Barker 2013.
simultaneous use of multiple technologies: Ophir, Nass, and Wagner 2009; NPR 2013.
One study of Microsoft employees: Lohr 2007.
236 *For example, one study:* Hinkley 2014.
Another study: Tiebrio et al. 2014.
Mark Bauerlein: Bauerlein 2009.
Distracted: Jackson and McKibben 2008.
The Big Disconnect: Steiner-Adair and Barker 2013.
Elias Aboujaoude: Aboujaoude 2011.
"freezing them in teen brain mode": George 2008.
237 *Sherry Turkle:* Turkle 2011; TED 2012.
Tibetan monks: Kaufman 2005; Davidson and Lutz 2008.
American Academy of Pediatrics: American Academy of Pediatrics 2013.
238 *Richard Louv:* Louv 2013a.
239 *Alison Gopnik:* TED 2011.
240 *In contrast, being outdoors:* Kaplan and De Young 2002.
241 *Richard Louv highlights:* Louv 2013b.
243 *Digital photography:* Fitzsimmons 2012.
244 *Miranda Andersen:* Andersen and Andersen 2013; see also YouTube video of *The Child in Nature*: https://www.youtube.com/watch?v=wsIYWEodnzo, accessed May 28, 2013.
245 *Google Earth:* www.earth.google.com.
Yonder: http://www.yonder.it.

"Dinosaur Train": http://pbskids.org/dinosaurtrain/.
247 *Nature Rocks:* www.naturerocks.org.
248 *Name That Shark, Bird Brains, and Be Bear-Aware:* National Wildlife Federation, Animal and nature games for kids. http://www.nwf.org/kids /games.aspx, accessed November 9, 2014.
I stood on a blustery hilltop: This distance learning event was conducted through the "Scientists in Action" program of the Denver Museum of Nature & Science. This marvelous program connects students around the USA with scientists doing real work in real time, often in remote places.
249 biomimicry: http://biomimicry.net.
251 *Janine Benyus:* Benyus 1997.

10. The Rewilding Revolution

257 *David Orr:* Orr 2007.
apocalyptic films: Wikipedia 2012.
fear of nuclear war has decreased: Ehrenfield 2002.
259 *William McDonough:* McDonough and Braungart 2013.
thrivability: http://thrivable.net.
260 *Peter Kahn:* Kahn Jr. and Friedman 1995.
261 *Richard Louv:* Louv 2011.
Bringing Nature Home: Tallamy 2007.
264 *more than 80 percent of North Americans:* United Nations Environment Programme, Regional Office for North America 2014.
Le Corbusier: Quoted in McDonough and Braungart 2002.
many more, often contentious human encounters: Sterba 2012.
265 *Living Building Challenge:* http://living-future.org/lbc.
biophilic cities: Beatley 2010.
"absolutely essential to living": Biophilic Cities Network homepage, http: //biophiliccities.org. See also a similar, parallel effort called the Wild Cities Project: http://wild10.org/en/program/the-global-foru/working-coalitions /wild-cities.
266 *Chicago Wilderness:* http://www.chicagowilderness.org.
Bay Area Open Space Council: http://openspacecouncil.org.
the Intertwine Alliance: http://theintertwine.org.
Amigos de los Rios: http://www.amigosdelosrios.org.
Homegrown National Park: This term, originally coined by Doug Tallamy, was adopted by the Toronto project: https://www.facebook.com/Home grownNationalPark, accessed August 4, 2014.
267 *What does this place want to be:* I thank my friend Antonio Pares for sharing this powerful question with me, and for filling me in on how such questions are currently influencing the architectural world.
Yellowstone to Yukon Initiative: http://y2y.net; see also Hannibal 2012.
the focus is less on big carnivores: An exception is my hometown of Van-

couver, British Columia, where grizzly bears have been moving ever closer to urban areas in recent years.

268 *a good place to start is with the arrival of humans:* Flannery 2001. There is an intense, ongoing academic debate about the timing of human arrival in the New World, with some estimates pushing this event back to at least 20,000 years ago. Lacking solid evidence of the latter, I am sticking here with the generally accepted view.

J. B. MacKinnon: MacKinnon 2013. The phrase "We always eat the big ones first" is borrowed here from MacKinnon's fine book.

270 *many rewilding proponents:* Foreman 2004.

273 *"collective impact":* Kania and Kramer 2011, 2013.

275 *more than 132,000 schools:* Danks 2014.

276 *the Sun Ray Library:* Lantry 2014.

282 *Project Milkweed:* http://www.xerces.org/milkweed/

284 *National Get Outdoors Day:* http://www.nationalgetoutdoorsday.org.

Epilogue

293 *In the words of poet Rainer Maria Rilke:* Barrows and Macy 2005, p. 45.

Bibliography

Aas, J. A., B. J. Paster, L. N. Stokes, I. Olsen, and F. E. Dewhirst. 2005. "Defining the Normal Bacterial Flora of the Oral Cavity." *Journal of Clinical Microbiology* 43(11):5721–5732.

Aboujaoude, E. 2011. *Virtually You: The Dangerous Powers of the E-Personality.* New York: W. W. Norton.

Abram, D. 1996. *The Spell of the Sensuous.* New York: Vintage Books.

———. 2011. "Storytelling and Wonder: On the Rejuvenation of Oral Culture." http://www.wildethics.org/essays/storytelling_and_wonder.html, accessed July 4, 2014.

Allmon, W. D. 2010. "The 'God Spectrum' and the Uneven Search for a Consistent View of the Natural World." In J. S. Schneiderman and W. A. Allmon (eds.), *For the Rock Record: Geologists on Intelligent Design.* Berkeley, CA: University of California Press, pp. 180–219.

American Academy of Pediatrics. 2012. "Kids and Vitamin D Deficiency." http://www.aap.org/en-us/about-the-aap/aap-press-room/Pages/Kids-and-Vitamin-D-Deficiency.aspx, accessed July 15, 2014. This press release summarizes recent research on the startling increase in severe vitamin D deficiency.

———. 2013. "Managing Media: We Need a Plan." http://www.aap.org/en-us/about-the-aap/aap-press-room/Pages/Managing-Media-We-Need-a-Plan.aspx, accessed June 29, 2014.

Andersen, M., and P. Andersen. 2013. *The Child in Nature*, a film by Miranda Andersen, 13, about Nature-Deficit Disorder. Interviewed on the New Nature Movement blog, Children & Nature Network, February 4, 2013. http://blog.childrenandnature.org/2013/02/04/the-child-in-nature-a-new-film-by-miranda-andersen-13/, accessed June 9, 2014.

Angier, N. 2011. The hormone surge of middle childhood. *New York Times.* December 26, 2011. http://www.nytimes.com/2011/12/27/science/now-we-are-six

-the-hormone-surge-of-middle-childhood.html?pagewanted=all, accessed April 18, 2014.

Auden, W. H. 1947. Introduction. In J. Betjeman, *Slick But Not Streamlined*. New York: Doubleday.

Barker, S. B., and A. R. Wolen. 2008. "The Benefits of Human-Companion Animal Interaction: A Review." *Journal of Veterinary Medical Education* 35(4): 487–495.

Barrows, A., and J. Macy (translators). 2005. *Rilke's Book of Hours: Love Poems to God*. New York: Riverhead.

Barth, G. 1990. *Fleeting Moments: Nature and Culture in American History*. Oxford, UK: Oxford University Press.

Bauerlein, M. 2009. *The Dumbest Generation: How the Digital Age Stupefies Young Americans and Jeopardizes Our Future*. New York: Tarcher.

Baylor, B. 1997. *The Other Way to Listen*. New York: Aladdin.

Beatley, T. 2010. *Biophilic Cities: Integrating Nature into Urban Design and Planning*. Washington, DC: Island Press.

Beck, A. M., and A. H. Katcher. 2003. "Future Directions in Human-Animal Bond Research." *American Behavioral Scientist* 43:79–93.

Benyus, J. 1997. *Biomimicry: Innovation Inspired by Nature*. New York: William Morrow & Company.

Berman, M .G., J. Jonides, and S. Kaplan. 2008. "The Cognitive Benefits of Interacting with Nature." *Psychological Science* 19(12):1207–1212.

Berry, T. 1990. *The Dream of the Earth*. San Francisco, CA: Sierra Club Books.

Bixler, R. D., M. E. Floyd, and W. E. Hammutt. 2002. "Environmental Socialization: Qualitative Tests of the Childhood Play Hypothesis." *Environment and Behavior* 34(6):795– 818.

Bridle, S. 2003. "Comprehensive Compassion: An Interview with Brian Swimme." *What Is Enlightenment?* Issue 19 (February 7). http://www.thegreatstory.org /SwimmeWIE.pdf, accessed April 15, 2014.

Broad, K. D., J. P. Curley, and E. B. Keverne. 2006. "Mother-Infant Bonding and the Evolution of Mammalian Social Relationships." *Philosophical Transactions of the Royal Society B*, 361:2199–2214.

Broda, H. W. 2011. *Moving the Classroom Outdoors: Schoolyard-Enhanced Learning in Action*. Portland, ME: Stenhouse.

Brody, J. E. 2009. "Babies Know: A Little Dirt Is Good for You." *New York Times*, January 26, 2009. http://www.nytimes.com/2009/01/27/health/27brod.html?_r =o, accessed July 16, 2014.

———. 2010. "Head Out for a Daily Dose of Green Space." *New York Times*, November 29, 2010. http://www.nytimes.com/2010/11/30/health/30brody.html, accessed April 2, 2014; NPR 2014.

Brown, L. R. 2009. *Plan B 4.0: Mobilizing to Save Civilization*. New York: W. W. Norton.

Buchsbaum, D., A. Gopnik, T. L. Griffiths, and P. Shafto. 2011. "Children's Imitation of Causal Action Sequences Is Influenced by Statistical and Pedagogical Evidence." *Cognition* 120:331–340.

Burnette, M. 2010. "What Mom Really Wants for Mother's Day." National Wildlife Federation, May 5, 2010. http://www.nwf.org/news-and-magazines/media-center/news-by-topic/get-outside/2010/04-30-10-ideas-for-mothers-day.aspx, accessed May 26, 2014.

Cain, V. 2012. "Professor Carter's Collection." *Common-Place* 12(2):1–20. http://www.common-place.org/vol-12/no-02/cain/, accessed August 1, 2014.

Capra, F. 1996. *The Web of Life: A New Scientific Understanding of Living Systems*. New York: Anchor Books.

Carmona, R. 2004. "The Growing Epidemic of Childhood Obesity." Statement to the Subcommittee on Competition, Infrastructure, and Foreign Commerce, March 2, 2004 (revised January 8, 2007). http://www.surgeongeneral.gov/news/testimony/childobesity03022004.html, accessed June 25, 2014.

Carson, R. 1955. *The Edge of the Sea*. Boston: Houghton Mifflin.

———. 1998. *The Sense of Wonder*. New York: Harper Collins. (Originally published in a 1956 issue of *Woman's Home Companion* under the title, "Help Your Child to Wonder.")

———. 2002. *Silent Spring*. Boston: Mariner Books. (Originally published in 1962 by Houghton Mifflin.)

Casey, B. J., and K. Caudle. 2013. "The Teenage Brain: Self Control." *Current Directions in Psychological Science* 22(2):82–87. doi: 10.1177/0963721413480170.

Centers for Disease Control and Prevention. "Faststats: Obesity and Overweight." http://www.cdc.gov/nchs/fastats/obesity-overweight.htm, accessed July 27, 2014.

———. "Attention-Deficit / Hyperactivity Disorder (ADHD)." http://www.cdc.gov/ncbddd/adhd/data.html, accessed August 10, 2014.

Chaisson, E. 2006. *Epic of Evolution: Seven Ages of the Cosmos*. Columbia University Press, New York.

Charles, C. 2012. "Addressing Children's Nature-Deficit Disorder: Bold Actions by Conservation Leaders Worldwide." IUCN, November 4, 2012. http://www.iucn.org/news_homepage/news_by_date/?11412/Addressing-Childrens-Nature-Deficit-Disorder-Bold-Actions-by-Conservation-Leaders-Worldwide, accessed January 4, 2014.

Charles, C., and A. Senauer. 2010. "Health Benefits to Children from Contact with the Outdoors and Nature." Children & Nature Network. http://www.childrenandnature.org/downloads/C&NNHealthBenefits2012.pdf.

Chawla, L. 1986. "Ecstatic Places." *Children's Environments Quarterly* 3(4):18–23.

———. 1992. "Childhood Place Attachments." In I. Altmann and S. Low (eds.), *Place Attachment*. New York: Plenum, pp. 63–86.

———. 1999. "Life Paths into Effective Environmental Action." *Journal of Environmental Education* 31(1):15–26.

Chawla, L., and V. Derr. 2012. "The Development of Conservation Behaviors in Childhood and Youth. In Susan D. Clayton (ed.), *The Oxford Handbook of Environmental and Conservation Psychology*. Oxford, UK: Oxford University Press, pp. 527–555.

Chawla, L., K. Keena, I. Pevec, and E. Stanley. 2014. "Green Schoolyards As Ha-

vens from Stress and Resources for Resilience in Childhood and Adolescence."
Health and Place 28:1–13.

Children & Nature Network. 2012. "Health Benefits to Children from Contact
with the Outdoors and Nature." http://www.childrenandnature.org/downloads
/CNNHealthBenefits2012.pdf.

Christian, D. 2004. *Maps of Time: An Introduction to Big History*. Berkeley, CA:
University of California Press.

Clark, K. 1969. *Civilisation: A Personal View*. London: John Murray.

Clayton, S. 2003. "Environmental Identity: A Conceptual and an Operational Definition." In S. Clayton and S. Opotow (eds.), *The Psychological Significance of
Nature*. Cambridge, MA: MIT Press, pp. 45–66.

CNN Travel. 2013. "Are Museums Still Relevant?" CNN Travel, August 22, 2013.
http://travel.cnn.com/are-museums-still-relevant-today-543771, accessed October 3, 2014.

Cobb, E. 1977. *The Ecology of Imagination in Childhood*. New York: Columbia
University Press.

Comstock, A. B. 1911. *Handbook of Nature Study*. New York: Comstock Publishing.

Conniff, R. 2013. "Microbes: The Trillions of Creatures Governing Your Health."
Smithsonian.com, May 2013. http://www.smithsonianmag.com/science-nature
/microbes-the-trillions-of-creatures-governing-your-health-37413457/, accessed
July 27, 2014.

Cornell, J. 1998. *Sharing Nature With Children*, Second Edition. Nevada City, CA:
Dawn Publications.

Coyle, K. J. 2010. *Back to School, Back Outside: How Outdoor Education and
Outdoor School Time Create High Performance Students*. National Wildlife
Federation Report, September 2010. http://www.nwf.org/pdf/Be%20Out%20
There/Back%20to%20School%20full%20report.pdf, accessed July 8, 2014.

Danks, S. G. 2012. *Asphalt to Ecosystems: Design Ideas for Schoolyard Transformation*. Oakland, CA: New Village Press.

———. 2014. "Trends That Give Us Hope: The Power and Potential of Green Schoolyards." The New Nature Movement blog, Children & Nature Network, February 7, 2014. http://blog.childrenandnature.org/2014/02/07/trends-that-give
-us-hope-the-power-and-potential-of-green-schoolyards/, accessed August 3,
2014.

David Suzuki Foundation. 2014. "Connecting with Nature" education guide. http://
www.davidsuzuki.org/what-you-can-do/connecting-with-nature-education
-guide/, accessed October 3, 2014.

Davidson, R. J., and A. Lutz. 2008. "Buddha's Brain: Neuroplasticity and Meditation." *IEEE Signal Processing Magazine* 25(1):174–176.

Davis, W. 2009. *The Wayfinders: Why Ancient Wisdom Matters in the Modern
World*. Toronto: House of Anansi.

Derbyshire, D. 2007. "How Children Lost the Right to Roam in Four Generations."
Daily Mail, June 15, 2007. http://www.dailymail.co.uk/news/article-462091/
How-children-lost-right-roam-generations.html, accessed September 4, 2014.

Dewey, J. 1938. *Experience and Education*. New York: Kappa Delta Pi.

Discover Wildlife. 2012. "David Attenborough on Life in Cold Blood: Exclusive Interview." *BBC Wildlife* magazine website, September 13, 2012. http://www.discoverwildlife.com/animals/david-attenborough-life-cold-blood-exclusive-interview, accessed February 18, 2014.

Duffy, M., and D. Duffy. 2002. *Children of the Universe. Cosmic Education in the Montessori Elementary Classroom*. Holidaysburg, PA: Parent Child Press.

Dunn, Rob. 2012. "Letting Biodiversity Get Under Our Skin." *Conservation*, http://conservationmagazine.org/2012/09/biodiversity-under-our-skin-2/, accessed August 14, 2014.

Eccles, J. S. 1999. "The Development of Children Ages 6–14." *The Future of Children* 9(2):30–44.

Ehrenfield, D. 2002. *Swimming Lessons: Keeping Afloat in the Age of Technology*. Oxford, UK: Oxford University Press.

Evans, E. M. 2000. "The Emergence of Beliefs about the Origins of Species in School-age Children." *Merrill-Palmer Quarterly: A Journal of Developmental Psychology* 46:221–254.

Evernden, N. 1993. *The Natural Alien: Humankind and Environment*, Second Edition. Toronto: University of Toronto Press.

Fitzsimmons, D. 2012. "Wild-snapping: Digital Photography Helps Tech-savvy Kids Focus on Nature." The New Nature Movement blog, Children & Nature Network, November 18, 2012. http://blog.childrenandnature.org/2012/11/18/wild-snapping-digital-photography-helps-techno-savvy-kids-focus-on-nature/, accessed June 9, 2014.

Fjortoft, I. 2001. "The Natural Environment As a Playground for Children: The Impact of Outdoor Play Activities in Pre-Primary School Children." *Early Childhood Education Journal* 29(2):111–117.

Flannery, T. 2001. *The Eternal Frontier: An Ecological History of North America and Its Peoples*. New York: Grove Press.

Foreman, D. 2004. *Rewilding North America: A Vision for Conservation in the 21st Century*. Washington, DC: Island Press.

Fraser, J., J. E. Heimlich, and V. Yocco. 2010. "American Beliefs Associated with Encouraging Children's Nature Experience Opportunities." Prepared for the Children & Nature Network, Project Grow Outside. Edgewater, MD: Institute for Learning Innovation. http://www.childrenandnature.org/documents/C118/.

Frehsée, N. 2014. "Shinrin Yoku: The Japanese Practice That Could Transform Your Day." *Huffington Post*, July 23, 2014. http://www.huffingtonpost.com/2014/07/23/shinrin-yoku-health-benefits_n_5599635.html?ncid=fcbklnkushpmg00000023&ir=Good+News, accessed November 3, 2014.

Frumkin, H. 2012. "Building the Science Base: Ecopsychology Meets Clinical Epidemiology." In P. Kahn and P. Hasbach (eds.), *Ecopsychology: Science, Totems, and the Technological Species*. Cambridge, MA: MIT Press, pp. 141–172.

Fuselli, P., and N. L. Yanchar. 2012. "Preventing playground injuries." *Pediatrics and Child Health*, 17(6):328-330. http://www.cps.ca/documents/position/playground-injuries, accessed November 9, 2014.

George, L. 2008. "Dumbed Down." *Maclean's*, November 6, 2008. http://www
.macleans.ca/society/health/dumbed-down/, accessed June 29, 2014.

Gilding, P. 2011. *The Great Disruption: Why the Climate Crisis Will Bring On
the End of Shopping and the Birth of a New World*. New York: Bloomsbury.

Ginsburg, K., the Committee on Communications, and the Committee on Psycho-
social Aspects of Child and Family Health. 2007. "The Importance of Play in
Promoting Healthy Child Development and Maintaining Strong Parent-Child
Bonds." American Academy of Pediatrics. http://www.aap.org/pressroom/play
FINAL.pdf, accessed June 18, 2014.

Gopnik, A. 2009. *The Philosophical Baby: What Children's Minds Tell Us About
Truth, Love, and the Meaning of Life*. New York: Picador.

——. 2012a. "Scientific Thinking in Young Children: Theoretical Advances, Empirical Research, and Policy Implications." *Science* 337:1623–1627.

——. 2012b. "What's Wrong with the Teenage Mind?" *Wall Street Journal*, January 28, 2012. http://online.wsj.com/news/articles/SB1000142405297020380 6
504577181351486558984, accessed June 18, 2014.

Gottschall, J. 2012. *The Storytelling Animal: How Stories Make Us Human*. Boston: Houghton Mifflin Harcourt.

Gould, S. J. 1993. "Unenchanted Evening." *Eight Little Piggies: Reflections in Natural History*. New York: W. W. Norton.

Haller, R. L., and C. L. Kramer. 2006. *Horticultural Therapy Methods: Making
Connections in Health Care, Human Service, and Community Programs*. Philadelphia: Haworth Press.

Handwerk, B. 2008. "Half of Humanity Will Live in Cities By Year's End." *National Geographic*, March 13, 2008. http://news.nationalgeographic.com
/news/2008/03/080313-cities.html, accessed July 27, 2014.

Hannibal, M. E. 2012. *The Spine of the Continent: The Race to Save America's
Last, Best Wilderness*. Guilford, CT: Lion's Press.

Hanski, I., et al. 2012. "Environmental Biodiversity, Human Microbiota, and
Allergy Are Interrelated." *Proceedings of the National Academy of Sciences*
109(21):8334–8339. doi/10.1073/pnas.1205624109.

Haught, J. F. 2008. *God After Darwin: A Theology of Evolution*. Boulder, CO:
Westview Press.

Hinkley, T. 2014. "Electronic Media Use Increased Risk of Poor Well-being
Among Young Children." *JAMA Pediatrics*, published online March 17, 2014.
doi:10.1001/jamapediatrics.2014.94.

Hirsh-Pasek, K., and R. M. Golinkoff. 2003. *Einstein Never Used Flashcards: How
Our Children Really Learn—And Why They Need to Play More and Memorize
Less*. Emmaus, PA: Rodale.

Hofferth, S., and J. Sandberg. 1999. "Changes in American Children's Time,
1981–1997." Population Studies Center, University of Michigan Institute for
Social Research, September 11, 2000. http://www.psc.isr.umich.edu/pubs/pdf
/rr00-456.pdf.

Hughes, B. 2012. *Evolutionary Playwork*. London: Routledge.

Hurtado, A. M., and K. Hill. 1992. "Paternal Effects on Child Survivorship Among

Ache and Hiwi Hunter-Gatherers: Implications for Modeling Pair-Bond Stability." In B. Hewlett (ed.), *Father-Child Relations: Cultural and Biosocial Contexts*. New York: Hawthorne, pp. 31–56.

Hutchinson, G. E. 1962. *The Enchanted Voyage: And Other Studies*. New Haven, CT: Yale University Press.

Jackson, M., and B. McKibben. 2008. *Distracted: The Erosion of Attention and Coming Dark Age*. Amherst, NY: Prometheus.

Jensen, E. 2000. "Moving with the Brain in Mind." *The Science of Learning* 58(3):34–37.

Johnson, K. 2013. "National Parks Try to Appeal to Minorities." *New York Times*, September 5, 2013. http://www.nytimes.com/2013/09/06/us/national-parks-try -to-appeal-to-minorities.html?hp&_r=0, accessed August 3, 2014.

Johnson, R. A. 2010. "Psychosocial and Therapeutic Aspects of Human-Animal Interaction." In P. M. Rabinwitz and L. A. Conti (eds.), *Human-Animal Medicine: Clinical Approaches to Zoonoses, Toxicants and Other Shared Health Risks*. Maryland Heights, MO: Saunders Elsevier, pp. 24–36.

Juster, F. T., et al. 2004. "Changing Times of American Youth: 1981–2003." Institute for Social Research, University of Michigan, Child Development Supplement, November 2014. http://ns.umich.edu/Releases/2004/Nov04/teen_time_report .pdf.

Kahn, P. H., Jr. 1999. *The Human Relationship with Nature: Development and Culture*. Cambridge, MA: MIT Press.

———. 2011. *Technological Nature: Adaptation and the Future of Human Life*. Cambridge, MA: MIT Press.

Kahn, P. H., Jr., and B. Friedman. 1995. "Environmental Views and Values of Children in an Inner-city Black Community." *Child Development* 66:1403–1417.

Kahn, P. H., Jr., and S. R. Kellert, eds. 2002. *Children and Nature: Psychological, Sociocultural, and Evolutionary Investigations*. Cambridge, MA: MIT Press.

Kania, J., and M. Kramer. 2011. "Collective Impact." *Stanford Social Innovation Review*, Winter 2011. http://www.ssireview.org/pdf/2011_WI_Feature_Kania .pdf, accessed August 5, 2014.

———. 2013. "Embracing Emergence: How Collective Impact Addresses Complexity." *Stanford Social Innovation Review*, January 21, 2013. http://www .ssireview.org/blog/entry/embracing_emergence_how_collective_impact _addresses_complexity, accessed August 5, 2014.

Kaplan, H. S., P. L. Hooper, and M. Gurven. 2009. "The Evolutionary and Ecological Roots of Human Social Organization." *Philosophical Transactions of the Royal Society* 364:3289–3299.

Kaplan, R., and R. De Young. 2002. "Toward a Better Understanding of Prosocial Behavior: The Role of Evolution and Directed Attention." *Behavioral and Brain Sciences* 13(2):263–264.

Kaplan, R., and S. Kaplan. 2002. "Adolescents and the Natural Environment: A Time Out?" In P. H. Kahn Jr. and S. R. Kellert (eds.), *Children and Nature: Psychological, Sociocultural, and Evolutionary Investigations*. Cambridge, MA: MIT Press, pp. 229–257.

Kaufman, M. 2005. "Meditation Gives Brain a Change, Study Finds." *Washington Post*, January 3, 2005. http://www.washingtonpost.com/wp-dyn/articles /A43006-2005Jan2.html, accessed June 4, 2014.

Keeler, R. 2008. *Natural Playscapes*. Redmond, WA: Exchange Press.

Kellert, S. R. 2002. "Experiencing Nature: Affective, Cognitive, and Evaluative Development in Children." In P. H. Kahn Jr. and S. R. Kellert (eds.), *Children and Nature: Psychological, Sociocultural, and Evolutionary Investigations*. Cambridge, MA: MIT Press, pp. 117–152.

Kellert, S. R., and V. Derr. 1998. *National Study of Outdoor Wilderness Experience*. New Haven, CT: Yale University. http://www.childrenandnature.org /downloads/kellert.complete.text.pdf, accessed May 5, 2014.

Kellert, S. R., and E. O. Wilson, eds. 1993. *The Biophilia Hypothesis*. Washington, DC: Island Press.

Khalil, K. 2014. "Exploring the Nature of Zoos and Aquariums." The New Nature Movement blog, Children & Nature Network, July 22, 2014. http://blog .childrenandnature.org/2014/07/22/exploring-the-nature-of-zoos-now-theyre -offering-new-opportunities-for-children/, accessed October 3, 2014.

King's College London. 2011. "Understanding the Diverse Benefits of Learning in Natural Environments." http://www.lotc.org.uk/wp-content/uploads/2011/09 /KCL-LINE-benefits-final-version.pdf, accessed September 15, 2014.

Koch, W. 2006. "Nature Programs' Goal: No Child Left Inside." *USA Today*, November 22. http://usatoday30.usatoday.com/news/nation/2006-11-21-no -child-left-inside_x.htm, accessed May 12, 2014.

Konner, M. 2010. *The Evolution of Childhood*. Cambridge, MA: Belknap.

Kuo, F. E. 2001. "Coping with Poverty: Impacts of Environment and Attention in the Inner City." *Environment and Behavior* 33(1):5–34.

Kuo, F. E., and W. C. Sullivan. 2001a. "Aggression and Violence in the Inner City: Effects of Environment via Mental Fatigue." *Environment and Behavior* 33(4):543–571.

———. 2001b. "Environment and Crime in the Inner City: Does Vegetation Reduce Crime?" *Environment and Behavior* 33(3):343–367.

Lantry, K. 2014. Getting out in nature at the Sun Ray Library. Spotlight on St. Paul. http://www.spotlightsaintpaul.com/2014/07/getting-out-in-nature-at-sun-ray-library.html, accessed November 9, 2014.

Largo-Wight, E. 2011. "Cultivating Healthy Places and Communities: Evidenced-based Nature Contact Recommendations." *International Journal of Environmental Health Research* 21(1):41–61.

Larned, W. T. 1997. *North American Indian Tales*. Mineola, NY: Dover.

Lear, L. 2009 (reprint). *Rachel Carson: Witness for Nature*. Boston: Mariner.

Leslie, C. W. 2010. *The Nature Connection: An Outdoor Workbook for Kids, Families and Classrooms*. North Adams, MA: Storey Publishing.

Leslie, C. W., and C. Roth. 2000. *Keeping a Nature Journal: Discover a Whole New Way of Seeing the World Around You*. North Adams, MA: Storey Publishing.

Lester, S., and M. Maudsley. 2006. *Play, Naturally: A Review of Children's Natural Play*. Children's Play Council, volume 3. http://www.playengland.org.uk/media /130593/play-naturally.pdf.

Lipman, S. L. 2012. *Fed Up with Frenzy: Slow Parenting in a Fast-Moving World.* Naperville, IL: Sourcebooks.

Liu, J. H. 2011. "The 5 Best Toys of All Time." *Wired,* January 31. http://archive.wired .com/geekdad/2011/01/the-5-best-toys-of-all-time/, accessed July 21, 2014.

Lohr, S. 2007. Slow down, brave multitasker, and don't read this in traffic. *New York Times,* March 25, 2007. http://www.nytimes.com/2007/03/25 /business/25multi.html?_r=2&pagewanted=all&, accessed November 7, 2014.

Lopez, B. 2012. "Children in the Woods." In J. Dunlap and S. R. Kellert (eds.), *Companions in Wonder: Children and Adults Exploring Nature Together.* Cambridge, MA: MIT Press, pp. 137–139.

Louv, R. 2006. *Last Child in the Woods: Saving Our Children from Nature-Deficit Disorder.* Chapel Hill, NC: Algonquin Books.

——. 2011. *The Nature Principle: Human Restoration and the End of Nature-Deficit Disorder.* Chapel Hill, NC: Algonquin Books.

——. 2013a. "High Tech High Nature: How Families Can Use Electronics to Explore the Outdoors." The New Nature Movement blog, Children & Nature Network, October 11, 2013. http://blog.childrenandnature.org/2013/10/11 /high-tech-high-nature-how-families-can-use-electronics-to-explore-the-out doors/, accessed May 12, 2014.

——. 2013b. "The Hybrid Mind: The More High-Tech Schools Become, the More Nature They Need." The New Nature Movement blog, Children & Nature Network, November 18, 2013. http://blog.childrenandnature.org/2013/11/18 /the-hybrid-mind-the-more-high-tech-schools-become-the-more-nature-they -need/, accessed June 6, 2014.

——. 2014a. "Hummingbird Parents: Seven Actions Parents Can Take to Re-duce Risk and Still Get Their Kids Outside." The New Nature Movement blog, Children & Nature Network, March 10, 2014. http://blog.childrenandnature .org/2014/03/10/seven-actions-parents-can-take-to-increase-outdoor-safety/, accessed May 26, 2014.

——. 2014b. "The Natural Teacher, Back to School: 10 Ways You Can Add Vi-tamin 'N' to the Classroom and Beyond." The New Nature Movement blog, Children & Nature Network, August 25, 2014. http://blog.childrenandnature .org/2014/08/25/the-natural-teacher-10-ways-you-can-add-vitamin-n-to-your -classroom-beyond/, accessed August 27, 2014.

Lynch, S. V., et al. 2014. "Effects of Early-Life Exposure to Allergens and Bacteria on Recurrent Wheeze and Atopy in Urban Children." *Journal of Allergy and Clinical Immunology,* http://dx.doi.org/10.1016/j.jaci.2014.04.018, accessed August 15, 2014.

MacKinnon, J. B. 2013. *The Once and Future World: Nature As It Was, As It Is, As It Could Be.* Toronto: Random House Canada.

Macy, J. 2007. *World As Lover, World As Self: Courage for Global Justice and Ecological Renewal.* Berkeley, CA: Parallax Press.

Malone, K., and P. Tranter. 2003. "Children's Environmental Learning and the Use, Design and Management of Schoolgrounds." *Children, Youth and Envi-ronments* 13(2). http://www.colorado.edu/journals/cye/13_2/Malone_Tranter /ChildrensEnvLearning.htm.

Marshall, P. 1992. *Nature's Web: An Exploration of Ecological Thinking*. New York: Simon & Schuster.

Martinez, D. 2004. "Indigenous Science: The Cultivated Landscape of North America." In K. Ausubel (ed.), *Nature's Operating Instructions: The True Biotechnologies*. San Francisco, CA: Sierra Club Books, pp. 80–91.

McDonough, P. 2009. "TV Viewing Among Kids at an Eight-Year High." The Nielsen Company, October 26. http://www.nielsen.com/us/en/insights/news/2009/tv-viewing-among-kids-at-an-eight-year-high.html, accessed July 12, 2014.

McDonough, W., and M. Braungart. 2002. "Buildings Like Trees, Cities Like Forests." McDonough Innovation: Design for the Circular Economy. http://www.mcdonough.com/speaking-writing/buildings-like-trees-cities-like-forests/#.U-pNRFb1Hcs, accessed July 30, 2014.

———. 2013. *The Upcycle: Beyond Sustainability—Designing for Abundance*. New York: North Point Press.

McGonigal, J. 2011. *Reality Is Broken: Why Games Make Us Better and How They Can Change the World*. London: Penguin Books.

Mercogliano, C. 2007. *In Defense of Childhood: Protecting Kids' Inner Wildness*. Boston: Beacon Press.

Micheva, K. D., B. Busse, N. C. Weiler, N. O'Rourke, and S. J. Smith. 2010. "Single-Synapse Analysis of a Diverse Synapse Population: Proteomic Imaging Methods and Markers." *Neuron* 68 (4):639–653.

Mock, D. W., and M. Fujioka. 1990. "Monogamy and Long-term Pair Bonding in Vertebrates." *Trends in Ecology and Evolution* 5(2):39–43.

Moore, E. O. 1981. "A Prison Environment's Effect on Health Care Service Demands." *Journal of Environmental Systems* 11:17–34.

Moore, R. C. 1986. "Childhood's Domain: Play and Spaces in Childhood Development." London: Croom Helm.

Moore, R. C., and H. H. Wong. 1997. *Natural Learning: Creating Environments for Rediscovering Nature's Way of Teaching*. Berkeley, CA: MIG Communications.

Morgan, J., and D. L. Anderson. 2002. *Born With a Bang: The Universe Tells Our Cosmic Story*. Book 1 of the Universe Series. Nevada City, CA: Dawn Publications.

———. 2003. *From Lava to Life: The Universe Tells Our Earth Story*. Book 2 of the Universe Series. Nevada City, CA: Dawn Publications.

———. 2006. *Mammals Who Morph: The Universe Tells Our Evolution Story*. Book 3 of the Universe Series. Nevada City, CA: Dawn Publications.

Moss, S. 2013. "Natural Childhood." Report for the National Trust, Britain. http://www.nationaltrust.org.uk/document-1355766991839/, accessed August 2, 2014.

Munoz, S. A. 2009. "Children in the Outdoors: A Literature Review." Council for Learning Outside the Classroom. http://www.lotc.org.uk/2011/03/children-in-the-outdoors-a-literature-review/.

Murphy, T. 2011. "Stem Education—It's Elementary." *US News & World Report*, August 29. http://www.usnews.com/news/articles/2011/08/29/stem-education--its-elementary, accessed June 19, 2014.

Myers, O. E., Jr. 2007. *The Significance of Children and Animals: Social Development and Our Connections to Other Species,* Second Edition. West Layfayette, IN: Purdue University Press.

Nabhan, G. P., and S. A. Trimble. 1995. *The Geography of Childhood: Why Children Need Wild Places.* Boston: Beacon Press.

National Wildlife Federation. 2010. "Whole Child: Developing Mind, Body and Spirit through Outdoor Play." http://www.nwf.org/~/media/PDFs/Be%20Out%20There/BeOutThere_WholeChild_V2.ashx, accessed June 30, 2014.

Nelson, M. K. (ed.). 2008. *Original Instructions: Indigenous Teachings for a Sustainable Future.* Rochester, NY: Bear & Company.

NPR. 2013. "The Myth of Multitasking." Interview with Psychologist Clifford Nass, May 10. http://www.npr.org/2013/05/10/182861382/the-myth-of-multitasking, accessed June 30, 2014.

———. 2014. "To Make Children Healthier, a Doctor Prescribes a Trip to the Park." Interview with physician Dr. Robert Zarr, July 14. http://www.npr.org/blogs/health/2014/07/14/327338918/to-make-children-healthier-a-doctor-prescribes-a-trip-to-the-park?utm_source=npr_email_a_friend&utm_medium=email&utm_content=20140716&utm_campaign=storyshare&utm_term=, accessed July 16, 2014.

Oellers, W. 2008. "Opening Minds Through Learning Outdoors." *Connect* 21(5):12.

Ophir, E., C. Nass, and A. D. Wagner. 2009. "Cognitive Control in Media Multitaskers." *Proceedings of the National Academy of Sciences* 106(37):15583–15587. http://www.ncbi.nlm.nih.gov/pmc/articles/PMC2747164/, accessed May 3, 2014.

Orr, D. W. 1992. *Ecological Literacy: Education and the Transition to a Postmodern World.* Albany, NY: SUNY Press.

———. 1994. *Earth in Mind: On Education, Environment, and the Human Prospect.* Washington, DC: Island Press.

———. 2007. "Optimism and Hope in a Hotter Time." *Conservation Biology* 21(6):1392–1395.

Outdoor Foundation. 2013. *Outdoor Participation Report.* http://www.outdoorfoundation.org/pdf/ResearchParticipation2013.pdf, accessed October 5, 2014.

Park, S.-H., and R. H. Mattson. 2008. "Effects of Flowering and Foliage Plants in Hospital Rooms on Patients Recovering from Abdominal Surgery." *Horticultural Technology* 18:563–568.

Peat, F. D. 2002. *Blackfoot Physics: A Journey into the Native American Universe.* Boston: Weiser.

Place-based Education Evaluation Collaborative. 2010. *The Benefits of Place-based Education: A Report from the Place-based Education Evaluation Collaborative* (Second Edition). http://www.peecworks.org/PEEC/Benefits_of_PBE-PEEC_2008_web.pdf, accessed February 2, 2014.

Pyle, R. M. 1998. *The Thunder Tree: Lessons from an Urban Wildland.* Guilford, CT: Lyons Press.

———. 2001. "The Rise and Fall of Natural History." *Orion* 20(4):16–23.

Quammen, D. 2003. *Monster of God: The Man-Eating Predator in the Jungles of History and the Mind.* New York: W. W. Norton.

Richtel, M. 2010. "Hooked on Gadgets, and Paying a Mental Price." *New York Times,* June 7. http://www.nytimes.com/2010/06/07/technology/07brain.html, accessed May 12, 2014.

Rideout, V., U. G. Foehr, and D. F. Roberts. 2010. "Generation M2: Media in the Lives of 8- to 18-Year-Olds." Kaiser Family Foundation study. http://kaiserfamilyfoundation.files.wordpress.com/2013/01/8010.pdf, accessed July 27, 2014.

Rifkin, J. 2009. *The Empathic Civilization: The Race to Global Consciousness in a World in Crisis.* New York: Tarcher.

Rogoff, B., M. Sellers, S. Pirrotta, N. Fox, and S. White. 1975. "Age of Assignment of Roles and Responsibilities in Children: A Cross-cultural Survey." *Human Development* 18:353–369.

Rosin, H. 2014. "The Overprotected Kid." *Atlantic,* April. http://www.theatlantic.com/features/archive/2014/03/hey-parents-leave-those-kids-alone/358631/, accessed June 12, 2014.

Ruebush, M. 2009. *Why Dirt Is Good: 5 Ways to Make Germs Your Friends.* New York: Kaplan.

Sam, M. 2008. "Ethics from the Land: Traditional Protocols and the Maintenance of Peace." In M. K. Nelson (ed.), *Original Instructions: Indigenous Teachings for a Sustainable Future.* Rochester, NY: Bear & Company, pp. 39–41.

Sampson, S. D. 2006. "Evoliteracy." In J. Brockman (ed.), *Intelligent Thought.* New York: Knopf, pp. 216–231.

———. 2012. "The Topophilia Hypothesis: Ecopsychology Meets Evolutionary Psychology." In P. H. Kahn and P. H. Hasbach (eds.), *Ecopsychology: Science Totems, and the Technological Species.* Boston: MIT Press.

Sanders, S. R. 1997. "Most Human Art." *Georgia Review/Utne Reader,* September/October.

San Francisco Unified School District, Science Department. 2014. "Spotlight on 2014 BioBlitz!" April 11 blog post. http://www.sfusdscience.org/blog/spotlight-on-2014-bioblitz, accessed June 29, 2014.

Sebba, R. 1991. "The Landscapes of Childhood: The Reflections of Childhood's Environment in Adult Memories and in Children's Attitudes." *Environment and Behavior* 23(4):395–422.

Seed, J., and J. Macy. 1998. *Thinking Like a Mountain: Towards a Council of All Beings.* Bagriola Island, BC: New Society.

Selhub, E. M., and A. C. Logan. 2012. *Your Brain on Nature: The Science of Nature's Influence on Your Health, Happiness, and Vitality.* Mississauga, ON: John Wiley & Sons.

Semali, L. M., and J. L. Kincheloe (eds.), 1999. *What Is Indigenous Knowledge: Voices from the Academy.* New York: Routledge.

Settee, P. 2008. "Indigenous Knowledge As the Basis for Our Future." In M. K. Nelson (ed.), *Original Instructions: Indigenous Teachings for a Sustainable Future.* Rochester, NY: Bear & Company, pp. 42–47.

Shattuck, R. 1980. *The Forbidden Experiment: The Story of the Wild Boy of Aveyron*. New York: Kodansha International.

Shepard, P. 1998. *Nature and Madness*. Athens, GA: University of Georgia Press.

Smith, T. M., et al. 2010. "Dental Evidence for Ontogenetic Differences Between Modern Humans and Neanderthals." *Proceedings of the National Academy of Science* 107(49):20923–20928.

Smithstein, S. 2010. "As We Get Wired, We Get Re-wired." *Psychology Today*, June 10. http://www.psychologytoday.com/blog/what-the-wild-things-are/201006/we-get-wired-we-get-re-wired, accessed May 11, 2014.

Sobel, D. 1996. *Beyond Ecophobia: Reclaiming the Heart in Nature Education*. Great Barrington, MA: Orion Society.

———. 2004. *Place-Based Education: Connecting Classrooms and Communities*. Great Barrington, MA: Orion Society.

———. 2008. *Childhood and Nature: Design Principles for Educators*. Portland, ME: Stenhouse.

———. 2011. *Wild Play: Parenting Adventures in the Great Outdoors*. San Francisco, CA: Sierra Club Books.

Sobel, D. M., J. B. Tenenbaum, and A. Gopnik. 2004. "Children's Causal Inferences from Indirect Evidence: Backwards Blocking and Bayesian Reasoning in Preschoolers." *Cognitive Science* 28(3):303–333.

Spangler, D. 1986. "The New Storytellers." *In Context*, Winter 1985/86:39–43.

Speth, J. G. 2008. *The Bridge at the Edge of the World: Capitalism, the Environment, and Crossing from Crisis to Sustainability*. New Haven, CT: Yale University Press.

Stage of Life. 2012. "Teens and Nature—Trends, Statistics, and Essays." Stage of Life trend report. http://www.stageoflife.com/TeensandNature.aspx, accessed July 18, 2014.

Standing, E. M. 1998. *Maria Montessori: Her Life and Work*. New York: Plume.

Steiner-Adair, C., and T. H. Barker. 2013. *The Big Disconnect: Protecting Childhood and Family Relationships in the Digital Age*. New York: Harper.

Sterba, J. 2012. *Nature Wars: The Incredible Story of How Wildlife Comebacks Turned Backyards into Battlegrounds*. New York: Crown.

Stone, M. K. 2009. *Smart by Nature: Schooling for Sustainability*. Berkeley, CA: Watershed Media, University of California Press.

Suzuki, D. 1997. *The Sacred Balance: Rediscovering Our Place in Nature*. Vancouver, BC: Greystone Books.

———. 2014. "Learning in Nature Is Good for Teachers and Students." David Suzuki Foundation, Science Matters blog. http://www.davidsuzuki.org/blogs/science-matters/2014/09/learning-in-nature-is-good-for-teachers-and-students/, accessed September 15, 2014.

Swimme, B. 1996. *The Hidden Heart of the Cosmos*. Maryknoll, NY: Orbis.

Swimme, B., and T. Berry. 1992. *The Universe Story: From the Primordial Flaring Forth to Ecozoic Era*. New York: Harper Collins.

Swimme, B., and M. E. Tucker. 2011. *Journey of the Universe*. New Haven, CT: Yale University Press.

Tallamy, D. W. 2007. *Bringing Nature Home: How You Can Sustain Wildlife with Native Plants*. Portland, OR: Timber Press.

Tattersall, I. 2009. "Human Origins: Out of Africa." *Proceedings of the National Academy of Sciences* 106(38):16018–16021.

Taylor, A. F., and F. E. Kuo. 2011. "Could Exposure to Everyday Green Spaces Help Treat ADHD? Evidence from Children's Play Settings." *Applied Psychology: Health and Well Being* 3(3):281–303.

Taylor, A. F., F. E. Kuo, and W. C. Sullivan. 2002. "Views of Nature and Self-Discipline: Evidence from Inner City Children." *Journal of Environmental Psychology* 22:49–63.

Taylor, A. F., A. Wiley, F. E. Kuo, and W. C. Sullivan. 1998. "Growing Up in the Inner City: Green Spaces As Places to Grow." *Environment and Behavior* 30(1):3–27.

TED. 2011. "What Do Babies Think?" Talk by Alison Gopnik. http://www.ted .com/talks/alison_gopnik_what_do_babies_thinkhttp://www.ted.com/talks /alison_gopnik_what_do_babies_think, accessed May 15, 2014.

———. 2012. Connected, but alone? Talk by Sherry Turkle. http://www.ted.com /talks/sherry_turkle_alone_together.html?utm_source=newsletter_weekly_2012 -0403&utm_campaign=newsletter_weekly&utm_medium=email, accessed June 29, 2014.

The Nature Conservancy. 2014a. "Nature Works Everywhere." Teacher resources. https://www.natureworkseverywhere.org/#resources, accessed October 3, 2014.

The Nature Conservancy. 2014b. "New Survey Shows Gravity of a Growing, Global Parental Concern: Kids Aren't Spending Enough Time in Nature." http://www.prweb.com/releases/2014/04/prweb11730801.htm, accessed June 4, 2014.

Tiebrio, S., et al. 2014. "Parental Monitoring of Children's Media Consumption: The Long-term Influences on Body Mass Index in Children." *JAMA Pediatrics*, May. http://archpedi.jamanetwork.com/article.aspx?articleid=1844042.

Tough, P. 2012. *How Children Succeed: Grit, Curiosity, and the Hidden Power of Character*. Boston: Houghton Mifflin Harcourt.

Tsunetsugu, Y., B.-J. Park, and Y. Miyzaki. 2010. "Trends in Research Related to 'Shinrin-yoku' (Taking in the Atmosphere or Forest Bathing) in Japan." *Environmental Health and Preventative Medicine* 15(1):27–37.

Tuan, Y.-F. 1990 [1974]. *Topophilia: A Study of Environmental Perceptions, Attitudes, and Values*. New York: Columbia University Press.

Turkle, S. 2011. *Alone Together. Why We Expect More from Technology and Less from Each Other*. New York: Basic Books.

Turner, J. 2000. *Teewinot: Climbing and Contemplating the Teton Range*. New York: St. Martin's.

Ulrich, R. S. 1984. "View Through a Window May Influence Recovery from Surgery." *Science* 224:420–421.

United Nations Environment Programme, Regional Office for North America. 2014. "North American Cities: Facts and Figures." http://www.rona.unep.org /cities/north_american_cities_keyfacts.html, accessed June 27, 2014.

Walsh, F. 2009. "Human-Animal Bonds I: The Relational Significance of Companion Animals." *Family Process* 48:462–480.

Ward, J. 2008. *I Love Dirt!: 52 Activities to Help You & Your Kids Discover the Wonders of Nature.* Boston: Trumpeter.

Wells, N. M., and K. S. Lekies. 2006. "Nature and the Life Course: Pathways from Childhood Nature Experiences to Adult Environmentalism." *Children, Youth and Environments* 16(1):1–25.

Whitaker, M. 2010. "Pulling the Covers Off Blanket Statements." Guest blog post for Bethe Almeras' Grass Stain Guru. http://grassstainguru.com/2010/07/21/pulling-the-covers-off-blanket-statements/, accessed June 18, 2014.

Whitehead, J. W. 2004. "Ritalin Nation: Are We Killing Our Children?" The Rutherford Institute, June 14. https://www.rutherford.org/publications_resources/john_whiteheads_commentary/ritalin_nation_are_we_killing_our_children, accessed August 10, 2014.

Wikipedia. 2012. List of apocalyptic films. http://en.wikipedia.org/wiki/List_of_apocalyptic_films, accessed June 12, 2014.

Williams, J. A., Jr., C. Podeschi, N. Palmer, P. Schwadel, and D. Meyler. 2012. "The Human-Environment Dialog in Award-winning Children's Picture Books. *Sociological Inquiry* 82(1):145–159.

Wilson, E. O. 1984. *Biophilia: The Human Bond with Other Species.* Boston: Harvard University Press.

———. 2006. *The Creation: An Appeal to Save Life on Earth.* New York: W. W. Norton.

Witmer, J. T., and C. S. Anderson. 1994. *How to Establish a High School Service Learning Program.* Alexandria, VA: Association for Supervision and Curriculum Development. Info about the book at http://www.ascd.org/Publications/Books/Overview/How-to-Establish-a-High-School-Service-Learning-Program.aspx, accessed August 23, 2014.

World Bank. 2013. *Turn Down the Heat: Climate Extremes, Regional Impacts, and the Case for Resilience.* A report for the World Bank by the Potsdam Institute for Climate Impact Research and Climate Analytics. Washington, DC: World Bank. License: Creative Commons Attribution—NonCommercial–NoDerivatives 3.0 Unported license (CC BY-NC-ND 3.0).

Xu, F., and V. Garcia. 2008. "Intuitive Statistics by 8-Month-Old Infants." *Proceedings of the National Academy of Sciences* 105(13):5012–5015.

Young, J. 2012. *What the Robin Knows: How Birds Reveal the Secrets of the Natural World.* Boston: Houghton Mifflin Harcourt.

Young, J., E. Haas, and E. McGown. 2010. *Coyote's Guide to Connecting With Nature,* Second Edition. Shelton, WA: Owlink.

Index